The Tomb of Tutankhamen

"It would be difficult to describe our emotions when for the first time the light of our powerful electric lamps flooded the Burial Chamber, illuminating the walls on which were painted representatives of Amentit, the catafalque drawn on a sled by the chief nobles of the land, King Ay before the Osiride Tutankhamen and lighting up the immense shrine overlaid with gold . . ."

The discovery of Tutankhamen's tomb in 1922 is a landmark in archaeological history and certainly the most important single find in Egypt's Valley of the Kings. Unlike that of more illustrious Pharaohs the tomb of the boy-king Tutankhamen had lain unmolested by grave-robbers for more than three thousand years. To its discoverers it yielded a treasure of unimagined magnificence, ranging from chariots, chairs and caskets to the great sepulchral shrine of "the Lord of the West."

The story of this discovery, first published by instalments between 1923 and 1933, is here told by Howard Carter who led the work of excavation. Not only does he provide a brilliant portrait of the life and death of an 18th Dynasty Pharaoh, but he also communicates the feeling of awe and excitement which spurred the explorers as the tomb yielded up its extraordinary riches.

The text is complemented by Harry Burton's contemporary photographs, and a selection of more recent colour photographs which show the treasures as they may be seen today.

Overleaf: the second golden coffin

The Tomb of Tutankhamen

Howard Carter

with 17 color plates and 65
monochrome illustrations
and two appendices

E. P. DUTTON & CO., INC., NEW YORK

First published in this edition in U.S.A. in 1972 by E. P. Dutton & Co., Inc.
First published in this edition in Great Britain in 1972 by Sphere Books Ltd.

Library of Congress Catalog Card Number: 72-77218

SBN: 0–525–22080–1

Printed in Great Britain by
Acorn Typesetting & Litho Services Limited
Feltham, Middlesex, England.

Contents

Publisher's note

Howard Carter discovered the tomb of Tutankhamen in 1922. The original edition of this book appeared in three volumes: Volume I, of which A. C. Mace, then Associate Curator at the Metropolitan Museum of Art, New York, was co-author, was published in 1923, Volume II in 1927 and Volume III in 1933.

The prefaces to all three volumes have been omitted since their immediate relevance is past. Nor was it possible to include from Volume I, Lady Burghclere's biographical sketch of her father, Lord Carnarvon; from Volume II, the introduction on Egyptian art and three of the five appendices; or from Volume III, the introduction, the facts and theories relating to the kings involved in the Aten heresy, and both appendices.

At the time of the discovery Harry Burton, of the Metropolitan Museum of Art, New York, photographed every stage of the excavation and every object. Photographs from his original negatives have been used to illustrate this edition, and the publishers are grateful to the Griffith Institute, Ashmolean Museum, Oxford, for supplying them and for their permission to reproduce them. The illustrations on pages 58, 66, 67 and 87 are by kind permission of *The Times*.

Acknowledgements for the colour plates are due to:

Plate 1 photograph by George Rainbird©copyright George Rainbird, London

Plates 5, 9, 10, 12, 15, photographs by F. L. Kenett©copyright George Rainbird Ltd., London

Plate 2 Middle East Archive/G. W. Allan, London

Plate 4 Middle East Archive/G. W. Allan, London

Plate 7 Middle East Archive, London

Plate 8 Middle East Archive, London

Plates 3, 11 and 14, Pierre Tetrel, Paris

Plates 6, 13 and 16, Scala, Florence

Joy Law selected the illustrations and was responsible for the overall design of this edition.

Dedication

With the full sympathy of my collaborator, Mr. Mace, I dedicate this account of the discovery of the tomb of Tutankhamen to the memory of my beloved friend and colleague, LORD CARNARVON, who died in the hour of his triumph. But for his untiring generosity and constant encouragement our labours could never have been crowned with success. His judgement in ancient art has rarely been equalled. His efforts, which have done so much to extend our knowledge of Egyptology, will ever be honoured in history, and by me his memory will always be cherished.

The golden throne

1

The King and The Queen

A FEW PRELIMINARY words about Tutankhamen, the king whose name the whole world knows, and who in that sense probably needs an introduction less than anyone in history. He was the son-in-law, as everyone knows, of that most written-about, and probably most over-rated, of all the Egyptian Pharaohs, the heretic king Akhenaten. Of his parentage we know nothing. He may have been of the blood royal and had some indirect claim to the throne on his own account. He may on the other hand have been a mere commoner. The point is immaterial, for, by his marriage to a king's daughter, he at once, by Egyptian law of succession, became a potential heir to the throne. A hazardous and uncomfortable position it must have been to fill at this particular stage of his country's history. Abroad, the Empire founded in the fifteenth century B.C. by Thothmes III, and held, with difficulty it is true, but still held, by succeeding monarchs, had crumpled up like a pricked balloon. At home dissatisfaction was rife. The priests of the ancient faith, who had seen their gods flouted and their very livelihood compromised, were straining at the leash, only waiting the most convenient moment to slip it altogether: the soldier class, condemned to a mortified inaction, were seething with discontent, and apt for any form of excitement: the foreign *harim* element, women who had been introduced into the Court and into the families of soldiers in such large numbers since the wars of conquest, were now, at a time of weakness, a sure and certain focus of intrigue: the manufacturers and merchants, as foreign trade declined and home credit was diverted to a local and extremely circumscribed area, were rapidly becoming sullen and discontented: the common populace, intolerant of change, grieving, many of them, at the loss of their old familiar gods, and ready enough to attribute any loss, deprivation, or misfortune, to the jealous intervention of these offended deities, were changing slowly from bewilderment to active resentment at the new heaven and new earth that had been decreed for them. And through it all Akhenaten, Gallio of Gallios, dreamt his life away at Tell el Amarna.

The question of a successor was a vital one for the whole country, and we may be sure that intrigue was rampant. Of male heirs there was none, and interest centres on a group of little girls, the eldest of whom could not have been more than fifteen at the time of her father's death. Young as she was, this eldest princess, Mertaten by name, had already been married some little while, for in the last year or two of Akhenaten's reign we find her husband associated with him as co-regent, a vain attempt to avert the crisis which even the arch-dreamer Akhenaten must have felt to be inevitable. Her taste of queenship was but a short one, for Smenkhkare, her husband, died within a short while of Akhenaten. He may even, as evidence in this tomb seems to show, have predeceased him, and it is quite possible that he met his death at the hands of a rival faction. In any case he disappears, and his wife with him, and the throne was open to the next claimant.

The second daughter, Maktaten, died unmarried in Akhenaten's lifetime. The third, Ankhesenpaaten, was married to Tutankhaten as he then was, the Tutankhamen with whom we are now so familiar. Just when this marriage took place is not certain. It may have been in Akhenaten's lifetime, or it may have been contracted hastily immediately after his death, to legalize his claim to the throne. In any event they were but children. Ankhesenpaaten was born in the eighth year of her father's reign, and therefore cannot have been more than ten; and we have reason to believe, from internal evidence in the tomb, that Tutankhamen himself was little more than a boy. Clearly in the first years of this reign of children there must have been a power behind the throne, and we can be tolerably certain who this power was. In all countries, but more particularly in those of the Orient, it is a wise rule, in cases of doubtful or weak succession, to pay particular attention to the movements of the most powerful Court official. In the Tell el Amarna Court this was a certain Ay, Chief Priest, Court Chamberlain, and practically Court everything else. He himself was a close personal friend of Akhenaten's, and his wife Tyi was nurse to the royal wife Nefertiti, so we may be quite sure there was nothing that went on in the palace that they did not know. Now, looking ahead a little, we find that it was this same Ay who secured the throne himself after Tutankhamen's death. We also know, from the occurrence of his cartouche in the sepulchral chamber of the newly found tomb, that he made himself responsible for the burial ceremonies of Tutankhamen, even if he himself did not actually construct the tomb. It is quite unprecedented in the Valley to find the name of a succeeding king upon the walls of his predecessor's sepulchral monument. The fact that it was so in this case seems to imply a special relationship between the two, and we shall probably be safe in assuming that it was Ay who was largely responsible for establishing the boy king upon the throne. Quite possibly he had designs upon it himself already, but, not feeling secure enough for the moment, preferred to bide his time and utilize the opportunities he would undoubtedly have, as minister to a young and inexperienced sovereign, to consolidate his position. It is interesting to speculate, and when we remember that Ay in his turn was supplanted by another of the leading officials of Akhenaten's reign, the General Horemheb, and that neither of them had any real claim to the throne, we can be reasonably sure that in this little by-way of history, from 1375 to 1350 B.C., there was a well-set stage for dramatic happenings.

However, as self-respecting historians, let us put aside the tempting "might have beens" and "probablys" and come back to the cold hard facts of history. What do we really know about this Tutankhamen with whom we have become so surprisingly familiar? Remarkably little, when you come right down to it. In the present state of our knowledge we might say with truth that the one outstanding feature of his life was the fact that he died and was buried. Of the man himself—if indeed he ever arrived at the dignity of manhood—and of his personal character we know nothing. Of the events of his short reign we can glean a little, a very little, from the monuments. We know, for instance, that at some time during his reign he abandoned the heretic capital of his father-in-law, and removed the Court back to Thebes. That he began as an Aten worshipper, and reverted to the old religion, is evident from his name Tutankhaten, changed to Tutankhamen, and from the fact that he made some slight additions and restorations to the temples of the old gods at Thebes. There is also a stela in the Cairo Museum, which originally stood in one of the Karnak temples, in which he refers to these temple restorations in somewhat grandiloquent language. "I found," he says, "the temples fallen into ruin, with their holy places overthrown, and their courts overgrown with weeds. I reconstructed their sanctuaries, I re-endowed the temples, and made them gifts of all precious things. I cast statues of the gods in gold and electrum, decorated with lapis lazuli and all fine stones."[1] We do not know at what particular period in his reign this change of religion took place, nor whether it was due to personal feeling or was dictated to him for political reasons. We know from the tomb of one of his officials that certain tribes in Syria and in the Sudan were subject to him and brought him tribute, and on many of the objects in his own tomb we see him trampling with great gusto on prisoners of war, and shooting them by hundreds from his chariot, but we must by no means take for granted that he ever in actual fact took the field himself. Egyptian monarchs were singularly tolerant of such polite fictions.

That pretty well exhausts the facts of his life as we know them from the monuments. From his tomb, so far, there is singularly little to add. We are getting to know to the last detail what he had, but of what he was and what he did we are still sadly to seek. There is nothing yet to give us the exact length of his reign. Six years we knew before as a minimum: much more than that it cannot have been. We can only hope that the inner chambers will be more communicative. His body, if, as we hope and expect, it still lies beneath the shrines within the sepulchre, will at least tell us his age at death, and may possibly give us some clue to the circumstances.

Just a word as to his wife, Ankhesenpaaten as she was known originally, and Ankhesenamen after the reversion to Thebes. As the one through whom the king inherited, she was a person of considerable importance, and he makes due acknowledgment of the fact by the frequency with which her name and person appear upon the tomb furniture. A graceful figure she was, too, unless her portraits do her more than justice, and her friendly relations with her husband are insisted on in true Tell el Amarna style. There are two particularly charming representations of her. In one, on the back of the throne, she anoints her husband with perfume: in the other, she accompanies him on a shooting expedition, and is represented crouching at his feet, handing him an arrow with one hand, and with the other pointing out to him a particularly fat duck which she fears may escape his notice. Charming pictures these, and pathetic, too, when we remember that at seventeen or eighteen years of age the wife was left a widow. Well, perhaps. On the other hand, if we know our Orient, perhaps not, for to this story there is a sequel, provided for us by a number of tablets, found some years ago in the ruins of Boghozkeui, and only recently deciphered. An interesting little tale of intrigue it outlines, and in a few words we get a clearer picture of Queen Ankhesenamen than Tutankhamen was able to achieve for himself in his entire equipment of funeral furniture.

She was, it seems, a lady of some force of character. The idea of retiring into the background in favour of a new queen did not appeal to her, and immediately upon the death of her husband she began to scheme. She had, we may presume, at least two months' grace, the time that must elapse between Tutankhamen's death and burial, for until the last king was buried it was hardly likely that the new one would take over the reins. Now, in the past two or three reigns there had been constant intermarriages between the royal houses of Egypt and Asia. One of Ankhesenamen's sisters had been sent in marriage to a foreign court, and many Egyptologists think that her own mother was an Asiatic princess. It was not surprising then, that in this crisis she should look abroad for help, and we find her writing a letter to the King of the Hittites in the following terms: "My husband is dead and I am told that you have grown-up sons. Send me one of them, and I will make him my husband, and he shall be king over Egypt."

It was a shrewd move on her part, for there was no real heir to the throne in Egypt, and the swift dispatch of a Hittite prince, with a reasonable force to back him up, would probably have brought off a very successful coup. Promptitude, however, was the one essential, and here the queen was reckoning without the Hittite king. Hurry in any matter was well outside his calculations. It would never do to be rushed into a scheme of this sort without due deliberation, and how did he know that the letter was not a trap? So he summoned his counsellors and the matter was talked over at length. Eventually it was decided to send a messenger to Egypt to investigate the truth of the story. "Where," he writes in his reply—and you can see him patting himself on the back for his shrewdness—"is the son of the late king, and what has become of him?"

Now, it took some fourteen days for a messenger to go from one country to the other, so the poor queen's feelings can be imagined, when, after a month's waiting, she received, in answer to her request, not a prince and a husband, but a dilatory futile letter. In despair she writes again: "Why should I deceive you? I have no son, and my husband is dead. Send me a son of yours and I will make him king." The Hittite king now decides to accede to her request and to send a son, but it is evidently too late. The time had gone by. The document breaks off here, and it is left to our imagination to fill in the rest of the story.

Did the Hittite prince ever start for Egypt, and how far did he get? Did Ay, the new king, get wind of Ankhesenamen's schemings and take effectual steps to bring them to naught? We shall never know. In any case the queen disappears from the scene and we hear of her no more. It is a fascinating little tale. Had the plot succeeded there would never have been a Rameses the Great.

The cords with the royal necropolis seal binding the doors of the second shrine

2

The Valley and the Tomb

THE VALLEY OF THE TOMBS of the Kings—the very name is full of romance, and of all Egypt's wonders there is none, I suppose, that makes a more instant appeal to the imagination. Here, in this lonely valley head, remote from every sound of life, with the "Horn," the highest peak in the Theban hills, standing sentinel like a natural pyramid above them, lay thirty or more kings, among them the greatest Egypt ever knew. Thirty were buried here. Now, probably, but two remain—Amenhetep II—whose mummy may be seen by the curious lying in his sarcophagus—and Tutankhamen, who still remains intact beneath his golden shrine. There, when the claims of science have been satisfied, we hope to leave him lying.

I do not propose to attempt a word picture of the Valley itself—that has been done too often in the past few months. I would like, however, to devote a certain amount of time to its history, for that is essential to a proper understanding of our present tomb.

Tucked away in a corner at the extreme end of the Valley, half concealed by a projecting bastion of rock, lies the entrance to a very unostentatious tomb. It is easily overlooked and rarely visited, but it has a very special interest as being the first ever constructed in the Valley. More than that: it is notable as an experiment in a new theory of tomb design. To the Egyptian it was a matter of vital importance that his body should rest inviolate in the place constructed for it, and this earlier kings had thought to ensure by erecting over it a very mountain of stone. It was also essential to a mummy's well-being that it should be fully equipped against every need, and, in the case of a luxurious and display-loving Oriental monarch, this would naturally involve a lavish use of gold and other treasure. The result was obvious enough. The very magnificence of the monument was its undoing, and within a few generations at most the mummy would be disturbed and its treasure stolen. Various expedients were tried; the entrance passage—naturally the weak spot in a pyramid—was plugged with granite monoliths weighing many tons; false passages were constructed; secret doors were contrived; everything that ingenuity could suggest or wealth could purchase was employed. Vain labour all of it, for by patience and perseverance the tomb robber in every case surmounted the difficulties that were set to baffle him. Moreover, the success of these expedients, and therefore the safety of the monument itself, was largely dependent on the good will of the mason who carried out the work, and the architect who designed it. Careless workmanship would leave a danger point in the best planned defences, and, in private tombs at any rate, we know that an ingress for plunderers was sometimes contrived by the officials who planned the work.

Efforts to secure the guarding of the royal monument were equally unavailing. A king might leave enormous endowments—as a matter of fact each king did—for the upkeep of large companies of pyramid officials and guardians, but after a time these very officials were ready enough to connive at the plundering of the monument they were paid to guard, while the endowments were sure, at the end of the dynasty at latest, to be diverted by some subsequent king to other purposes. At the beginning of the Eighteenth Dynasty there was hardly a king's tomb in the whole of Egypt that had not been rifled—a somewhat grisly thought to the monarch who was choosing the site for his own last resting place. Thothmes I evidently found it so, and devoted a good deal of thought to the problem, and as a result we get the lonely little tomb at the head of the Valley. Secrecy was to be the solution to the problem.

A preliminary step in this direction had been taken by his predecessor, Amenhetep I, who made his tomb some distance away from his funerary temple, on the summit of the Drah Abu'l Negga foothills, hidden beneath a stone, but this was carrying it a good deal further. It was a drastic break with tradition, and we may be sure that he hesitated long before he made the decision. In the first place his pride would suffer, for love of ostentation was ingrained in every Egyptian monarch and in his tomb more than anywhere else he was accustomed to display it. Then, too, the new arrangement would seem likely to cause a certain amount of inconvenience to his mummy. The early funerary monuments had always, in immediate proximity to the actual place of burial, a temple in which the due ceremonies were performed at the various yearly festivals, and daily offerings were made. Now there was to be no monument over the tomb itself, and the funerary temple in which the offerings were made was to be situated a mile or so away, on the other side of the hill. It was certainly not a convenient arrangement, but it was necessary if the secrecy of the tomb was to be kept, and secrecy King Thothmes had decided on, as the one chance of escaping the fate of his predecessors.

The construction of this hidden tomb was entrusted by Thothmes to Ineni, his chief architect, and in the biography which was inscribed on the wall of his funerary chapel Ineni has put on record the secrecy with which the work was carried out. "I superintended the excavation of the cliff tomb of His Majesty," he tells us, "alone, no one seeing, no one hearing." Unfortunately he omits to tell us anything about the workmen he employed. It is sufficiently obvious that a hundred or more labourers with a knowledge of the king's dearest secret would never be allowed at large, and we can be quite sure that Ineni found some effectual means of stopping their mouths. Conceivably the work was carried out by prisoners of war, who were slaughtered at its completion.

How long the secret of this particular tomb held we do not know. Probably not long, for what secret was ever kept in Egypt? At the time of its discovery in 1899 little remained in it but the massive stone sarcophagus, and the king himself was moved, as we know, first of all to the tomb of his daughter Hatshepsut, and subsequently, with the other royal mummies, to Deir el Bahari. In any case, whether the hiding of the tomb was temporarily successful or not, a new fashion had been set, and the remaining kings of this Dynasty, together with those of the Nineteenth and Twentieth, were all buried in the Valley.

The idea of secrecy did not long prevail. From the nature of things it could not, and the later kings seem to have accepted the fact, and gone back to the old plan of making their tombs conspicuous. Now that it had become the established custom to place all the royal tombs within a very restricted area they may have thought that tomb robbery was securely provided against, seeing that it was very much to the reigning king's interest to see that the royal burial site was protected. If they did, they mightily deceived themselves. We know from internal evidence that Tutankhamen's tomb was entered by robbers within ten, or at most fifteen, years of his death. We also know, from *graffiti* in the tomb of Thothmes IV, that that monarch too had suffered at the hands of plunderers within a very few years of his burial, for we find King Horemheb in the eighth year of his reign issuing instructions to a certain high official named Maya to "renew the burial of King Thothmes IV, justified, in the Precious Habitation in Western Thebes." They must have been bold spirits who made the venture: they were evidently in a great hurry, and we have reason to believe that they were caught in the act. If so, we may be sure they died deaths that were lingering and ingenious.

Strange sights the Valley must have seen, and desperate the ventures that took place in it. One can imagine the plotting for days beforehand, the secret rendezvous on the cliff by night, the bribing or drugging of the cemetery guards, and then the desperate burrowing in the dark, the scramble through a small hole into the burial chamber, the hectic search by a glimmering light for treasure that was portable, and the return home at dawn laden with booty. We can imagine these things, and at the same time we can realize how inevitable it all was. By providing his mummy with the elaborate and costly outfit which he thought essential to its dignity, the king was himself compassing its destruction. The temptation was too great. Wealth beyond the dreams of avarice lay there at the disposal of whoever should find the means to reach it, and sooner or later the tomb robber was bound to win through.

For a few generations, under the powerful kings of the Eighteenth and Nineteenth Dynasties, the Valley tombs must have been reasonably secure. Plundering on a big scale would be impossible without the connivance of the officials concerned. In the Twentieth Dynasty it was quite another story. There were weaklings on the throne, a fact of which the official classes, as ever, were quick to take advantage. Cemetery guardians became lax and venial, and a regular orgy of grave-robbing seems to have set in. This is a fact of which we have actual first-hand evidence, for there have come down to us, dating from the reign of Rameses IX, a series of papyri dealing with this very subject, with reports of investigations into charges of tomb robbery, and accounts of the trial of the criminals concerned. They are extraordinarily interesting documents. We get from them, in addition to very valuable information about the tombs, something which Egyptian documents as a rule singularly lack, a story with a real human element in it, and we are enabled to see right into the minds of a group of officials who lived in Thebes three thousand years ago.

The leading characters in the story are three, Khamwese, the vizier, or governor of the district, Peser, the mayor of that part of the city which lay on the east bank, and Pewero, the mayor of the western side, *ex-officio* guardian of the necropolis. The two latter were evidently, one might say naturally, on bad terms: each was jealous of the other. Consequently, Peser was not ill pleased to receive one day reports of tomb-plundering on an extensive scale that was going on on the western bank. Here was a chance to get his rival into trouble, so he hastened to report the matter to the vizier, giving, somewhat foolishly, exact figures as to the tombs which had been entered—ten royal tombs, four tombs of the priestesses of Amen, and a long list of private tombs.

On the following day Khamwese sent a party of officials across the river to confer with Pewero, and to investigate the charges. The results of their investigations were as follows. Of the ten royal tombs, one was found to have been actually broken into, and attempts had been made on two of the others. Of the priestesses' tombs, two were pillaged and two were intact. The private tombs had all been plundered. These facts were hailed by Pewero as a complete vindication of his administration, an opinion which the vizier apparently endorsed. The plundering of the private tombs was cynically admitted, but what of that? To people of our class what do the tombs of private individuals matter? Of the four priestesses' tombs two were plundered and two were not. Balance the one against the other, and what cause has anyone to grumble? Of the ten royal tombs mentioned by Peser only one had actually been entered: only one out of ten, so clearly his whole story was a tissue of lies! Thus Pewero, on the principle, apparently, that if you are accused of ten murders and are only found guilty of one, you leave the court without a stain on your character.

As a celebration of his triumph Pewero collected next day "the inspectors, the necropolis administrators, the workmen, the police, and all the labourers of the necropolis" and sent them as a body to the east side, with instructions to make a triumphant parade throughout the town generally, but particularly in the neighbourhood of Peser's house. You may be sure they carried out this latter part of their instructions quite faithfully. Peser bore it as long as he could, but at last his feelings got too much for him, and in an altercation with one of the western officials he announced his intention, in front of witnesses, of reporting the whole matter to the king himself. This was a fatal error, of which his rival was quick to take advantage. In a letter to the vizier he accused the unfortunate Peser—first, of questioning the good faith of a commission appointed by his direct superior, and secondly, of going over the head of that superior, and stating his case directly to the king, a proceeding at which the virtuous Pewero threw up his hands in horror, as contrary to all custom and subversive of all discipline. This was the end of Peser. The offended vizier summoned a court, a court in which the unhappy man, as a judge, was bound himself to sit, and in it he was tried for perjury and found guilty.

That in brief is the story: it is told at full length in volume IV, par. 499 ff., of Breasted's *Ancient Records of Egypt*. It is tolerably clear from it that both the mayor and the vizier were themselves implicated in the robberies in question. The investigation they made was evidently a blind, for within a year or two of these proceedings we find other cases of tomb-robbing cropping up in the Court records, and at least one of the tombs in question occurs in Peser's original list.

The leading spirits in this company of cemetery thieves seem to have been a gang of eight men, five of whose names have come down to us—the stone-cutter Hapi, the artisan Iramen, the peasant Amenemheb, the water-carrier Kemwese, and the negro slave Ehenefer. They were eventually apprehended on the charge of having desecrated the royal tomb referred to in the investigation, and we have a full account of their trial. It began, according to custom, by beating the prisoners "with a double rod, smiting their feet and their hands," to assist their memories. Under this stimulus they made full confession. The opening sentences in the confession are mutilated in the text, but they evidently describe how the thieves tunnelled through the rock to the burial chamber, and found the king and queen in their sarcophagi: "We penetrated them all, we found her resting likewise." The text goes on:

> "We opened their coffins, and their coverings in which they were. We found the august mummy of this king. . . . There was a numerous list of amulets and ornaments of gold at its throat; its head had a mask of gold upon it; the august mummy of this king was overlaid with gold throughout. Its coverings were wrought with gold and silver, within and without; inlaid with every costly stone. We stripped off the gold, which we found on the august mummy of this god, and its amulets and ornaments which were at its throat, and the covering wherein it rested. We found the king's wife likewise; we stripped off all that we found on her likewise. We set fire to their coverings. We stole their furniture, which we found with them, being vases of gold, silver, and bronze. We divided, and made the gold which we found on these two gods, on their mummies, and the amulets, ornaments and coverings, into eight parts."[1]

On this confession they were found guilty, and removed to the house of detention, until such time as the king himself might determine their punishment.

In spite of this trial and a number of others of a similar character, matters in the Valley went rapidly from bad to worse. The tombs of Amenhetep III, Seti I, and Rameses II, are mentioned in the court records as having been broken into, and in the following Dynasty all attempts at guarding the tombs seem to have been abandoned, and we find the royal mummies being moved about from sepulchre to sepulchre in a desperate effort to preserve them. Rameses III, for instance, was disturbed and reburied three times at least in this Dynasty, and other kings known to have been transferred included Ahmes, Amenhetep I, Thothmes II, and even Rameses the Great himself. In this last case the docket states:

> "Year 17, third month of the second season, day 6, day of bringing Osiris, King Usermare-Setepnere (Rameses II), to bury him again, in the tomb of Osiris, King Menmareseti (I): by the High Priest of Amen, Paynezem."

A reign or two later we find Seti I and Rameses II being moved from this tomb and re-buried in the tomb of Queen Inhapi; and in the same reign we get a reference to the tomb we have been using as our laboratory this year:

> "Day of bringing King Menpehtire (Rameses I) out from the tomb of King Menmareseti (II), in order to bring him into the tomb of Inhapi, which is in the Great Place, wherein King Amenhetep rests."

No fewer than thirteen of the royal mummies found their way at one time or another to the tomb of Amenhetep II, and here they were allowed to remain. The other kings were eventually collected from their various hiding places, taken out of the Valley altogether, and placed in a well-hidden tomb cut in the Deir el Bahari cliff. This was the final move, for by some accident the exact locality of the tomb was lost, and the mummies remained in peace for nearly three thousand years.

Throughout all these troublous times in the Twentieth and Twenty-first Dynasties there is no mention of Tutankhamen and his tomb. He had not escaped altogether—his tomb, as we have already noted, having been entered within a very few years of his death—but he was lucky enough to escape the ruthless plundering of the later period. For some reason his tomb had been overlooked. It was situated in a very low-lying part of the Valley, and a heavy rain storm might well have washed away all trace of its entrance. Or again, it may owe its safety to the fact that a number of huts, for the use of workmen who were employed in excavating the tomb of a later king, were built immediately above it.

With the passing of the mummies the history of the Valley, as known to us from ancient Egyptian sources, comes to an end. Five hundred years had passed since Thothmes I had constructed his modest little tomb there, and, surely in the whole world's history, there is no small plot of ground that had five hundred years of more romantic story to record. From now on we are to imagine a deserted valley, spirit-haunted doubtless to the Egyptian, its cavernous galleries plundered and empty, the entrances of many of them open, to become the home of fox, desert owl, or colonies of bats. Yet, plundered, deserted and desolate as were its tombs, the romance of it was not yet wholly gone. It still remained the sacred Valley of the Kings, and crowds of the sentimental and the curious must still have gone to visit it. Some of its tombs, indeed, were actually re-used in the time of Osorkon I (about 900 B.C.) for the burial of priestesses.

References to its rock-hewn passages are numerous in classical authors, and that many of them were still accessible to visitors in their day is evident from the reprehensible manner in which, like John Smith, 1878, they carved their names upon the walls. A certain Philetairos, son of Ammonios, who inscribed his name in several places on the walls of the tomb in which we had our lunch, intrigued me not a little during the winter, though perhaps it would have been better not to mention the fact, lest I seem to countenance the beastly habits of the John Smiths.

One final picture, before the mist of the Middle Ages settles down upon the Valley, and hides it from our view. There is something about the atmosphere of Egypt—most people experience it I think—that attunes one's mind to solitude, and that is probably one of the reasons why, after the conversion of the country to Christianity, so many of its inhabitants turned with enthusiasm to the hermit's life. The country itself, with its equable climate, its narrow strip of cultivable land, and its desert hills on either side, honeycombed with natural and artificial caverns, was well adapted to such a purpose. Shelter and seclusion were readily obtainable, and that within easy reach of the outer world, and the ordinary means of subsistence. In the early centuries of the Christian era there must have been thousands who forsook the world and adopted the contemplative life, and in the rock-cut sepulchres upon the desert hills we find their traces everywhere. Such an ideal spot as the Valley of the Kings could hardly pass unnoticed, and in the II–IV centuries A.D. we find a colony of anchorites in full possession, the open tombs in use as cells, and one transformed into a church.

This, then, is our final glimpse of the Valley in ancient times, and a strange incongruous picture it presents. Magnificence and royal pride have been replaced by humble poverty. The "precious habitation" of the king has narrowed to a hermit's cell.

The road to the tombs of the kings

3

The Valley in modern times

FOR OUR FIRST REAL DESCRIPTION of the Valley in modern times we must turn to the pages of Richard Pococke, an English traveller who in 1743 published *A Description of the East* in several volumes. His account is extremely interesting, and, considering the hurried nature of his visit, extraordinarily accurate. Here is his description of the approach to the Valley:

> The Sheik furnished me with horses, and we set out to go to Biban-el-Meluke, and went about a mile to the north, in a sort of street, on each side of which the rocky ground about ten feet high has rooms cut into it, some of them being supported with pillars; and, as there is not the least sign in the plain of private buildings, I thought that these in the very earliest times might serve as houses, and be the first invention after tents, and contrived as better shelter from wind, and cold of the nights. It is a sort of gravelly stone, and the doors are cut regularly to the street.[1] We then turned to the north west, enter'd in between the high rocky hills, and went in a very narrow valley. We after turn'd towards the south, and then to the north west, going in all between the mountains about a mile or a mile and a half . . . We came to a part that is wider, being a round opening like an amphitheatre and ascended by a narrow step passage about ten feet high, which seems to have been broken down thro' the rock, the ancient passage being probably from the Memnonium under the hills, and it may be from the grottos I enter'd on the other side. By this passage we came to Biban-el-Meluke, or Bab-el-Meluke, that is, the gate or court of the kings, being the sepulchres of the Kings of Thebes.[2]

The tradition of a secret passage through the hills to the Deir el Bahari side of the cliff is still to be found among the natives, and to the present day there are archaeologists who subscribe to it. There is, however, little or no basis for the theory, and certainly not a vestige of proof.

Pococke then goes on to an account of such of the tombs as were accessible at the time of his visit. He mentions fourteen in all, and most of them are recognizable from his description. Of five of them, those of Rameses IV, Rameses VI, Rameses XII, Seti II, and the tomb commenced by Tausert and finished by Setnekht, he gives the entire plan. In the case of four—Merenptah, Rameses III, Amenmeses and Rameses XI—he only planned the outer galleries and chambers, the inner chambers evidently being inaccessible; and the remaining five he speaks of as "stopped up."[3] It is evident from Pococke's narrative that he was not able to devote as much time to his visit as he would have liked. The Valley was not a safe spot to linger in, for the pious anchorite we left in possession had given place to a horde of bandits, who dwelt among the Kurna hills, and terrorized the whole country-side. "The Sheik also was in haste to go," he remarks, "being afraid, as I imagine, lest the people should have opportunity to gather together if we staid out long."

These Theban bandits were notorious, and we find frequent mention of them in the tales of eighteenth-century travellers. Norden, who visited Thebes in 1737, but who never got nearer the Valley than the Ramasseum—he seems to have thought himself lucky to have got so far—describes them thus:

> "These people occupy, at present, the grottos, which are seen in great numbers in the neighbouring mountains. They obey no one; they are lodged so high, that they discover at a distance if anyone comes to attack them. Then, if they think themselves strong enough, they descend into the plain, to dispute the ground; if not, they keep themselves under shelter in their grottos, or they retire deeper into the mountains, whither you would have no great desire to follow them."[4]

Bruce, who visited the Valley in 1769, also suffered at the hands of these bandits, and puts on record a somewhat drastic, but fruitless, attempt, made by one of the native governors, to curb their activities:

> "A number of robbers, who much resemble our gypsies, live in the holes of the mountains above Thebes. They are all outlaws, punished with death if elsewhere found. Osman Bey, an ancient governor of Girge, unable to suffer any longer the disorders committed by these people, ordered a quantity of dried faggots to be brought together, and, with his soldiers, took possession of the face of the mountain, where the greatest number of these wretches were: he then ordered all their caves to be filled with this dry brushwood, to which he set fire, so that most of them were destroyed; but they have since recruited their numbers without changing their manners."[5]

In the course of this visit Bruce made copies of the figures of harpers in the tomb of Rameses III, a tomb which still goes by his name, but his labours were brought to an abrupt conclusion. Finding that it was his intention to spend the night in the tomb, and continue his researches in the morning, his guides were seized with terror, "With great clamour and marks of discontent, they dashed their torches against the largest harp, and made the best of their way out of the cave, leaving me and my people in the dark; and all the way as they went, they made dreadful denunciations of tragical events that were immediately to follow, upon their departure from the cave." That their terror was genuine and not ill-founded, Bruce was soon to discover, for as he rode down the Valley in the gathering darkness, he was attacked by a party of the bandits, who lay in wait for him, and hurled stones at him from the side of the cliff. With the aid of his gun and his servant's blunderbuss he managed to beat them off, but, on arriving at his boat, he thought it prudent to cast off at once, and made no attempt to repeat his visit.

Nor did even the magic of Napoleon's name suffice to curb the arrogance of these Theban bandits, for the members of his scientific commission who visited Thebes in the last days of the century were molested, and even fired upon. They succeeded, however, in making a complete survey of all the tombs then open, and also carried out a small amount of excavation.

Let us pass on now to 1815, and make the acquaintance of one of the most remarkable men in the whole history of Egyptology. In the early years of the century, a young Italian giant, Belzoni by name, was earning a precarious income in England by performing feats of strength at fairs and circuses. Born in Padua, of a respectable family of Roman extraction, he had been intended for the priesthood, but a roving disposition, combined with the internal troubles in Italy at that period, had driven him to seek his fortune abroad. We happened recently upon a reference to him in his pre-Egyptian days, in one of "Rainy Day" Smith's books of reminiscences, where the author describes how he was carried round the stage, with a group of other people, by the "strong man" Belzoni. In the intervals of circus work Belzoni seems to have studied engineering, and in 1815 he thought he saw a chance of making his fortune by introducing into Egypt a hydraulic wheel, which would, he claimed, do four times the work of the ordinary native appliance. With this in view, he made his way to Egypt, contrived an introduction to Mohammed Ali the "Bashaw," and in the garden of the palace actually set up his wheel. According to Belzoni it was a great success, but the Egyptians refused to have anything to do with it, and he found himself stranded in Egypt.

Then, through the traveller Burchardt, he got an introduction to Salt, the British Consul-General in Egypt, and contracted with him to bring the "colossal Memnion bust" (Rameses II, now in the British Museum) from Luxor to Alexandria. This was in 1815, and the next five years he spent in Egypt, excavating and collecting antiquities, first for Salt, and afterwards on his own account, and quarrelling with rival excavators, notably Drovetti, who represented the French Consul. Those were the great days of excavating. Anything to which a fancy was taken, from a scarab to an obelisk, was just appropriated, and if there was a difference of opinion with a brother excavator one laid for him with a gun.

Belzoni's account of his experiences in Egypt, published in 1820, is one of the most fascinating books in the whole of Egyptian literature, and I should like to quote from it at length—how, for instance, he dropped an obelisk in the Nile and fished it out again, and the full story of his various squabbles. We must confine ourselves, however, to his actual work in the Valley. Here he discovered and cleared a number of tombs, including those of Ay, Mentuherkhepeshef, Rameses I, and Seti I. In the last named he found the magnificent alabaster sarcophagus which is now in the Soane Museum in London.

This was the first occasion on which excavations on a large scale had ever been made in the Valley, and we must give Belzoni full credit for the manner in which they were carried out. There are episodes which give the modern excavator rather a shock, as, for example, when he describes his method of dealing with sealed doorways—by means of a battering ram—but on the whole the work was extraordinarily good. It is perhaps worth recording the fact that Belzoni, like everyone else who has ever dug in the Valley, was of the opinion that he had absolutely exhausted its possibilities. "It is my firm opinion," he states, "that in the Valley of Beban el Malook, there are no more (tombs) than are now known, in consequence of my late discoveries; for, previously to my quitting that place, I exerted all my humble abilities in endeavouring to find another tomb, but could not succeed; and what is a still greater proof, independent of my own researches, after I quitted the place, Mr. Salt, the British Consul, resided there four months and laboured in like manner in vain to find another."

In 1820 Belzoni returned to England, and gave an exhibition of his treasures, including the alabaster sarcophagus and a model of the tomb of Seti, in a building which had been erected in Piccadilly in 1812, a building which many of us can still remember—the Egyptian Hall. He never returned to Egypt, but died a few years later on an expedition to Timbuctoo.

For twenty years after Belzoni's day the Valley was well exploited, and published records come thick and fast. We shall not have space here to do more than mention a few of the names —Salt, Champollion, Burton, Hay, Head, Rosellini, Wilkinson, who numbered the tombs, Rawlinson, Rhind. In 1844 the great German expedition under Lepsius made a complete survey of the Valley, and cleared the tomb of Rameses II, and part of the tomb of Merenptah. Hereafter comes a gap; the German expedition was supposed to have exhausted the possibilities, and nothing more of any consequence was done in the Valley until the very end of the century.

In this period, however, just outside the Valley, there occurred one of the most important events in the whole of its history. In the preceding chapter we told how the various royal mummies were collected from their hiding-places, and deposited all together in a rock cleft at Deir el Bahari. There for nearly three thousand years they had rested, and there, in the summer of 1875, they were found by the members of a Kurna family, the Abd-el-Rasuls. It was in the thirteenth century B.C. that the inhabitants of this village first adopted the trade of tomb-robbing, and it is a trade that they have adhered to steadfastly ever since. Their activities are curbed at the present day, but they still search on the sly in out-of-the-way corners, and occasionally make a rich strike. On this occasion the find was too big to handle. It was obviously impossible to clear the tomb of its contents, so the whole family was sworn to secrecy, and its heads determined to leave the find where it was, and to draw on it from time to time as they needed money. Incredible as it may seem the secret was kept for six years, and the family, with a banking account of forty or more dead Pharaohs to draw upon, grew rich.

It soon became manifest, from objects which came into the market, that there had been a rich find of royal material somewhere, but it was not until 1881 that it was possible to trace the sale of the objects to the Abd-el-Rasul family. Even then it was difficult to prove anything. The head of the family was arrested and subjected by the Mudir of Keneh, the notorious Daoud Pasha, whose methods of administering justice were unorthodox but effectual, to an examination. Naturally he denied the charge, and equally naturally the village of Kurna rose as one man and protested that in a strictly honest community the Abd-el-Rasul family were of all men the most honest. He was released provisionally for lack of evidence, but his interview with Daoud seems to have shaken him. Interviews with Daoud usually did have that effect.

One of our older workmen told us once of an experience of his in his younger days. He had been by trade a thief, and in the exercise of his calling had been apprehended and brought before the Mudir. It was a hot day, and his nerves were shaken right at the start by finding the Mudir taking his ease in a large earthenware jar of water. From this unconventional seat of justice Daoud had looked at him—just looked at him—"and as his eyes went through me I felt my bones turning to water within me. Then very quietly he said to me, 'This is the first time you have appeared before me. You are dismissed, but—be very, very careful that you do not appear a second time,' and I was so terrified that I changed my trade and never did."

Some effect of this sort must have been produced on the Abd-el-Rasul family, for a month later one of its members went to the Mudir and made full confession. News was telegraphed at once to Cairo, Emile Brugsch Bey of the Museum was sent up to investigate and take charge, and on the 5th of July, 1881, the long-kept secret was revealed to him. It must have been an amazing experience. There, huddled together in a shallow, ill-cut grave, lay the most powerful monarchs of the ancient East, kings whose names were familiar to the whole world, but whom no one in their wildest moments had ever dreamt of seeing. There they had remained, where the priests in secrecy had hurriedly brought them that dark night three thousand years ago; and on their coffins and mummies, neatly docketed, were the records of their journeyings from one hiding-place to another. Some had been re-wrapped, and two or three in the course of their many wanderings had contrived to change their coffins. In forty-eight hours—we don't do things quite so hastily nowadays—the tomb was cleared; the kings were embarked upon the Museum barge; and within fifteen days of Brugsch Bey's arrival in Luxor, they were landed in Cairo and were deposited in the Museum.

It is a familiar story, but worth repeating, that as the barge made its way down the river the men of the neighbouring villages fired guns as for a funeral, while the women followed along the bank, tearing their hair, and uttering that shrill quavering cry of mourning for the dead, a cry that has doubtless come right down from the days of the Pharaohs themselves.

To return to the Valley. In 1898, acting on information supplied by local officials, M. Loret, then Director-General of the Service of Antiquities, opened up several new royal tombs, including those of Thothmes I, Thothmes III, and Amenhetep II. This last was a very important discovery. We have already stated that in the Twenty-first Dynasty thirteen royal mummies had found sanctuary in this Amenhetep's tomb, and here in 1898 the thirteen were found. It was but their mummies that remained. The wealth, which in their power they had lavished on their funerals, had long since vanished, but at least they had been spared the last indignity. The tomb had been entered, it is true; it had been robbed, and the greater part of the funeral equipment had been plundered and broken, but it had escaped the wholesale destruction that the other royal tombs had undergone, and the mummies remained intact. The body of Amenhetep himself still lay within its own sarcophagus, where it had rested for more than three thousand years. Very rightly the Government, at the representation of Sir William Garstin, decided against its removal. The tomb was barred and bolted, a guard was placed upon it, and there the king was left in peace.

Unfortunately there is a sequel to this story. Within a year or two of the discovery the tomb was broken into by a party of modern tomb-robbers, doubtless with the connivance of the guard, and the mummy was removed from its sarcophagus and searched for treasure. The thieves were subsequently tracked down by the Chief Inspector of Antiquities, and arrested, although he was unable to secure their conviction at the hands of the native court. The whole proceedings, as set forth in the official report, remind one very forcibly of the records of ancient tomb robbery described in the preceding chapter, and we are forced to the conclusion that in many ways the Egyptian of the present day differs little from his ancestor in the reign of Rameses IX.

One moral we can draw from this episode, and we commend it to the critics who call us vandals for taking objects from the tombs. By removing antiquities to museums we are really assuring their safety: left *in situ* they would inevitably, sooner or later, become the prey of thieves, and that, for all practical purposes, would be the end of them.

In 1902 permission to dig in the Valley under Government supervision was granted to an American, Mr. Theodore Davis, and he subsequently excavated there for twelve consecutive seasons. His principal finds are known to most of us. They include the tombs of Thothmes IV, Hatshepsut, Siptah, Yua and Thua—great-grandfather and grandmother these of Tutankhamen's queen—Horemheb, and a vault, not a real tomb, devised for the transfer of the burial of Akhenaten from its original tomb at Tell el Amarna. This cache comprised the mummy and coffin of the heretic king, a very small part of his funerary equipment, and portions of the sepulchral shrine of his mother Tyi. In 1914 Mr. Davis's concession reverted to us, and the story of the tomb of Tutankhamen really begins.

4

Our prefatory work at Thebes

EVER SINCE my first visit to Egypt in 1890 it had been my ambition to dig in the Valley, and when, at the invitation of Sir William Garstin and Sir Gaston Maspero, I began to excavate for Lord Carnarvon in 1907, it was our joint hope that eventually we might be able to get a concession there. I had, as a matter of fact, when Inspector of the Antiquities Department, found, and superintended the clearing of, two tombs in the Valley for Mr. Theodore Davis, and this had made me the more anxious to work there under a regular concession. For the moment it was impossible, and for seven years we dug with varying fortune in other parts of the Theban necropolis. The results of the first five of these years have been published in *Five Years' Explorations at Thebes*, a joint volume brought out by Lord Carnarvon and myself in 1912.

In 1914 our discovery of the tomb of Amenhetep I, on the summit of the Drah abu'l Negga foothills, once more turned our attention valleywards, and we awaited our chance with some impatience. Mr. Theodore Davis, who still held the concession, had already published the fact that he considered the Valley exhausted, and that there were no more tombs to be found, a statement corroborated by the fact that in his last two seasons he did very little work in the Valley proper, but spent most of his time excavating in the approach thereto, in the neighbouring north valley, where he hoped to find the tombs of the priest kings and of the Eighteenth Dynasty queens, and in the mounds surrounding the temple of Medinet Habu. Nevertheless he was loath to give up the site, and it was not until June 1914, that we actually received the long-coveted concession. Sir Gaston Maspero, Director of the Antiquities Department, who signed our concession, agreed with Mr. Davis that the site was exhausted, and told us frankly that he did not consider that it would repay further investigation. We remembered, however, that nearly a hundred years earlier Belzoni had made a similar claim, and refused to be convinced. We had made a thorough investigation of the site, and were quite sure that there were areas, covered by the dumps of previous excavators, which had never been properly examined.

Clearly enough we saw that very heavy work lay before us, and that many thousands of tons of surface debris would have to be removed before we could hope to find anything; but there was always the chance that a tomb might reward us in the end, and, even if there was nothing else to go upon, it was a chance that we were quite willing to take. As a matter of fact we had something more, and, at the risk of being accused of *post actum* prescience, I will state that we had definite hopes of finding the tomb of one particular king, and that king Tutankhamen.

To explain the reasons for this belief of ours we must turn to the published pages of Mr. Davis's excavations. Towards the end of his work in the Valley he had found, hidden under a rock, a faience cup which bore the name of Tutankhamen. In the same region he came upon a small pit-tomb, in which were found an unnamed alabaster statuette, possibly of Ay, and a broken wooden box, in which were fragments of gold foil, bearing the figures and names of Tutankhamen and his queen. On the basis of these fragments of gold he claimed that he had actually found the burial place of Tutankhamen. The theory was quite untenable, for the pit-tomb in question was small and insignificant, of a type that might very well belong to a member of the royal household in the Ramesside period, but ludicrously inadequate for a king's burial in the Eighteenth Dynasty. Obviously, the royal material found in it had been placed there at some later period, and had nothing to do with the tomb itself.

Some little distance eastward from this tomb, he had also found in one of his earlier years of work (1907–8), buried in an irregular hole cut in the side of the rock, a cache of large pottery jars, with sealed mouths, and hieratic inscriptions upon their shoulders. A cursory examination was made of their contents, and as these seemed to consist merely of broken pottery, bundles of linen, and other oddments, Mr. Davis refused to be interested in them, and they were laid aside and stacked away in the store-room of his Valley house. There, some while afterwards, Mr. Winlock noticed them, and immediately realized their importance. With Mr. Davis's consent the entire collection of jars was packed and sent to the Metropolitan Museum of Art, New York, and there Mr. Winlock made a thorough examination of their contents. Extraordinarily interesting they proved to be. There were clay seals, some bearing the name of Tutankhamen and others the impression of the royal necropolis seal, fragments of magnificent painted pottery vases, linen head-shawls—one inscribed with the latest known date of Tutankhamen's reign— floral collars, of the kind represented as worn by mourners in burial scenes, and a mass of other miscellaneous objects; the whole representing, apparently, the material which had been used during the funeral ceremonies of Tutankhamen, and afterwards gathered together and stacked away within the jars.

We had thus three distinct pieces of evidence—the faience cup found beneath the rock, the gold foil from the small pit-tomb, and this important cache of funerary material—which seemed definitely to connect Tutankhamen with this particular part of the Valley. To these must be added a fourth. It was in the near vicinity of these other finds that Mr. Davis had discovered the famous Akhenaten cache. This contained the funerary remains of heretic royalties, brought hurriedly from Tell el Amarna and hidden here for safety, and that it was Tutankhamen himself who was responsible for their removal and reburial we can be reasonably sure from the fact that a number of his clay seals were found.

With all this evidence before us we were thoroughly convinced in our own minds that the tomb of Tutankhamen was still to find, and that it ought to be situated not far from the centre of the Valley. In any case, whether we found Tutankhamen or not, we felt that a systematic and exhaustive search of the inner valley presented reasonable chances of success, and we were in the act of completing our plans for an elaborate campaign in the season of 1914–15 when war broke out, and for the time being all our plans had to be left in abeyance.

War-work claimed most of my time for the next few years, but there were occasional intervals in which I was able to carry out small pieces of excavation. In February 1915, for example, I made a complete clearance of the interior of the tomb of Amenhetep III, partially excavated in 1799 by M. Devilliers, one of the members of Napoleon's "Commission d'Égypte," and re-excavated later by Mr. Theodore Davis. In the course of this work we made the interesting discovery, from the evidence of intact foundation-deposits outside the entrance, and from other material found within the tomb, that it had been originally designed by Thothmes IV, and that Queen Tyi had actually been buried there.

The following year, while on a short holiday at Luxor, I found myself involved quite unexpectedly in another piece of work. The absence of officials owing to the war, to say nothing of the

Hatshepsut's cleft tomb

general demoralization caused by the war itself, had naturally created a great revival of activity on the part of the local native tomb robbers, and prospecting parties were out in all directions. News came into the village one afternoon that a find had been made in a lonely and unfrequented region on the western side of the mountain above the Valley of the Kings. Immediately a rival party of diggers armed themselves and made their way to the spot, and in the lively engagement that ensued the original party were beaten and driven off, vowing vengeance.

To avert further trouble the notables of the village came to me and asked me to take action. It was already late in the afternoon, so I hastily collected the few of my workmen who had escaped the Army Labour Levies, and with the necessary materials set out for the scene of action, an expedition involving a climb of more than 1,800 feet over the Kurna hills by moonlight. It was midnight when we arrived on the scene, and the guide pointed out to me the end of a rope which dangled sheer down the face of a cliff. Listening, we could hear the robbers actually at work, so I first severed their rope, thereby cutting off their means of escape, and then, making secure a good stout rope of my own, I lowered myself down the cliff. Shinning down a rope at midnight, into a nestful of industrious tomb-robbers, is a pastime which at least does not lack excitement. There were eight at work, and when I reached the bottom there was an awkward moment or two. I gave them the alternative of clearing out by means of my rope, or else of staying where they were without a rope at all, and eventually they saw reason and departed. The rest of the night I spent on the spot, and, as soon as it was light enough, climbed down into the tomb again to make a thorough investigation.

The tomb was in a most remarkable situation. Its entrance was contrived in the bottom of a natural water-worn cleft, 130 feet from the top of the cliff, and 220 feet above the valley bed, and so cunningly concealed that neither from the top nor the bottom could the slightest trace of it be seen. From the entrance a lateral passage ran straight into the face of the cliff, a distance of some 55 feet, after which it turned at right angles, and a short passage, cut on a sharp slope, led down into a chamber about 18 feet square. The whole place was full of rubbish from top to bottom, and through this rubbish the robbers had burrowed a tunnel over 90 feet long, just big enough for a man to crawl through.

It was an interesting discovery, and might turn out to be very important, so I determined to make a complete clearance. Twenty days it took, working night and day with relays of workmen, and an extraordinarily difficult job it proved. The method of gaining access to the tomb by means of a rope from the top was unsatisfactory, for it was not a very safe proceeding at best, and it necessitated, moreover, a stiff climb from the valley. Obviously means of access from the valley-bottom would be preferable, and this we contrived by erecting sheers at the entrance to the tomb, so that by a running tackle we could pull ourselves up or let ourselves down. It was not a very comfortable operation even then, and I personally always made the descent in a net.

Excitement among the workmen ruled high as the work progressed, for surely a place so well concealed must contain a wonderful treasure, and great was their disappointment when it proved that the tomb had neither been finished nor occupied. The only thing of value it contained was a large sarcophagus of crystalline sandstone, like the tomb, unfinished, with inscriptions which showed it to have been intended for Queen Hatshepsut. Presumably this masterful lady had had the tomb constructed for herself as wife of King Thothmes II. Later, when she seized the throne and ruled actually as a king, it was clearly necessary for her to have her tomb in the Valley like all the other kings—as a matter of fact I found it there myself in 1903—and the present tomb was abandoned. She would have been better advised to hold to her original plan. In this secret spot her mummy would have had a reasonable chance of avoiding disturbance: in the Valley it had none. A king she would be, and a king's fate she shared.

In the autumn of 1917 our real campaign in the Valley opened. The difficulty was to know where to begin, for mountains of rubbish thrown out by previous excavators encumbered the ground in all directions, and no sort of record had ever been kept as to which areas had been properly excavated and which had not. Clearly the only satisfactory thing to do was to dig systematically right down to bedrock, and I suggested to Lord Carnarvon that we take as a starting point the triangle of ground defined by the tombs of Rameses II, Merenptah, and Rameses VI, the area in which we hoped the tomb of Tutankhamen might be situated.

It was rather a desperate undertaking, the site being piled high with enormous heaps of thrown-out rubbish, but I had reason to believe that the ground beneath had never been touched, and a strong conviction that we should find a tomb there. In the course of the season's work we cleared a considerable part of the upper layers of this area, and advanced our excavations right up to the foot of the tomb of Rameses VI. Here we came on a series of workmen's huts, built over masses of flint boulders, the latter usually indicating in the Valley the near proximity of a tomb. Our natural impulse was to enlarge our clearing in this direction, but by doing this we should have cut off all access to the tomb of Rameses above, to visitors one of the most popular tombs in the whole Valley. We determined to await a more convenient opportunity. So far the only results from our work were some *ostraca*,[1] interesting but not exciting.

We resumed our work in this region in the season of 1919–20. Our first need was to break fresh ground for a dump, and in the course of this preliminary work we lighted on some small deposits of Rameses IV, near the entrance to his tomb. The idea this year was to clear the whole of the remaining part of the triangle already mentioned, so we started in with a fairly large

Workmen's huts above Tutankhamen's tomb

gang of workmen. By the time Lord and Lady Carnarvon arrived in March the whole of the top debris had been removed, and we were ready to clear down into what we believed to be virgin ground below. We soon had proof that we were right, for we presently came upon a small cache containing thirteen alabaster jars, bearing the names of Rameses II and Merenptah, probably from the tomb of the latter. As this was the nearest approach to a real find that we had yet made in the Valley, we were naturally somewhat excited, and Lady Carnarvon, I remember, insisted on digging out these jars—beautiful specimens they were—with her own hands.

With the exception of the ground covered by the workmen's huts, we had now exhausted the whole of our triangular area, and had found no tomb. I was still hopeful, but we decided to leave this particular section until, by making a very early start in the autumn, we could accomplish it without causing inconvenience to visitors.

For our next attempt we selected the small lateral valley in which the tomb of Thothmes III was situated. This occupied us throughout the whole of the two following seasons, and, though nothing intrinsically valuable was found, we discovered an interesting archaeological fact. The actual tomb in which Thothmes III was buried had been found by Loret in 1898, hidden in a cleft in an inaccessible spot some way up the face of the cliff. Excavating in the valley below, we came upon the beginning of a tomb, by its foundation deposits originally intended for the same king. Presumably, while the work on this low-level tomb was in progress, it occurred to Thothmes or to his architect that the cleft in the rock above was a better site. It certainly presented better chances of concealment, if that were the reason for the change; though probably the more plausible explanation would be that one of the torrential downpours of rain which visit Luxor occasionally may have flooded out the lower tomb, and suggested to Thothmes that his mummy would have a more comfortable resting-place on a higher level.

Near by, at the entrance to another abandoned tomb, we came upon foundation-deposits of his wife Merytrehatshepsut, sister of the great queen of that name. Whether we are to infer that she was buried there is a moot point, for it would be contrary to all custom to find a queen in the Valley. In any case the tomb was afterwards appropriated by the Theban official, Sennefer.

We had now dug in the Valley for several seasons with extremely scanty results, and it became a much debated question whether we should continue the work, or try for a more profitable site elsewhere. After these barren years were we justified in going on with it? My own feeling was that so long as a single area of untouched ground remained the risk was worth taking. It is true that you may find less in more time in the Valley than in any other site in Egypt, but, on the other hand, if a lucky strike be made, you will be repaid for years and years of dull and unprofitable work.

There was still, moreover, the combination of flint boulders and workmen's huts at the foot of the tomb of Rameses VI to be investigated, and I had always had a kind of superstitious feeling that in that particular corner of the Valley one of the missing kings, possibly Tutankhamen, might be found. Certainly the stratification of the debris there should indicate a tomb. Eventually we decided to devote a final season to the Valley, and, by making an early start, to cut off access to the tomb of Rameses VI, if that should prove necessary, at a time when it would cause least inconvenience to visitors. That brings us to the present season and the results that are known to everyone.

5

The finding of the Tomb

THE HISTORY of the Valley, as I have endeavoured to show in former chapters, has never lacked the dramatic element, and in this, the latest episode, it has held to its traditions. For consider the circumstances. This was to be our final season in the Valley. Six full seasons we had excavated there, and season after season had drawn a blank; we had worked for months at a stretch and found nothing, and only an excavator knows how desperately depressing that can be; we had almost made up our minds that we were beaten, and were preparing to leave the Valley and try our luck elsewhere; and then—hardly had we set hoe to ground in our last despairing effort than we made a discovery that far exceeded our wildest dreams. Surely, never before in the whole history of excavation has a full digging season been compressed within the space of five days.

Let me try and tell the story of it all. It will not be easy, for the dramatic suddenness of the initial discovery left me in a dazed condition, and the months that have followed have been so crowded with incident that I have hardly had time to think. Setting it down on paper will perhaps give me a chance to realize what has happened and all that it means.

I arrived in Luxor on 28 October, and by 1 November I had enrolled my workmen and was ready to begin. Our former excavations had stopped short at the north-east corner of the tomb of Rameses VI, and from this point I started trenching southwards. It will be remembered that in this area there were a number of roughly constructed workmen's huts, used probably by the labourers in the tomb of Rameses. These huts, built about three feet above bed-rock, covered the whole area in front of the Ramesside tomb, and continued in a southerly direction to join up with a similar group of huts on the opposite side of the Valley, discovered by Davis in connexion with his work on the Akhenaten cache. By the evening of 3 November we had laid bare a sufficient number of these huts for experimental purposes, so, after we had planned and noted them, they were removed, and we were ready to clear away the three feet of soil that lay beneath them.

Hardly had I arrived on the work next morning (4 November) than the unusual silence, due to the stoppage of the work, made me realize that something out of the ordinary had happened, and I was greeted by the announcement that a step cut in the rock had been discovered underneath the very first hut to be attacked. This seemed too good to be true, but a short amount of extra clearing revealed the fact that we were actually in the entrance of a steep cut in the rock, some thirteen feet below the entrance to the tomb of Rameses VI, and a similar depth from the present bed level of the Valley. The manner of cutting was that of the sunken stairway entrance so common in the Valley, and I almost dared to hope that we had found our tomb at last. Work continued feverishly throughout the whole of that day and the morning of the next, but it was not until the afternoon of 5 November that we succeeded in clearing away the masses of rubbish that overlay the cut, and were able to demarcate the upper edges of the stairway on all its four sides.

It was clear by now beyond any question that we actually had before us the entrance to a tomb, but doubts, born of previous disappointments, persisted in creeping in. There was always the horrible possibility, suggested by our experience in the Thothmes III Valley, that the tomb was an unfinished one, never completed and never used: if it had been finished there was the depressing probability that it had been completely plundered in ancient times. On the other hand, there was just the chance of an untouched or only partially plundered tomb, and it was with ill-suppressed excitement that I watched the descending steps of the staircase, as one by one they came to light. The cutting was excavated in the side of a small hillock, and, as the work progressed, its western edge receded under the slope of the rock until it was, first partially, and then completely, roofed in, and became a passage, 10 feet high by 6 feet wide. Work progressed more rapidly now; step succeeded step, and at the level of the twelfth, towards sunset, there was disclosed the upper part of a doorway, blocked, plastered, and sealed.

A sealed doorway—it was actually true, then! Our years of patient labour were to be rewarded after all, and I think my first feeling was one of congratulation that my faith in the Valley had not been unjustified. With excitement growing to fever heat I searched the seal impressions on the door for evidence of the identity of the owner, but could find no name: the only decipherable ones were those of the well-known royal necropolis seal, the jackal and nine captives. Two facts, however, were clear: first, the employment of this royal seal was certain evidence that the tomb had been constructed for a person of very high standing; and second, that the sealed door was entirely screened from above by workmen's huts of the Twentieth Dynasty was sufficiently clear proof that at least from that date it had never been entered. With that for the moment I had to be content.

While examining the seals I noticed, at the top of the doorway, where some of the plaster had fallen away, a heavy wooden lintel. Under this, to assure myself of the method by which the doorway had been blocked, I made a small peephole, just large enough to insert an electric torch, and discovered that the passage beyond the door was filled completely from floor to ceiling with stones and rubble—additional proof this of the care with which the tomb had been protected.

It was a thrilling moment for an excavator. Alone, save for my native workmen, I found myself, after years of comparatively unproductive labour, on the threshold of what might prove to be a magnificent discovery. Anything, literally anything, might lie beyond that passage, and it needed all my self-control to keep from breaking down the doorway, and investigating then and there.

One thing puzzled me, and that was the smallness of the opening in comparison with the ordinary Valley tombs. The design was certainly of the Eighteenth Dynasty. Could it be the tomb of a noble buried here by royal consent? Was it a royal cache, a hiding-place to which a mummy and its equipment had been removed for safety? Or was it actually the tomb of the king for whom I had spent so many years in search?

Once more I examined the seal impressions for a clue, but on the part of the door so far laid bare only those of the royal necropolis seal already mentioned were clear enough to read. Had I but known that a few inches lower down there was a perfectly clear and distinct impression of the seal of Tutankhamen, the king I most desired to find, I would have cleared on, had a much better night's rest in consequence, and saved myself nearly three weeks of uncertainty. It was late, however, and darkness was already upon us. With some reluctance I re-closed the small

The tombs of Rameses VI and Tutankhamen

hole that I had made, filled in our excavation for protection during the night, selected the most trustworthy of my workmen—themselves almost as excited as I was—to watch all night above the tomb, and so home by moonlight, riding down the Valley.

Naturally my wish was to go straight ahead with our clearing to find out the full extent of the discovery, but Lord Carnarvon was in England, and in fairness to him I had to delay matters until he could come. Accordingly, on the morning of 6 November I sent him the following cable: "At last have made wonderful discovery in Valley; a magnificent tomb with seals intact; re-covered same for your arrival; congratulations."

My next task was to secure the doorway against interference until such time as it could finally be reopened. This we did by filling our excavation up again to surface level, and rolling on top of it the large flint boulders of which the workmen's huts had been composed. By the evening of the same day, exactly forty-eight hours after we had discovered the first step of the staircase, this was accomplished. The tomb had vanished. So far as the appearance of the ground was concerned there never had been any tomb, and I found it hard to persuade myself at times that the whole episode had not been a dream.

I was soon to be reassured on this point. News travels fast in Egypt, and within two days of the discovery congratulations, inquiries, and offers of help descended upon me in a steady stream from all directions. It became clear, even at this early stage, that I was in for a job that could not be tackled single-handed, so I wired to Callender, who had helped me on various previous occasions, asking him if possible to join me without delay, and to my relief he arrived on the very next day. On the 8th I had received two messages from Lord Carnarvon in answer to my cable, the first of which read, "Possibly come soon," and the second, received a little later, "Propose arrive Alexandria 20th."

We had thus nearly a fortnight's grace, and we devoted it to making preparations of various kinds, so that when the time of reopening came, we should be able, with the least possible delay, to handle any situation that might arise. On the night of the 18th I went to Cairo for three days, to meet Lord Carnarvon and make a number of necessary purchases, returning to Luxor on the 21st. On the 23rd Lord Carnarvon arrived in Luxor with his daughter, Lady Evelyn Herbert, his devoted companion in all his Egyptian work, and everything was in hand for the beginning of the second chapter of the discovery of the tomb. Callender had been busy all day clearing away the upper layer of rubbish, so that by morning we should be able to get into the staircase without any delay.

By the afternoon of the 24th the whole staircase was clear, sixteen steps in all, and we were able to make a proper examination of the sealed doorway. On the lower part the seal impressions were much clearer, and we were able without any difficulty to make out on several of them the name of Tutankhamen. This added enormously to the interest of the discovery. If we had found, as seemed almost certain, the tomb of that shadowy monarch, whose tenure of the throne coincided with one of the most interesting periods in the whole of Egyptian history, we should indeed have reason to congratulate ourselves.

With heightened interest, if that were possible, we renewed our investigation of the doorway. Here for the first time a disquieting element made its appearance. Now that the whole door was exposed to light it was possible to discern a fact that had hitherto escaped notice—that there had been two successive openings and re-closings of a part of its surface: furthermore, that the sealing originally discovered, the jackal and nine captives, had been applied to the re-closed portions, whereas the sealings of Tutankhamen covered the untouched part of the doorway, and were therefore those with which the tomb had been originally secured. The tomb then was not absolutely intact, as we had hoped. Plunderers had entered it, and entered it more than once—from the evidence of the huts above, plunderers of a date not later than the reign of

The "mannequin" of Tutankhamen

Seal impressions

Rameses VI—but that they had not rifled it completely was evident from the fact that it had been re-sealed.[1]

Then came another puzzle. In the lower strata of rubbish that filled the staircase we found masses of broken potsherds and boxes, the latter bearing the names of Akhenaten, Smenkhkare and Tutankhamen, and, what was much more upsetting, a scarab of Thothmes III and a fragment with the name of Amenhetep III. Why this mixture of names? The balance of evidence so far would seem to indicate a cache rather than a tomb, and at this stage in the proceedings we inclined more and more to the opinion that we were about to find a miscellaneous collection of objects of the Eighteenth Dynasty kings, brought from Tell el Amarna by Tutankhamen and deposited here for safety.

So matters stood on the evening of the 24th. On the following day the sealed doorway was to be removed, so Callender set carpenters to work making a heavy wooden grille to be set up in its place. Mr. Engelbach, Chief Inspector of the Antiquities Department, paid us a visit during the afternoon, and witnessed part of the final clearing of rubbish from the doorway.

On the morning of the 25th the seal impressions on the doorway were carefully noted and photographed, and then we removed the actual blocking of the door, consisting of rough stones carefully built from floor to lintel, and heavily plastered on their outer faces to take the seal impressions.

This disclosed the beginning of a descending passage (not a staircase), the same width as the entrance stairway, and nearly seven feet high. As I had already discovered from my hole in the doorway, it was filled completely with stone and rubble, probably the chip from its own excavation. This filling, like the doorway, showed distinct signs of more than one opening and re-closing of the tomb, the untouched part consisting of clean white chip, mingled with dust, whereas the disturbed part was composed mainly of dark flint. It was clear that an irregular tunnel had been cut through the original filling at the upper corner on the left side, a tunnel corresponding in position with that of the hole in the doorway.

As we cleared the passage we found, mixed with the rubble of the lower levels, broken potsherds, jar sealings, alabaster jars, whole and broken, vases of painted pottery, numerous fragments of smaller articles, and water skins, these last having obviously been used to bring up the water needed for the plastering of the doorways. These were clear evidence of plundering, and we eyed them askance. By night we had cleared a considerable distance down the passage, but as yet saw no sign of second doorway or of chamber.

The day following (26 November) was the day of days, the most wonderful that I have ever lived through, and certainly one whose like I can never hope to see again. Throughout the morning the work of clearing continued, slowly perforce, on account of the delicate objects that were mixed with the filling. Then, in the middle of the afternoon, thirty feet down from the outer door, we came upon a second sealed doorway, almost an exact replica of the first. The seal impressions in this case were less distinct, but still recognizable as those of Tutankhamen and of the royal necropolis. Here again the signs of opening and re-closing were clearly marked upon the plaster. We were firmly convinced by this time that it was a cache that we were about to open, and not a tomb. The arrangement of stairway, entrance passage and doors reminded us very forcibly of the cache of Akhenaten and Tyi material found in the very near vicinity of the present excavation by Davis, and the fact that Tutankhamen's seals occurred there likewise seemed almost certain proof that we were right in our conjecture. We were soon to know. There lay the sealed doorway, and behind it was the answer to the question.

Slowly, desperately slowly it seemed to us as we watched, the remains of passage debris that encumbered the lower part of the doorway were removed, until at last we had the whole door clear before us. The decisive moment had arrived. With trembling hands I made a tiny breach in the upper left-hand corner. Darkness and blank space, as far as an iron testing-rod could reach, showed that whatever lay beyond was empty, and not filled like the passage we had just cleared. Candle tests were applied as a precaution against possible foul gases, and then, widening the hole a little, I inserted the candle and peered in, Lord Carnarvon, Lady Evelyn and Callender standing anxiously beside me to hear the verdict. At first I could see nothing, the hot air escaping from the chamber causing the candle flame to flicker, but presently, as my eyes grew accustomed to the light, details of the room within emerged slowly from the mist, strange animals, statues, and gold—everywhere the glint of gold. For the moment—an eternity it must have seemed to the others standing by—I was struck dumb with amazement, and when Lord Carnarvon, unable to stand the suspense any longer, inquired anxiously, "Can you see anything?" it was all I could do to get out the words, "Yes, wonderful things." Then, widening the hole a little further, so that we both could see, we inserted an electric torch.

Overleaf: "wonderful things . . ."

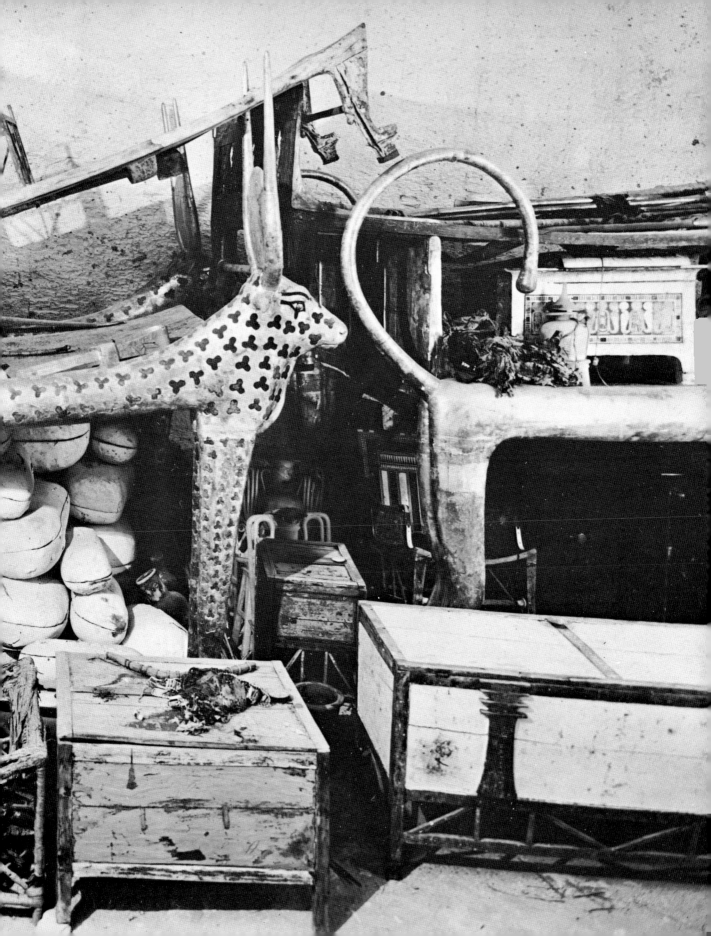

6

A preliminary investigation

I SUPPOSE MOST EXCAVATORS would confess to a feeling of awe—embarrassment almost—when they break into a chamber closed and sealed by pious hands so many centuries ago. For the moment, time as a factor in human life has lost its meaning. Three thousand, four thousand years maybe, have passed and gone since human feet last trod the floor on which you stand, and yet, as you note the signs of recent life around you—the half-filled bowl of mortar for the door, the blackened lamp, the finger-mark upon the freshly painted surface, the farewell garland dropped upon the threshold—you feel it might have been but yesterday. The very air you breathe, unchanged throughout the centuries, you share with those who laid the mummy to its rest. Time is annihilated by little intimate details such as these, and you feel an intruder.

That is perhaps the first and dominant sensation, but others follow thick and fast—the exhilaration of discovery, the fever of suspense, the almost overmastering impulse, born of curiosity, to break down seals and lift the lids of boxes, the thought—pure joy to the investigator—that you are about to add a page to history, or solve some problem of research, the strained expectancy—why not confess it?—of the treasure-seeker. Did these thoughts actually pass through our minds at the time, or have I imagined them since? I cannot tell. It was the discovery that my memory was blank, and not the mere desire for dramatic chapter-ending, that occasioned this digression.

Surely never before in the whole history of excavation had such an amazing sight been seen as the light of our torch revealed to us. The photographs which have subsequently been published were taken afterwards when the tomb had been opened and electric light installed. Let the reader imagine how the objects appeared to us as we looked down upon them from our spy-hole in the blocked doorway, casting the beam of light from our torch—the first light that had pierced the darkness of the chamber for three thousand years—from one group of objects to another, in a vain attempt to interpret the treasure that lay before us. The effect was bewildering, overwhelming. I suppose we had never formulated exactly in our minds just what we had expected or hoped to see, but certainly we had never dreamed of anything like this, a roomful—a whole museumful it seemed—of objects, some familiar, but some the like of which we had never seen, piled one upon another in seemingly endless profusion.

Gradually the scene grew clearer, and we could pick out individual objects. First, right opposite to us—we had been conscious of them all the while, but refused to believe in them—were three great gilt couches, their sides carved in the form of monstrous animals, curiously attenuated in body, as they had to be to serve their purpose, but with heads of startling realism. Uncanny beasts enough to look upon at any time: seen as we saw them, their brilliant gilded surfaces picked out of the darkness by our electric torch, as though by limelight, their heads throwing grotesque distorted shadows on the wall behind them, they were almost terrifying. Next, on the right, two statues caught and held our attention; two life-sized figures of a king in black, facing each other like sentinels, gold kilted, gold sandalled, armed with mace and staff, the protective sacred cobra upon their foreheads.

These were the dominant objects that caught the eye at first. Between them, around them, piled on top of them, there were countless others—exquisitely painted and inlaid caskets; alabaster vases, some beautifully carved in openwork designs; strange black shrines, from the open door of one a great gilt snake peeping out; bouquets of flowers or leaves; beds; chairs beautifully carved; a golden inlaid throne; a heap of curious white oviform boxes; staves of all shapes and designs; beneath our eyes, on the very threshold of the chamber, a beautiful lotiform cup of translucent alabaster; on the left a confused pile of overturned chariots, glistening with gold and inlay; and peeping from behind them another portrait of a king.

Such were some of the objects that lay before us. Whether we noted them all at the time I cannot say for certain, as our minds were in much too excited and confused a state to register accurately. Presently it dawned upon our bewildered brains that in all this medley of objects before us there was no coffin or trace of mummy, and the much-debated question of tomb or cache began to intrigue us afresh. With this question in view we re-examined the scene before us, and noticed for the first time that between the two black sentinel statues on the right there was another sealed doorway. The explanation gradually dawned upon us. We were but on the threshold of our discovery. What we saw was merely an antechamber. Behind the guarded door there were to be other chambers, possibly a succession of them, and in one of them, beyond any shadow of doubt, in all his magnificent panoply of death, we should find the Pharaoh lying.

We had seen enough, and our brains began to reel at the thought of the task in front of us. We re-closed the hole, locked the wooden grille that had been placed upon the first doorway, left our native staff on guard, mounted our donkeys and rode home down the Valley, strangely silent and subdued.

It was curious, as we talked things over in the evening, to find how conflicting our ideas were as to what we had seen. Each of us had noted something that the others had not, and it amazed us next day to discover how many and how obvious were the things that we had missed. Naturally, it was the sealed door between the statues that intrigued us most, and we debated far into the night the possibilities of what might lie behind it. A single chamber with the king's sarcophagus? That was the least we might expect. But why one chamber only? Why not a succession of passages and chambers, leading, in true Valley style, to an innermost shrine of all, the burial chamber? It might be so, and yet in plan the tomb was quite unlike the others. Visions of chamber after chamber, each crowded with objects like the one we had seen, passed through our minds and left us gasping for breath. Then came the thought of the plunderers again. Had they succeeded in penetrating this third doorway—seen from a distance it looked absolutely untouched—and, if so, what were our chances of finding the king's mummy intact? I think we slept but little, all of us, that night.

Next morning (27 November) we were early on the field, for there was much to be done. It was essential, before proceeding further with our examination, that we should have some more adequate means of illumination, so Callender began laying wires to connect us up with the main lighting system of the Valley. While this was in preparation we made careful notes of the seal-impressions upon the inner doorway and then removed its entire blocking. By noon everything was ready and Lord Carnarvon, Lady Evelyn, Callender and I entered the tomb and made a careful inspection of the first chamber (afterwards called the Antechamber). The evening before I had written to Mr. Engelbach, the Chief Inspector of the Antiquities Department, advising him of the progress of clearing, and asking him to come over and make an official inspection. Unfortunately he was at the moment in Kena on official business, so the local Antiquities Inspector, Ibraham Effendi, came in his stead.

By the aid of our powerful electric lamps many things that had been obscure to us on the previous day became clear, and we were able to make a more accurate estimate of the extent of our discovery. Our first objective was naturally the sealed door between the statues, and here a disappointment awaited us. Seen from a distance it presented all the appearance of an absolutely intact blocking, but close examination revealed the fact that a small breach had been made near the bottom, just wide enough to admit a boy or a slightly built man, and that the hole made had subsequently been filled up and re-sealed. We were not then to be the first. Here, too, the thieves had forestalled us, and it only remained to be seen how much damage they had had the opportunity or the time to effect.

Our natural impulse was to break down the door, and get to the bottom of the matter at once, but to do so would have entailed serious risk of damage to many of the objects in the Antechamber, a risk which we were by no means prepared to face. Nor could we move the objects in question out of the way, for it was imperative that a plan and complete photographic record should be made before anything was touched, and this was a task involving a considerable amount of time, even if we had had sufficient plant available—which we had not—to carry it through immediately. Reluctantly we decided to abandon the opening of this inner sealed door until we had cleared the Antechamber of all its contents. By doing this we should not only ensure the complete scientific record of the outer chamber which it was our duty to make, but should have a clear field for the removal of the door-blocking, a ticklish operation at best.

Having satisfied to some extent our curiosity about the sealed doorway, we could now turn our attention to the rest of the chamber, and make a more detailed examination of the objects which it contained. It was certainly an astounding experience. Here, packed tightly together in this little chamber, were scores of objects, any one of which would have filled us with excitement under ordinary circumstances, and been considered ample repayment for a full season's work. Some were of types well enough known to us; others were new and strange, and in some cases these were complete and perfect examples of objects whose appearance we had heretofore but guessed at from the evidence of tiny broken fragments found in other royal tombs.

Nor was it merely from a point of view of quantity that the find was so amazing. The period to which the tomb belongs is in many respects the most interesting in the whole history of Egyptian art, and we were prepared for beautiful things. What we were not prepared for was the astonishing vitality and animation which characterized certain of the objects. It was a revelation to us of unsuspected possibilities in Egyptian art, and we realized, even in this hasty preliminary survey, that a study of the material would involve a modification, if not a complete revolution, of all our old ideas. That, however, is a matter for the future. We shall get a clearer estimate of exact artistic values when we have cleared the whole tomb and have the complete contents before us.

One of the first things we noted in our survey was that all of the larger objects, and most of the smaller ones, were inscribed with the name of Tutankhamen. His, too, were the seals upon the innermost door, and therefore his, beyond any shadow of doubt, the mummy that ought to lie behind it. Next, while we were still excitedly calling each other from one object to another, came a new discovery. Peering beneath the southernmost of the three great couches, we noticed a small irregular hole in the wall. Here was yet another sealed doorway, and a plunderers' hole which, unlike the others, had never been repaired. Cautiously we crept under the couch, inserted our portable light, and there before us lay another chamber, rather smaller than the first, but even more crowded with objects.

The sealed door between the statues

The state of this inner room (afterwards called the Annexe) simply defies description. In the Antechamber there had been some sort of an attempt to tidy up after the plunderers' visit, but here everything was in confusion, just as they had left it. Nor did it take much imagination to picture them at their work. One—there would probably not have been room for more than one— had crept into the chamber, and had then hastily but systematically ransacked its entire contents, emptying boxes, throwing things aside, piling them one upon another, and occasionally passing objects through the hole to his companions for closer examination in the outer chamber. He had done his work just about as thoroughly as an earthquake. Not a single inch of floor space remains vacant, and it will be a matter of considerable difficulty, when the time for clearing comes, to know how to begin. So far we have not made any attempt to enter the chamber, but have contented outselves with taking stock from outside. Beautiful things it contains, too,

The state of the Annexe

smaller than those in the Antechamber for the most part, but many of them of exquisite work-manship. Several things remain in my mind particularly—a painted box, apparently quite as lovely as the one in the Antechamber; a wonderful chair of ivory, gold, wood, and leather-work; alabaster and faience vases of beautiful form; and a gaming board, in carved and coloured ivory.

I think the discovery of this second chamber, with its crowded contents, had a somewhat sobering effect upon us. Excitement had gripped us hitherto, and given us no pause for thought, but now for the first time we began to realize what a prodigious task we had in front of us, and what a responsibility it entailed. This was no ordinary find, to be disposed of in a normal season's work; nor was there any precedent to show us how to handle it. The thing was outside all experience, bewildering, and for the moment it seemed as though there were more to be done than any human agency could accomplish.

Moreover, the extent of our discovery had taken us by surprise, and we were wholly unprepared to deal with the multitude of objects that lay before us, many in a perishable condition, and needing careful preservative treatment before they could be touched. There were numberless things to be done before we could even begin the work of clearing. Vast stores of preservatives and packing material must be laid in; expert advice must be taken as to the best method of dealing with certain objects; provision must be made for a laboratory, some safe and sheltered spot in which the objects could be treated, catalogued and packed; a careful plan to scale must be made, and a complete photographic record taken, while everything was still in position; a dark-room must be contrived.

These were but a few of the problems that confronted us. Clearly, the first thing to be done was to render the tomb safe against robbery; we could then with easy minds work out our plans—plans which we realized by this time would involve, not one season only, but certainly two, and possibly three or four. We had our wooden grille at the entrance to the passage, but that was not enough, and I measured up the inner doorway for a gate of thick steel bars. Until we could get this made for us—and for this and for other reasons it was imperative for me to visit Cairo—we must go to the labour of filling in the tomb once more.

Meanwhile the news of the discovery had spread like wildfire, and all sorts of extraordinary and fanciful reports were going abroad concerning it; one story, that found considerable credence among the natives, being to the effect that three aeroplanes had landed in the Valley, and gone off to some destination unknown with loads of treasure. To overtake these rumours as far as possible, we decided on two things—first, to invite Lord Allenby and the various heads of the departments concerned to come and pay a visit to the tomb, and secondly, to send an authoritative account of the discovery to *The Times*. On the 29th, accordingly, we had an official opening of the tomb, at which were present Lady Allenby—Lord Allenby was unfortunately unable to leave Cairo—Abd el Aziz Bey Yehia, the Governor of the Province, Mohamed Bey Fahmy, Mamour of the District, and a number of other Egyptian notables and officials; and on the 30th Mr. Tottenham, Adviser to the Ministry of Public Works, and M. Pierre Lacau, Director-General of the Service of Antiquities, who had been unable to be present on the previous day, made their official inspection. Mr. Merton, *The Times* correspondent, was also present at the official opening, and sent the dispatch which created so much excitement at home.

On 3 December, after closing up the entrance doorway with heavy timber, the tomb was filled to surface level. Lord Carnarvon and Lady Evelyn left on the 4th, on their way to England, to conclude various arrangements there, preparatory to returning later in the season; and on the 6th, leaving Callender to watch over the tomb in my absence, I followed them to Cairo to make my purchases. My first care was the steel gate, and I ordered it the morning I arrived, under promise that it should be delivered within six days. The other purchases I took more leisurely, and a miscellaneous collection they were, including photographic material, chemicals, a motor-car, packing-boxes of every kind, with thirty-two bales of calico, more than a mile of wadding, and as much again of surgical bandages. Of these last two important items I was determined not to run short.

While in Cairo I had time to take stock of the position, and it became more and more clear to me that assistance—and that on a big scale—was necessary if the work in the tomb was to be carried out in a satisfactory manner. The question was, where to turn for this assistance. The first and pressing need was in photography, for nothing could be touched until a complete photographic record had been made, a task involving technical skill of the highest order. A day or two after I arrived in Cairo I received a cable of congratulation from Mr. Lythgoe, Curator of the Egyptian Department of the Metropolitan Museum of Art, New York, whose concession at Thebes ran in close proximity to our own, being only divided by the natural mountain wall, and in my reply I somewhat diffidently inquired whether it would be possible—for the immediate emergency, at any rate—to secure the assistance of Mr. Harry Burton, their photographic expert. He promptly cabled back, and his cable ought to go on record as an example of disinterested scientific co-operation: "Only too delighted to assist in any possible way. Please call on Burton and any other members of our staff."

This offer was subsequently most generously confirmed by the Trustees and the Director of the Metropolitan Museum, and on my return to Luxor I arranged with my friend Mr. Winlock, the director of the New York excavations on that concession, and who was to be the actual sufferer under the arrangement, not only that Mr. Burton should be transferred, but that Mr. Hall and Mr. Hauser, draughtsmen to the expedition, should devote such of their time as might be necessary to make a large-scale drawing of the Antechamber and its contents. Another member of the New York staff, Mr. Mace, director of their excavations on the pyramid field at Lisht, was also available, and at Mr. Lythgoe's suggestion cabled offering help. Thus no fewer than four members of the New York staff were for whole or part time associated in the work of the season. Without this generous help it would have been impossible to tackle the enormous task.

Another piece of luck befell me in Cairo. Mr. Lucas, Director of the Chemical Department of the Egyptian Goverment, was taking three months' leave prior to retiring from the Government on completion of service, and for this three months he generously offered to place his chemical knowledge at our disposal, an offer which, needless to say, I hastened to accept. That completed our regular working staff. In addition, Dr. Alan Gardiner kindly undertook to deal with any inscriptional material that might be found, and Professor Breasted, in a couple of visits, gave us much assistance in the difficult task of deciphering the seal impressions.

By 13 December the steel gate was finished and I had completed my purchases. I returned to Luxor, and on the 15th everything arrived safely in the Valley, delivery of the packages having been greatly expedited by the courtesy of the Egyptian State Railway officials, who permitted them to travel by express instead of on the slow freight train. On the 16th we opened up the tomb once more, and on the 17th the steel gate was set up in the door of the chamber and we were ready to begin work. On the 18th work was actually begun, Burton making his first experiments in the Antechamber, and Hall and Hauser making a start on their plan. Two days later Lucas arrived, and at once began experimenting on preservatives for the various objects.

On the 22nd, as the result of a good deal of clamour, permission to see the tomb was given to the Press, both European and native, and the opportunity was also afforded to a certain number of the native notables of Luxor, who had been disappointed at not receiving an invitation to the official opening. It had only been possible on that occasion to invite a very limited number, owing to a difficulty of ensuring the safety of the objects in the very narrow space that was available. On the 25th Mace arrived, and two days later, photographs and plans being sufficiently advanced, the first object was removed from the tomb.

The steel gate in position

7

A survey of the Antechamber

IN THIS CHAPTER we propose to make a detailed survey of the objects in the Antechamber, and it will give the reader a better idea of things if we make it systematically, and do not range backwards and forwards from one end of it to the other, as in the first excitement of discovery we naturally did. It was but a small room, some 26 feet by 12 feet, and we had to tread warily, for, though the officials had cleared for us a small alleyway in the centre, a single false step or hasty movement would have inflicted irreparable damage on one of the delicate objects with which we were surrounded.

In front of us, in the doorway—we had to step over it to get into the chamber—lay a beautiful wishing-cup. It was of pure semi-translucent alabaster, with lotus-flower handles on either side, supporting the kneeling figures which symbolize Eternity. Turning right as we entered, we noticed, first, a large cylindrical jar of alabaster; next, two funerary bouquets of leaves, one leaning against the wall, the other fallen; and in front of them, standing out into the chamber, a painted wooden casket. This last will probably rank as one of the greatest artistic treasures of the tomb, and on our first visit we found it hard to tear ourselves away from it. Its outer face was completely covered with gesso; upon this prepared surface there were a series of brilliantly coloured and exquisitely painted designs—hunting scenes upon the curved panels of the lid, battle scenes upon the sides, and upon the ends representations of the king in lion form, trampling his enemies under his feet. Descriptions give but a faint idea of the delicacy of the painting, which far surpasses anything of the kind that Egypt has yet produced. No photograph could do it justice, for even in the original a magnifying glass is essential to a due appreciation of the smaller details, such as the stippling of the lions' coats, or the decoration of the horses' trappings.

There is another remarkable thing about the painted scenes upon this box. The motives are Egyptian and the treatment Egyptian, and yet they leave an impression on your mind of something strangely non-Egyptian, and you cannot for the life of you explain exactly where the difference lies. They remind you of other things, too—the finest Persian miniatures, for instance —and there is a curious floating impression of Benozzo Gozzoli, due, maybe, to the gay little tufts of flowers which fill the vacant spaces. The contents of the box were a queer jumble. At the top there were a pair of rush and papyrus sandals, and a royal robe, completely covered with a decoration of beadwork and gold sequins. Beneath them were other decorated robes, one of which had had attached to it upwards of three thousand gold rosettes, three pairs of court sandals elaborately worked in gold, a gilt head-rest, and other miscellaneous objects. This was the first box we opened, and the ill-assorted nature of its contents—to say nothing

The painted wooden casket

of the manner in which they were crushed and bundled together—was a considerable puzzle to us. The reason of it became plain enough later, as we shall show in the following chapter.

Next, omitting some small unimportant objects, we came to the end (north) wall of the chamber. Here was the tantalizing sealed doorway, and on either side of it, mounting guard over the entrance, stood the life-size wooden statues of the king already described. Strange and imposing figures these, even as we first saw them, surrounded and half concealed by other objects: as they stand now in the empty chamber, with nothing in front of them to distract the eye, and beyond them, through the opened door, the golden shrine half visible, they present an appearance that is almost painfully impressive. Originally they were shrouded in shawls of linen, and this, too, must have added to the effect. One other point about this end wall, and an interesting one. Unlike the other walls of the chamber, its whole surface was covered with plaster, and a close examination revealed the fact that from top to bottom it was but a blind, a mere partition wall.

Turning now to the long (west) wall of the chamber, we found the whole of the wall-space occupied by the three great animal-sided couches, curious pieces of furniture which we knew from illustrations in the tomb paintings, but of which we had never seen actual examples before. The first was lion-headed, the second cow-headed, and the third had the head of a composite animal, half hippopotamus and half crocodile. Each was made in four pieces for convenience in carrying, the frame of the actual bed fitting by means of hook and staple to the animal sides, the feet of the animals themselves fitting into an open pedestal. As is usually the case in Egyptian beds, each had a foot panel but nothing at the head. Above, below, and around these couches, packed tightly together, and in some cases perched precariously one upon another, was a miscellany of smaller objects, of which we shall only have space here to mention the more important.

Thus, resting on the northernmost of the couches—the lion-headed one—there was a bed of ebony and woven cord, with a panel of household gods delightfully carved, and, resting upon this again, there were a collection of elaborately decorated staves, a quiverful of arrows, and a number of compound bows. One of these last was cased with gold and decorated with bands of inscription and animal motives in granulated work of almost inconceivable fineness—a masterpiece of jewellers' craft. Another, a double compound bow, terminated at either end in the carved figure of a captive, so arranged that their necks served as notches for the string, the pleasing idea being that every time the king used the bow he bow-strung a brace of captives. Between bed and couch there were four torch-holders of bronze and gold, absolutely new in type, one with its torch of twisted linen still in position in the oil-cup; a charmingly wrought alabaster libation vase; and, its lid resting askew, a casket, with decorative panels of brilliant turquoise blue faience and gold. This casket, as we found later in the laboratory, contained a number of interesting and valuable objects, among others a leopard-skin priestly robe, with decoration of gold and silver stars and gilt leopard-head, inlaid with coloured glass; a very large and beautifully worked scarab of gold and lapis lazuli blue glass; a buckle of sheet gold, with a decoration of hunting scenes applied in infinitesimally small granules; a sceptre in solid gold and lapis lazuli glass; beautifully coloured collarettes and necklaces of faience; and a handful of massive gold rings, twisted up in a fold of linen—of which more anon.

Beneath the couch, resting on the floor, stood a large chest, made of a delightful combination of ebony, ivory, and red wood, which contained a number of small vases of alabaster and glass; two black wooden shrines, each containing the gilt figure of a snake, emblem and standard of the tenth nome of Upper Egypt (Aphroditopolis); a delightful little chair, with decorative panels of ebony, ivory, and gold, too small for other than a child's use; two folding duck-stools, inlaid with ivory; and an alabaster box, with incised ornamentation filled in with pigments.

A long box of ebony and white painted wood, with trellis-worked stand and hinged lid, stood free upon the floor in front of the couch. Its contents were a curious mixture. At the top, crumpled together and stuffed in as packing, there were shirts and a number of the king's under-garments, whereas below, more or less orderly arranged upon the bottom of the box, there were sticks, bows, and a large number of arrows, the points of these last having all been broken off and stolen for their metal. As originally deposited, the box probably contained nothing but sticks, bows and arrows, and included not only those from the top of the bed already described, but a number of others which had been scattered in various quarters of the chamber. Some of the sticks were of very remarkable workmanship. One terminated in a curve, on which were fashioned the figures of a pair of captives, with tied arms and interlocked feet, the one an African, the other an Asiatic, their faces carved in ebony and ivory respectively. The latter figure is an almost painfully realistic piece of work. On another of the sticks a very effective decoration was contrived by arranging minute scales of iridescent beetle-wings in a pattern, while in others again there was an applied pattern of variegated barks. With the sticks there were a whip in ivory and four cubit measures. To the left of the couch, between it and the next one, there were a toilet table and a cluster of wonderful perfume jars in carved alabaster.

So much for the first couch. The second, the cow-headed one, facing us as we entered the chamber, was even more crowded. Resting precariously on top of it there was another bed of wood, painted white, and, balanced on top of this again, a rush-work chair, extraordinarily modern-looking in appearance and design, and an ebony and red-wood stool. Below the bed and resting actually on the framework of the couch, there were, among other things, an ornamental white stool, a curious rounded box of ivory and ebony veneer, and a pair of gilt *sistra* —instruments of music that are usually associated with Hathor, the goddess of joy and dancing.[1]

Detail from the cow-headed bed

Below, the centre space was occupied by a pile of oviform wooden cases, containing trussed ducks and a variety of other food offerings.

Standing on the floor in front of the couch there were two wooden boxes, one having a collarette and a pad of rings resting loose upon its lid; a large stool of rush-work, and a smaller one of wood and reed. The larger of the two boxes had an interesting and varied list of contents. A docket, written in hieratic on the lid, quotes seventeen objects of lapis lazuli blue, and within there were sixteen libation vases of blue faience, the seventeenth being found subsequently in another part of the chamber. In addition, thrown carelessly in, there were a number of other faience cups; a pair of electrum boomerangs, mounted at either end with blue faience; a beautiful little casket of carved ivory; a calcite wine-strainer; a very elaborate tapestry-woven garment; and the greater part of a corslet. This last—which we shall have occasion to describe at some length in Chapter 10—was composed of several thousand pieces of gold, glass, and faience, and there is no doubt that when it has been cleaned and its various parts assembled it will be the most imposing thing of its kind that Egypt has ever produced. Between this couch and the third one, tilted carelessly over on to its side, lay a magnificent cedarwood chair, elaborately and delicately carved, and embellished with gold.

We come now to the third couch, flanked by its pair of queer composite animals, with open mouths, and teeth and tongue of ivory. Resting on top of it in solitary state there was a large round-topped chest, with ebony frame and panels painted white. This was originally the chest of under-linen. It still contained a number of garments—loin-cloths, etc.—most of them folded and rolled into neat little bundles.[2] Below this couch stood another of the great artistic treasures of the tomb—perhaps the greatest so far taken out—a throne, overlaid with gold from top to bottom, and richly adorned with glass, faience, and stone inlay. Its legs, fashioned in feline form, were surmounted by lions' heads, fascinating in their strength and simplicity. Magnificent crowned and winged serpents formed the arms, and between the bars which supported the back there were six protective cobras, carved in wood, gilt and inlaid. It was the panel of the back, however, that was the chief glory of the throne, and I have no hesitation in claiming for it that it is the most beautiful thing that has yet been found in Egypt.

The scene is one of the halls of the palace, a room decorated with flower-garlanded pillars, frieze of *uraei* (royal cobras), and dado of conventional "recessed" panelling. Through a hole in the roof the sun shoots down his life-giving protective rays. The king himself sits in an unconventional attitude upon a cushioned throne, his arm thrown carelessly across its back. Before him stands the girlish figure of the queen, putting, apparently, the last touches to his toilet: in one hand she holds a small jar of scent or ointment, and with the other she gently anoints his shoulder or adds a touch of perfume to his collar. A simple homely little composition, but how instinct with life and feeling it is, and with what a sense of movement!

The colouring of the panel is extraordinarily vivid and effective. The face and other exposed portions of the bodies, both of king and queen, are of red glass, and the head-dresses of brilliant turquoise-like faience. The robes are of silver, dulled by age to an exquisite bloom. The crowns, collars, scarves, and other ornamental details of the panel are all inlaid, inlay of coloured glass and faience, of carnelian, and of a composition hitherto unknown—translucent fibrous calcite, underlaid with coloured paste, in appearance for all the world like *millefiori* glass. As background we have the sheet gold with which the throne was covered. In its original state, with gold and silver fresh and new, the throne must have been an absolutely dazzling sight—too dazzling, probably, for the eye of a Westerner, accustomed to drab skies and neutral tints: now, toned down a little by the tarnishing of the alloy, it presents a colour scheme that is extraordinarily attractive and harmonious.

Detail from the golden throne (see page 8)

Apart altogether from its artistic merit, the throne is an important historical document, the scenes upon it being actual illustrations of the politico-religious vacillations of the reign. In original conception—witness the human arms on the sun-disk in the back panel—they are based on pure Tell el Amarna Aten worship. The cartouches, however, are curiously mixed. In some of them the Aten element has been erased and the Amen form substituted, whereas in others the Aten remains unchallenged. It is curious, to say the least of it, that an object which bore such manifest signs of heresy upon it should be publicly buried in this, the stronghold of the Amen faith, and it is perhaps not without significance that on this particular part of the throne there were remains of a linen wrapping. It would appear that Tutankhamen's return to the ancient faith was not entirely a matter of conviction. He may have thought the throne too valuable a possession to destroy, and have kept it in one of the more private apartments of the palace; or, again, it is possible that the alteration in the Aten names was sufficient to appease the sectarians, and that there was no need for secrecy.

Upon the seat of the throne rested the footstool that originally stood before it, a stool of gilded wood and dark blue faience, with panels on the top and sides on which were represented captives, bound and prone. This was a very common convention in the East—"until I make thine enemies thy footstool," sings the Psalmist—and we may be sure that on certain occasions convention became actual fact.

Before the couch there were two stools, one of plain wood painted white, the other of ebony, ivory, and gold, its legs carved in the shape of ducks' heads, its top made in the semblance of leopard skin, with claws and spots of ivory—the finest example we know of its kind. Behind it, resting against the south wall of the chamber, there were a number of important objects. First came a shrine-shaped box with double doors, fastened by shooting bolts of ebony. This was entirely cased with thick sheet-gold, and on the gold, in delicate low relief, there were a series of little panels, depicting, in delightfully naïve fashion, a number of episodes in the daily life of king and queen. In all of these scenes the dominant note is that of friendly relationship between the husband and the wife, the unselfconscious friendliness that marks the Tell el Amarna school, and one would not be surprised to find that here, too, there had been a change in the cartouches from the Aten to the Amen. Within the shrine there was a pedestal, showing that it had originally contained a statuette: it may well have been a gold one, an object, unfortunately, too conspicuous for the plunderers to overlook. It also contained a necklace of enormous beads, gold, carnelian, green feldspar and blue glass, to which was attached a large gold pendant in the shape of a very rare snake goddess; and considerable portions of the corslet already referred to in our description of one of the earlier boxes.

Beside this shrine there was a large *shawabti* statuette of the king, carved, gilded, and painted, and a little farther along, peering out from behind the overturned body of a chariot, a statue of peculiar form, cut sharp off at waist and elbows. This was exactly life-size, and its body was painted white in evident imitation of a shirt; there can be very little doubt that it represents a mannequin, to which the king's robes, and possibly his collars, could be fitted. There were also in this same quarter of the chamber another toilet box and the scattered pieces of a gilt canopy or shrine. These last were of extremely light construction, and were made to fit rapidly one to another. The canopy was probably a travelling one, carried in the king's train wherever he went, and set up at a moment's notice to shield him from the sun.

The rest of the south wall and the whole of the east, as far as the entrance doorway, were taken up by the parts of no fewer than four chariots. They were heaped together in terrible confusion, the plunderers having evidently turned them this way and that, in their endeavours to secure the more valuable portions of the gold decoration which covered them. Theirs not the whole responsibility, however. The entrance passage was far too narrow to admit the ingress

The small golden shrine

of complete chariots, so, to enable them to get into the chamber, the axles were deliberately sawn in two, the wheels dismounted and piled together, and the dismembered bodies placed by themselves.

In the reassembling and restoration of these chariots we have a prodigious task ahead of us, but the results will be gorgeous enough to justify any amount of time that is bestowed upon them. From top to bottom they are covered with gold, every inch of which is decorated, either with embossed patterns and scenes upon the gold itself, or with inlaid designs in coloured glass and stone. The actual woodwork of the chariots is in good condition and needs but little treatment, but with the horse-trappings and other leather parts it is quite another story, the untanned leather having been affected by the damp and turned into a black, unpleasant-looking glue. Fortunately these leather parts were, in almost every instance, plated with gold, and from this gold, which is well preserved, we hope to be able to make a reconstruction of the harness. Mixed with the chariot parts there were a number of miscellaneous smaller objects, including alabaster jars, more sticks and bows, bead sandals, baskets, and a set of four horse-hair fly-whisks, with lion-head handles of gilded wood.

We have now made a complete tour of the Antechamber—a fairly comprehensive one, it seemed—and yet we find, by reference to our notes, that out of some six or seven hundred objects which it contained we have mentioned a scant hundred. Nothing but a complete catalogue, transcribed from our register cards, would give an adequate idea of the extent of the discovery, and in the present volume that is naturally out of the question. We must confine ourselves here to a more or less summary description of the principal finds, and reserve a detailed study of the objects for later publications. It would be impossible, in any case, to attempt such an account at the present moment, for there are months, possibly years, of reconstructive work ahead of us, if the material is to be treated as it deserves. We must remember, too, that we have dealt so far with but a single chamber. There are inner chambers still untouched, and we hope to find among their contents treasures far surpassing those with which the present volume is concerned.

The small golden shrine

8

Clearing the Antechamber

CLEARING THE OBJECTS from the Antechamber was like playing a gigantic game of spillikins. So crowded were they that it was a matter of extreme difficulty to move one without running serious risk of damaging others, and in some cases they were so inextricably tangled that an elaborate system of props and supports had to be devised to hold one object or group of objects in place while another was being removed. At such times life was a nightmare. One was afraid to move lest one should kick against a prop and bring the whole thing crashing down. Nor, in many cases, could one tell without experiment whether a particular object was strong enough to bear its own weight. Certain of the things were in beautiful condition, as strong as when they first were made, but others were in a most precarious state, and the problem constantly arose whether it would be better to apply preservative treatment to an object *in situ*, or to wait until it could be dealt with in more convenient surroundings in the laboratory. The latter course was adopted whenever possible, but there were cases in which the removal of an object without treatment would have meant almost certain destruction.

There were sandals, for instance, of patterned bead-work, of which the threading had entirely rotted away. As they lay on the floor of the chamber they looked in perfectly sound condition, but, try to pick one up, and it crumbled at the touch, and all you had for your pains was a handful of loose, meaningless beads. This was a clear case for treatment on the spot—a spirit stove, some paraffin wax, an hour or two to harden, and the sandal could be removed intact, and handled with the utmost freedom. The funerary bouquets again: without treatment as they stood they would have ceased to exist; subjected to three or four sprayings of celluloid solution they bore removal well, and were subsequently packed with scarcely any injury. Occasionally, particularly with the larger objects, it was found better to apply local treatment in the tomb, just sufficient to ensure a safe removal to the laboratory, where more drastic measures were possible. Each object presented a separate problem, and, as I said before, there were cases in which only experiment could show what the proper treatment was to be.

It was slow work, painfully slow, and nerve-racking at that, for one felt all the time a heavy weight of responsibility. Every excavator must, if he have any archaeological conscience at all. The things he finds are not his own property, to treat as he pleases, or neglect as he chooses. They are a direct legacy from the past to the present age, he but the privileged intermediary through whose hands they come; and if, by carelessness, slackness, or ignorance, he lessens the sum of knowledge that might have been obtained from them, he knows himself to be guilty of an archaeological crime of the first magnitude. Destruction of evidence is so painfully easy, and yet so hopelessly irreparable. Tired or pressed for time, you shirk a tedious piece of cleaning, or do it in a half-hearted, perfunctory sort of way, and you will perhaps have thrown away the one chance that will ever occur of gaining some important piece of knowledge.

Too many people—unfortunately there are so called archaeologists among them—are apparently under the impression that the object bought from a dealer's shop is just as valuable as one which has been found in actual excavation, and that until the object in question has been cleaned, entered in the books, marked with an accession number, and placed in a tidy museum case, it is not a proper subject for study at all. There was never a greater mistake. Field-work is all-important, and it is a sure and certain fact that if every excavation had been properly, systematically, and conscientiously carried out, our knowledge of Egyptian archaeology would be at least fifty per cent greater than it is. There are numberless derelict objects in the store-rooms of our museums which would give us valuable information could they but tell us whence they came, and box after box full of fragments which a few notes at the time of finding would have rendered capable of reconstruction.

Granting, then, that a heavy weight of responsibility must at all times rest upon the excavator, our own feelings on this occasion will easily be realized. It had been our privilege to find the most important collection of Egyptian antiquities that had ever seen the light, and it was for us to show that we were worthy of the trust. So many things there were that might go wrong. Danger of theft, for instance, was an ever-present anxiety. The whole countryside was agog with excitement about the tomb; all sorts of extravagant tales were current about the gold and jewels it contained; and, as past experience had shown, it was only too possible that there might be a serious attempt to raid the tomb by night. This possibility of robbery on a large scale was negatived, so far as was humanly possible, by a complicated system of guarding, there being present in the Valley, day and night, three independent groups of watchmen, each answerable to a different authority—the Government Antiquities Guards, a squad of soldiers supplied by the Mudir of Kena, and a selected group of the most trustworthy of our own staff. In addition, we had a heavy wooden grille at the entrance to the passage, and a massive steel gate at the inner doorway, each secured by four padlocked chains; and, that there might never be any mistake about these latter, the keys were in the permanent charge of one particular member of the European staff, who never parted with them for a moment, even to lend them to a colleague. Petty or casual theft we guarded against by doing all the handling of the objects ourselves.

Another and perhaps an even greater cause for anxiety was the condition of many of the objects. It was manifest with some of them that their very existence depended on careful manipulation and correct preservative treatment, and there were moments when our hearts were in our mouths. There were other worries, too—visitors, for instance, but I shall have quite a little to say about them later—and I fear that by the time the Antechamber was finished our nerves, to say nothing of our tempers, were in an extremely ragged state. But here am I talking about finishing before we have even begun. We must make a fresh start. It is not time to lose our tempers yet.

Obviously, our first and greatest need was photography. Before anything else was done, or anything moved, we must have a series of preliminary views, taken in panorama, to show the general appearance of the chamber. For lighting we had available two movable electric standards, giving 3,000 candle-power, and it was with these that all the photographic work in the tomb was done. Exposures were naturally rather slow, but the light was beautifully even, much more so than would have been afforded by flashlight—a dangerous process in such a crowded chamber—or reflected sunlight, which were the two possible alternatives. Fortunately for us, there was an uninscribed and empty tomb close by—the Davis cache tomb of Akhenaten. This we got permission from the Government to use as a dark room, and here Burton established himself. It was not too convenient in some ways, but it was worth while putting up with a little

Printed numbers on every object

inconvenience to have a dark room so close, for in the case of experimental exposures he could slip across and develop without moving his camera out of position. Moreover, these periodic dashes of his from tomb to tomb must have been a godsend to the crowd of curious visitors who kept vigil above the tomb, for there were many days during the winter in which it was the only excitement they had.

Our next step, after these preliminary photographs had been taken, was to devise an efficient method of registering the contents of the chamber, for it would be absolutely essential, later on, that we should have a ready means of ascertaining the exact part of the tomb from which any particular object might have come. Naturally, each object, or closely allied group of objects, would be given its own catalogue number, and would have that number securely attached to it when it was moved away from the chamber, but that was not enough, for the number might not indicate position. So far as possible, the numbers were to follow a definite order, beginning at the entrance doorway and working systematically round the chamber, but it was very certain that many objects now hidden would be found in the course of clearing, and have to be numbered out of turn. We got over the difficulty by placing printed numbers on every object and photographing them in small groups. Every number showed in at least one of the photographs, so that, by duplicating prints, we were able to place with the notes of every single object in our filing cabinets a print which showed at a glance its actual position in the tomb.

So far, so good, as far as the internal work in the tomb was concerned. Outside it, we had a still more difficult problem to solve, that of finding adequate working and storage space for the objects as they were removed. Three things were absolutely essential. In the first place we must have plenty of room. There would be boxes to unpack, notes and measurements to be taken, repairs to be carried out, experiments with various preservative materials to be made, and obviously we should require considerable table accommodation as well as ordinary storage space. Then, secondly, we must have a place that we could render thief-proof, for, as things were moved, the laboratory would come to be almost as great a source of danger as the tomb itself. Lastly, we must have seclusion. This may seem a less obvious need than the others, but we foresaw, and the winter's happenings proved us to be right, that unless we were out of sight of visitors' ordinary haunts we should be treated as a side-show, and should be unable to get any work done at all. Eventually we solved the problem by getting permission from the Government to take over the tomb of Seti II (No. 15 in the Valley catalogue). This certainly fulfilled the third of our requirements. It is not a tomb ordinarily visited by tourists, and its position, tucked away in a corner at the extreme end of the Valley, was exactly suitable to our purpose. No other tomb lay beyond it, so, without causing inconvenience to anyone, we could close to ordinary traffic the path that led to it, and thus secure complete privacy for ourselves.

It had other advantages, too. For one thing, it was so well sheltered by overhanging cliffs that at no time of day did the sun ever penetrate its doors, thus remaining comparatively cool even in the hottest of summer weather. There was also a considerable amount of open space in front of it, and this we utilized later as an open-air photographic studio and a carpenter's shop. We were somewhat restricted as to space, for the tomb was so long and narrow that all our work had to be done at the upper end of it, the lower part being useless except for storage purposes. It had also the disadvantage of being rather a long way from the scene of operations. These, however, were but minor drawbacks compared with the positive advantages which the tomb offered. We had a reasonable amount of room, we had privacy, and safety we ensured by putting up a many-padlocked steel gate, one and a half tons in weight.

One other point with regard to the laboratory work the reader should bear in mind. We were five hundred miles from anywhere, and, if we ran short of preservative materials, there might be considerable delay before we could secure a fresh supply. The Cairo shops furnished most of our needs, but there were certain chemicals of which we exhausted the entire Cairo stock before the winter was over, and other things which, in the first instance, could only be procured in England. Constant care and forethought were therefore necessary to prevent shortage and the consequent holding up of the work.

By 27 December all our preparations were made, and we were ready to make a start on the actual removal of the objects. We worked on a regular system of division of labour. Burton came first with his photographs of the numbered groups of objects; Hall and Hauser followed with their scale plan of the chamber, every object being drawn on the plan in projection; Callender and I did the preliminary noting and clearing, and superintended the removal of the objects to the laboratory; and there Mace and Lucas received them, and were responsible for the detail-noting, mending, and preservation.

The first object to be removed was the painted wooden casket. Then, working from north to south, and thus putting off the evil day when we should have to tackle the complicated tangle of chariots, we gradually disencumbered the great animal couches of the objects which surrounded them. Each object as it was removed was placed upon a padded wooden stretcher and securely fastened to it with bandages. Enormous numbers of these stretchers were required, for, to avoid double handling, they were in almost every case left permanently with the object, and not re-used. From time to time, when a sufficient number of stretchers had been filled— about once a day, on an average—a convoy was made up and dispatched under guard to the laboratory. This was the moment for which the crowd of watchers above the tomb were waiting. Out came the reporters' note-books, *click*, *click*, *click* went the cameras in every direction, and a lane had to be cleared for the procession to pass through. I suppose more films were wasted in the Valley last winter than in any other corresponding period of time since cameras were first invented. We in the laboratory had occasion once for a piece of old mummy cloth for experimental purposes; it was sent up to us in a stretcher, and it was photographed eight times before it got to us!

The removal and transport of the smaller objects was a comparatively simple matter, but it was quite otherwise when it came to the animal couches and the chariots. Each of the former was constructed in four pieces—the two animal sides, the bed proper, and the base to which the animals' feet were socketed. They were manifestly much too large to negotiate the narrow entrance passage, and must have been brought into the tomb in sections and assembled there. Indeed, strips of newer gold round the joints show where the damage they had incurred in handling had been made good after deposition. It was obvious that to get the couches out of the tomb we must take them apart again; no easy matter, for after three thousand years the bronze hooks had naturally set tight in the staples, and would not budge. We got them apart eventually, and with scarcely any damage, but it took no fewer than five of us to do it. Two supported the central part of the couch, two were responsible for the well-being of the animals, while the fifth, working from underneath, eased up the hooks, one after the other, with a lever.

Even when taken apart there was none too much room to get the side animals through the passage, and they needed very careful handling. However, we got them all out without accident, and packed them straight into boxes we had in readiness for them just outside the entrance to the tomb.

Most difficult of all to move were the chariots, which had suffered considerably from the treatment to which they had been subjected. It had not been possible to get them into the tomb whole in the first instance, for they were too wide for the entrance passage, and the wheels had had to be removed and the axles sawn off at one end. They had evidently been moved out of position and turned upside down by the plunderers, and in the subsequent tidying up the parts had been loosely stacked one upon another. Egyptian chariots are of very light construction,

A statue, secured with bandages, being removed on a padded wooden stretcher

and the rough usage which they had undergone made these extremely difficult to handle. There was another complication, in that the parts of the harness were made of undressed leather. Now this, if exposed to humidity, speedily resolves itself into glue, and that was what had happened here—the black glutinous mass which represented the trappings having run down over everything and dropped, not only on the other parts of the chariots themselves, but upon other objects which had nothing to do with them. Thus the leather has almost entirely perished, but, fortunately, as I have already stated, we have for reconstructional purposes the gold ornamentation with which it was covered.

Seven weeks in all it took us to clear the Antechamber, and thankful indeed were we when it was finished, and that without any kind of disaster befalling us. One scare we had. For two or three days the sky was very black, and it looked as though we were in for one of the heavy storms that occasionally visit Thebes. On such occasions rain comes down in torrents, and if the storm persists for any length of time the whole bed of the Valley becomes a raging flood. No power on earth could have kept our tomb from being flooded under these conditions, but, fortunately, though there must have been heavy rain somewhere in the district, we escaped with but a few drops. Certain correspondents indulged in some highly imaginative writing on the subject of this threatened storm. As a result of this and other distorted news we received a somewhat cryptic cable, sent presumably by a zealous student of the occult. It ran: "In the case of further trouble, pour milk, wine and honey on the threshold." Unfortunately, we had neither wine nor honey with us, so were unable to carry out the directions. In spite of our negligence, however, we escaped the further trouble. Perhaps we were given absent treatment.

In the course of our clearing we naturally accumulated a good deal of evidence with regard to the activities of the original tomb plunderers, and this will be as good a place as any to give a statement of the conclusions at which we arrived.

In the first place, we know from the sealings on the outer doorway that all the plundering was done within a very few years of the king's burial. We also know that the plunderers entered the tomb at least twice. There were broken scattered objects on the floor of the entrance passage and staircase, proving that at the time of the first attempt the passage-way between the inner and the outer sealed doors was empty. It is, I suppose, just possible that this preliminary plundering was done immediately after the funeral ceremonies. Thereafter the passage was entirely filled with stones and rubbish, and it was through a tunnel excavated in the upper left-hand corner of this filling that the subsequent attempts were made. At this final attempt the thieves had penetrated into all the chambers of the tomb, but their tunnel was only a narrow one, and clearly they could not have got away with any except the smaller objects.

Now as to internal evidence of the damage they had been able to effect. To begin with, there was a strange difference between the respective states in which the Antechamber and the Annexe had been left. In the latter, as we have described in the preceding chapter, everything was in confusion, and there was not a vacant inch of floor-space. It was quite evident that the plunderers had turned everything topsy-turvy, and that the present state of the chamber was precisely that in which they had left it. The Antechamber was quite different. There was a certain amount of confusion, it was true, but it was orderly confusion, and had it not been for the evidence of plundering afforded by the tunnel and the re-sealed doorways, one might have imagined at first view that there never had been any plundering, and that the confusion was due to Oriental carelessness at the time of the funeral.

However, when we commenced clearing, it quickly became manifest that this comparative orderliness was due to a process of hasty tidying-up, and that the plunderers had been just as busy here as they had in the Annexe. Parts of the same object were found in different quarters of the chamber; objects that should have been in boxes were lying on the floor or upon the couches; on the lid of one of the boxes there was a collar, intact but crumpled; behind the chariots, in an entirely inaccessible place, there was a box-lid, the box to which it belonged being far away, near the innermost door. Quite clearly the plunderers had scattered things here just as they had done in the Annexe, and someone had come after them and rearranged the chamber.

Later, when we came to unpack the boxes, we found still more circumstantial evidence. One, the long white box at the north end of the chamber, was half full of sticks, bows and arrows, and above, stuffed tightly in upon them, there was a mixed collection of the king's under-linen. Yet the metal points had been broken from all the arrows, and a few were found dropped upon the floor. Other sticks and bows that obviously belonged to this box were likewise scattered in the chamber. In another box there were a number of decorated robes, bundled together and thrust in anyhow, and mixed with them several pairs of sandals. So tightly had the contents of the box been stuffed, that the metal toe-thong of one of the sandals had pierced right through its own leather sole and penetrated that of another which lay beneath it. In still another box, jewellery and tiny statuettes had been packed on top of faience libation vases. Others, again, were half empty, or contained a mere jumble of odds and ends of cloth.

There was, moreover, certain evidence that this confusion was due to hasty repacking, and had nothing to do with the original arrangement of the boxes, for on the lids of several there were neat little dockets stating clearly what the contents should have been, and in only one case did the docket bear any sort of relation to the contents as they actually were. This particular docket called for "17 (unknown objects) of lapis lazuli colour." Within the box there were sixteen libation vases of dark blue faience, and a seventeenth was on the floor of the chamber some distance away. Eventually, in our final study of the material these dockets will be of great value. We shall be able, in a great many cases, to apportion out the objects to the boxes which originally contained them, and shall know exactly what is missing.

The best evidence of all was supplied by a very elaborate garment of faience, gold and inlay, comprising in one piece corslet, collar and pectoral. The largest portion of it was found in the box which contained the faience vases just mentioned; the pectoral and most of the collar were tucked away in the small gold shrine; and isolated pieces of it turned up in several other boxes, and were scattered all over the floor. There is nothing at present to show which of the boxes it originally belonged to, or even that it actually belonged to any of them. It is quite possible that the plunderers brought it from the innermost chamber to the better light of the Ante-chamber, and there deliberately pulled it to pieces.

From the facts at our disposal we can now reconstruct the whole sequence of events. A breach was first made in the upper left-hand corner of the first sealed door, just large enough to admit a man, and then the tunnelling began, the excavators working in a chain, passing the stones and baskets of earth back from one to another. Seven or eight hours' work might suffice to bring them to the second sealed door; a hole in this, and they were through. Then in the semi-darkness began a mad scramble for loot. Gold was their natural quarry, but it had to be in portable form, and it must have maddened them to see it glinting all around them, on plated objects which they could not move, and had not time to strip. Nor, in the dim light in which they were working, could they always distinguish between the real and the false, and many an object which they took for solid gold was found on closer examination to be but gilded wood, and was contemptuously thrown aside. The boxes were treated in very drastic fashion. Without exception they were dragged out into the centre of the room and ransacked, their contents being strewn about all over the floor. What valuables they found in them and made away with we may never know, but their search can have been but hurried and superficial, for many objects of solid gold were overlooked. One very valuable thing we know they did secure. Within the small gold shrine there was a pedestal of gilded wood, made for a statuette, with the imprint of the statuette's feet still marked upon it. The statuette itself was gone, and there can be very little doubt that it was a solid gold one, probably very similar to the gold statuette of Thothmes III, in the image of Amen, in the Carnarvon collection.

Next, the Antechamber having been thoroughly worked over, the thieves turned their attention to the Annexe, knocking a hole in its doorway just big enough to let them through, and overturning and ransacking its contents quite as thoroughly as they had done those of the outer chamber.

Then, and apparently not until then, they directed themselves towards the burial chamber, and made a very small hole in the sealed doorway which screened it from the Antechamber. How much damage they did there we shall know in due time, but, so far as we can tell at present, it was less than in the outer chambers. They may, indeed, have been disturbed at this particular stage in the proceedings, and there is a very interesting little piece of evidence that seems to bear the theory out.

It may be remembered that in our description of the objects in the Antechamber (chapter 7) we mentioned that one of the boxes contained a handful of solid gold rings tied up in a fold of

Plunderers' loot: the rings tied in a scarf

cloth. They were just the things to attract a thief, for their intrinsic value was considerable, and yet they could very easily be hidden away. Now, every visitor to Egypt will remember that if you give money to a *fellah* his ordinary proceeding will be to undo a portion of his head-shawl, put the coins in a fold of it, twist it round two or three times to hold the coins tight in place, and make it finally secure by looping the bag thus formed into a knot. These rings had been secured in exactly the same way—the same loose fold in the cloth, the same twisting round to form the bag, and the same loose knot. This, unquestionably, was the work of one of the thieves.

It was not his head-shawl that he had used—the *fellah* of the period wore no such garment—but one of the king's scarves which he had picked up in the tomb, and he had fastened them thus for convenience in carrying. How comes it then that the precious bundle of rings was left in the tomb, and not carried off? It was the very last thing that a thief would be likely to forget, and, in case of sudden alarm, it was not heavy enough to impede his flight, however hurried that might be. We are almost forced to the conclusion that the thieves were either trapped within the tomb, or overtaken in their flight—traced, in any case, with some of the plunder still upon them. If this be so, it explains the presence of certain other pieces of jewellery and gold-work too valuable to leave and too big to overlook.

In any case, the fact that a robbery had been committed got to the ears of the officials concerned, and they came to the tomb to investigate and make the damage good. For some reason they seem to have been in almost as great a hurry as the thieves, and their work of reparation was sadly scamped. The Annexe they left severely alone, not even taking the trouble to fill up the hole in the doorway. In the Antechamber the smaller objects with which the floor was covered were swept up, bundled together, and jammed—there is no other word—back into the boxes, no attempt being made to sort the material, or to put the objects into the boxes which had been originally intended for them. Some of the boxes were packed tight, others were left almost empty, and on one of the couches there were deposited two large bundles of cloth in which a miscellaneous collection of material had been wrapped. Nor even was all the small material gathered up. The sticks, bows and arrows were left in scattered groups; on the lid of a box were thrown a crumpled collar of pendants, and a pad of faience rings; and on the floor, one on one side of the chamber and one on the other, there was a pair of fragile bead-work sandals. The larger objects were pushed carelessly back against the walls, or stacked one upon another. Certainly no respect was shown, either to the objects themselves, or to the king whose property they were, and one wonders why, if they tidied up so badly, they took the trouble to tidy up at all. One thing we must credit them with. They did not do any pilfering, as they might easily have done, on their own account. We can be reasonably sure of that from the valuable objects, small and easily concealed, which they repacked into the boxes.

The Antechamber finished—so far, at least, as they intended to finish it—the hole in the innermost doorway was refilled, plastered, and stamped with the royal necropolis seal. Then, retracing their steps, they closed and sealed the Antechamber door, filled up the plunderers' tunnel through the passage-blocking, and made good the outer doorway. What further steps they took to prevent repetition of the crime we do not know, but probably they buried the whole entrance to the tomb deep out of sight. Better political conditions in the country might have prevented it for a time, but in the long run nothing but ignorance of its whereabouts could have saved it from further attempts at plundering; and very certain it is that, between the time of this re-closing and that of our discovery, no hand had touched the seals upon the door.

9

Visitors and the Press

A RCHAEOLOGY UNDER THE LIMELIGHT is a new and rather bewildering experience for most of us. In the past we have gone about our business happily enough, intensely interested in it ourselves, but not expecting other folk to be more than tepidly polite about it, and now all of a sudden we find the world takes an interest in us, an interest so intense and so avid for details that special correspondents at large salaries have to be sent to interview us, report our every movement, and hide round corners to surprise a secret out of us. It is, as I said, a little bewildering for us, not to say embarrassing, and we wonder sometimes just exactly how and why it has all come about. We may wonder, but I think it would puzzle anyone to give an exact answer to the question. One must suppose that at the time the discovery was made the general public was in a state of profound boredom with news of reparations, conferences and mandates, and craved for some new topic of conversation. The idea of buried treasure, too, is one that appeals to most of us. Whatever the reason, or combination of reasons, it is quite certain that, once the initial *Times* dispatch had been published, no power on earth could shelter us from the light of publicity that beat down upon us. We were helpless, and had to make the best of it.

The embarrassing side of it was soon brought home to us in no uncertain manner. Telegrams poured in from every quarter of the globe. Within a week or two letters began to follow them, a deluge of correspondence that has persisted ever since. Amazing literature some of it. Beginning with letters of congratulation, it went on to offers of assistance, ranging all the way from tomb-planning to personal valeting; requests for souvenirs—even a few grains of sand from above the tomb would be received so thankfully; fantastic money offers, from moving-picture rights to copyright on fashions of dress; advice on the preservation of antiquities, and the best method of appeasing evil spirits and elementals; press clippings; tracts; would-be facetious communications; stern denunciations of sacrilege; claims of relationship—surely you must be the cousin who lived in Camberwell in 1893, and whom we have never heard of since; and so on and so on. Fatuous communications of this sort came tumbling in upon us at the rate of ten or fifteen a day right through the winter. There is a whole sackful of them, and an interesting psychological study they would make if one had the time to give to them. What, for instance, is one to make of a person who solemnly inquires whether the discovery of the tomb throws any light on the alleged Belgian atrocities in the Congo?

Next came our friends the newspaper correspondents, who flocked to the Valley in large numbers and devoted all their social gifts—and they were considerable—towards dispelling any lingering remains of loneliness or desert boredom that we might still have left to us. They certainly did their work with some thoroughness, for each owed it to himself and to his paper to get daily information, and we in Egypt were delighted when we heard Lord Carnarvon's decision to place the whole matter of publicity in the hands of *The Times*.

Another, and perhaps the most serious of all the embarrassments that notoriety brought upon us, was the fatal attraction the tomb had for visitors. It was not that we wanted to be secretive, or had any objection to visitors as such—as a matter of fact, there are few things more pleasant than showing one's work to appreciative people—but as the situation developed it became very clear that, unless something was done to discourage it, we should spend the entire season playing showmen, and never get any work done at all. It was surely a new chapter in the history of the Valley. Tourist visitors it had always known, but heretofore it had been a business proceeding and not a garden party. Armed with guide-books, they had conscientiously visited as many tombs as time, or their dragoman, would allow them, bustled through their lunch, and been hurried off to a further debauch of sight-seeing elsewhere.

This winter, dragoman and time schedules were disregarded alike, and many of the ordinary sights were left unvisited. The tomb drew like a magnet. From a very early hour in the morning the pilgrimage began. Visitors arrived on donkeys, in sand-carts, and in two-horse cabs, and proceeded to make themselves at home in the Valley for the day. Round the top of the upper level of the tomb there was a low wall, and here they each staked out a claim and established themselves, waiting for something to happen. Sometimes it did, more often it did not, but it seemed to make no difference to their patience. There they would sit the whole morning, reading, talking, knitting, photographing the tomb and each other, quite satisfied if at the end they could get a glimpse of anything. Great was the excitement, always, when word was passed up that something was to be brought out of the tomb. Books and knitting were thrown aside, and the whole battery of cameras was cleared for action and directed at the entrance passage. We were really alarmed sometimes lest the whole wall should give way, and a crowd of visitors be precipitated into the mouth of the tomb. From above, it must really have been an imposing spectacle to see strange objects like the great gilt animals from the couches emerging gradually from the darkness into the light of day. We who were bringing them up were much too anxious about their safety in the narrow passage to think about such things ourselves, but a preliminary gasp and then a quick buzz of exclamations brought home to us the effect it had upon the watchers above.

To these, the casual visitors who contented themselves with watching from the top, there could be no objection, and, whenever possible, we brought things out of the tomb without covers for their special benefit. Our real embarrassment was caused by the numbers of people who, for one reason or another, had to be shown over the tomb itself. This was a difficulty that came upon us so gradually and insidiously that for a long time we none of us realized what the inevitable result must be, but in the end it brought the work practically to a standstill. At the beginning we had, of course, the formal inspections of the departmental officials concerned. These, naturally, we welcomed. In the same way we were always glad to receive other archaeologists. They had a right to visit the tomb, and we were delighted to show them everything there was to be seen. So far there was no difficulty, and there never would be any difficulty. It was with the letters of introduction that the trouble began. They were written, literally in hundreds, by our friends—we never realized before how many we had—by our friends' friends, by people who had a real claim upon us, and by people who had less than none; for diplomatic reasons, by Ministers or departmental officials in Cairo; to say nothing of self-written introductions, which either bluntly demanded admittance to the tomb or showed quite clearly and ingeniously how unreasonable it would be to refuse them. One ingenious person even intercepted a telegraph boy, and tried to make the delivery of the message an excuse for getting in. The desire to visit the tomb became an obsession with the tourist, and in the Luxor hotels the question of ways and means became a regular topic of conversation. Those who had seen the tomb boasted of the fact openly, and to many of those who had not it became a matter of personal pride to effect an introduction somehow. To such lengths were things carried that certain tourist agencies in America actually advertised a trip to Egypt to see the tomb.

All this, as may be imagined, put us in a very awkward position. There were certain visitors whom for diplomatic reasons we had to admit, and others whom we could not refuse without giving serious offence, not only to themselves, but to the third parties whose introduction they brought. Where were we to draw the line? Obviously something had to be done, for, as I said, the whole of the work in the tomb was being rapidly brought to a standstill. Eventually we solved the difficulty by running away. Ten days after the opening of the sealed door we filled up the tomb, locked and barred the laboratory, and disappeared for a week. This made a complete break. When we resumed work the tomb itself was irrevocably buried, and we made it a fixed rule that no visits were to be made to the laboratory at all.

Now this whole question of visitors is a matter of some delicacy. We have already got into a good deal of hot water over it, and have been accused of lack of consideration, ill manners, selfishness, boorishness, and quite a number of other things; so perhaps it would be as well to make a clear statement of the difficulties involved. These are two. In the first place, the presence of a number of visitors creates serious danger to the objects themselves, danger that we, who are responsible for them, have no right to let them undergo. How could it be otherwise? The tomb is small and crowded, and sooner or later—it actually happened more than once last year— a false step or hasty movement on the part of a visitor will do some piece of absolutely irreparable damage. It is not the fault of the visitor, for he does not and cannot know the exact position or condition of every object. It is our fault, for letting him be there. The unfortunate part of it is that the more interested and the more enthusiastic the visitor is, the more likely he is to be the cause of damage: he gets excited, and in his enthusiasm over one object he is very liable to step back into or knock against another. Even if no actual damage is caused, the passage of large parties of visitors through the tomb stirs up the dust, and that in itself is bad for the objects.

That is the first and obvious danger. The second, due to the loss of actual working time that visitors cause, is not so immediately apparent, but it is in some ways even more serious. This will seem a terribly exaggerated view to the individual visitor, who will wonder what difference the half-hour that he or she consumed could make to the whole season's work. Perfectly true, so far as that particular half-hour is concerned, but what of the other nine visitors, or groups of visitors, who come on the same day? By strict arithmetic he and they have occupied five hours of our working day; in actual fact, it is considerably more than five, for in the short intervals between visitors it is impossible to settle down to any serious piece of work. To all intents and purposes a complete day has been lost. Now, there were many days last season in which we actually did have ten parties of visitors, and if we had given way to every demand, and avoided any possibility of giving offence, there would not have been a day in which we did not far exceed the ten. In other words, there would have been whole weeks at a time in which no work was done at all. As it actually worked out last winter, we gave visitors a quarter of our working season. This resulted in our having to prolong our work into the hot weather a whole month longer than we had intended, and the heat of the Valley in May is not a thing to look forward to with equanimity, and is anything but inducive to good work.

There was much more at stake, however, than our own personal inconvenience: there was actual danger for the objects themselves. Delicate antiquities are extremely sensitive to any change of temperature, and have to be watched most carefully. In the present case the change from the close atmosphere of the Antechamber to the variable temperature outside, and the dry airiness of the tomb we used as a laboratory, was a very appreciable one, and certain of the

Visitors to the tomb

objects were affected by it. It was extremely important that preservatives should be applied at the very first possible moment, and in some cases there was need of experimental treatment which had to be watched very carefully. The danger of constant interruption is obvious, and I need not labour the point. What would a chemist think if you asked him to break off a delicate experiment to show you round his laboratory? What would be the feelings of a surgeon if you interrupted him in the middle of an operation? And what about the patient? For the matter of that, what would a business man say—what wouldn't he say?—if he had a succession of ten parties of visitors in the course of the morning, each expecting to be shown all over the office?

Yet, surely, the claims of archaeology for consideration are just as great as those of any other form of scientific research, or even—dare I say it?—of that of the sacred science of money-making itself. Why, because we carry on our work in unfrequented regions instead of in a crowded city, are we to be considered churlish for objecting to constant interruptions? I suppose the reason really is that in popular opinion archaeology is not work at all. Excavation is a sort of super-tourist amusement, carried out with the excavator's own money if he is rich enough, or with other people's money if he can persuade them to subscribe it, and all he has to do is to enjoy life in a beautiful winter climate and pay a gang of natives to find things for him. It is the dilettante archaeologist, the man who rarely does any work with his own hands, but as often as not is absent when the actual discovery is made, who is largely responsible for this opinion. The serious excavator's life is frequently monotonous and, as I hope to show in the next chapter, quite as hard-working as that of any other member of society.

I have written more than I intended on this subject, but really it is a very serious matter for us. We have an opportunity in this tomb such as no archaeologists ever had before, but if we are to take full advantage of it—and failure to do so will earn for us the just execration of every future generation of archaeologists—it is absolutely essential that we be left to carry on the work without interruption. It is not as if our visitors were all keen on archaeology, or even mildly interested in it. Too many of them are attracted by mere curiosity, or, even worse, by a desire to visit the tomb because it is the thing to do. They want to be able to talk at large about it to their friends at home, or crow over less fortunate tourists who have not managed to secure an introduction themselves. Can you imagine anything more maddening, when you are completely absorbed in a difficult problem, than to give up half an hour of your precious time to a visitor who has pulled every conceivable kind of wire to gain admittance, and then to hear him say quite audibly as he goes away "Well there wasn't much to see, after all"? That actually happened last winter—and more than once.

In the coming season there will in any case be much less for visitors to see. It will be absolutely impossible to get into the burial chamber, for every available inch of space will be occupied by scaffolding, and the removal of the shrine, section by section, will be much too ticklish an operation to admit of interruptions. In the laboratory we propose to deal with only one object at a time, which will be packed and got rid of as soon as we have finished with it. Six cases of objects from the tomb are already on exhibition in the Cairo Museum, and we would earnestly beg visitors to Egypt to content themselves with these, and with what they can see from the outside of the tomb, and not to set their hearts on getting into the tomb itself. Those who are genuinely interested in archaeology for its own sake will be the first to realize that the request is a reasonable one. The others, the idly curious, who look on the tomb as a side-show, and Tutankhamen as a mere topic of conversation, have no rights in the matter, and need no consideration. Whatever our discoveries next season may be, we trust that we may be allowed to deal with them in a proper and dignified manner.

A luncheon party at the tomb given by Lord Carnarvon

10

Work in the laboratory

THIS CHAPTER IS DEDICATED to those—and they are many—who think that an excavator spends his time basking in the sun, pleasantly exhilarated by watching other people work for him, and otherwise relieved from boredom by having baskets full of beautiful antiquities brought up from the bowels of the earth from time to time for him to look at. His actual life is very different, and, as there can be but few who know the details of it, it will be worth our while to give a general outline here before going into the question of the laboratory work of the past season. Incidentally, it will help to explain why this careful laboratory work was necessary.

In the first place, it must be clearly understood that there is never any question of having basketfuls of objects brought to the excavator for him to look at; the first and most important rule in excavating is that the archaeologist must remove every antiquity from the ground with his own hands. So much depends upon it. Quite apart from the question of possible damage that might be caused by clumsy fingers, it is very essential that you see the object *in situ*, to gain any evidence you can from the position in which it lies, and the relationship it bears to objects near it. For example, there may very likely be dating evidence. How many pieces there are in museums with vague "probably Middle Kingdom" kind of labels, which, by reference to the objects with which they were found, might easily have been assigned accurately to the Dynasty to which they belonged, or even to the reign of some particular king. There will, again, be evidence of arrangement to be secured, evidence that may show the use for which some particular object was made, or give the details for its ultimate reconstruction.

Take, for instance, the tiny fragments of serrated flint which are found in such enormous quantities in town sites of the Middle Kingdom. We can guess their use, and with the label "sickle flints" they make not uninteresting museum material. Now find, as I have done, a complete sickle lying in the ground, its wooden parts in such condition that a touch will destroy the evidence of its ever having been a sickle at all. Two courses are open to you. By careful handling and the use of preservatives you may be able to get your sickle out of the ground intact, or, if it is too far gone for that, you can at least take the measurements and notes that will enable you to construct the wood anew. In either case you get a complete museum object, worth, archaeologically, a thousand times more than the handful of disconnected pieces of flint that you would otherwise have secured. This is a simple illustration of the importance of field evidence: we shall have other and more striking instances to record when we come to deal with the different classes of material.

One other matter before we pass on. By noting the exact position of an object, or group of objects, you can not infrequently secure evidence that will enable you to make a find of similar objects elsewhere. Foundation deposits are a case in point. In every construction the arrangement of the deposits followed a regular system, and, having found one, it is a simple matter to put your finger upon the others.

An excavator, then, must see every object in position, must make careful notes before it is moved, and, if necessary, must apply preservative treatment on the spot. Obviously, under these conditions it is all-important for you to keep in close touch with your excavations. Holiday trips and days off are out of the question. While the work is actually running you must be on the spot all day, and available at all hours of the day. Your workmen must know where to find you at any given moment, and must have a perfectly clear understanding that the news of a discovery must be passed on to you without any delay.

In the case of an important discovery you will probably know something has happened before you actually get the report, for—in Egypt particularly—the news will have spread almost instantaneously, and have had a curious psychological effect upon your entire gang of workmen. They will be working differently, not necessarily harder, but differently, and much more silently. The ordinary work-songs will have ceased. A smaller discovery you will frequently sense in advance from the behaviour of the man who brings the message. Nothing would induce him to come straight to you and tell you openly what he has found. At all costs he must make a mystery of it, so he hovers about in a thoroughly self-conscious manner, thereby advertising to the world at large exactly what has happened, and eventually makes himself still more conspicuous by beckoning you aside and whispering his news. Even then it will be difficult to get any but the vaguest of reports out of him, and it will probably not be until you have reached the actual spot that you find out exactly what has been found. This is due largely to an Egyptian's love of mystery for its own sake. The same man will tell his friends all about the find on the first opportunity, but it is part of the game to pretend that they must know nothing about it at the time. Partly, too, to excitement. Not that he takes any real interest in the objects themselves, but because he looks on them in the light of a gamble. Most excavators work on what is known as the *baksheesh* system: that is to say, they pay their workmen rewards, over and above their wages, for anything they find. It is not an ideal arrangement, but it has two advantages: it helps to ensure the safety of the objects, particularly the small, easily concealed ones, which may be most valuable to you for dating purposes; and it makes the men keener about their work, and more careful about the manner in which they carry it out, the reward being more for the safe handling than for the value of the object.

For these, and for many other reasons which we could mention, it is all-important for you to keep close to your work, and, even if nothing is being found at the moment, you will not have much time to be idle. To begin with, every tomb, every building, every broken wall even, must be noted, and if you are dealing with pit-tombs this may involve considerable gymnastic exercise. The pits may range anywhere from ten to a hundred and twenty feet in depth, and I calculated once that in the course of a single season I had climbed, hand over hand, up half a mile of rope. Then there is photography. Every object of any archaeological value must be photographed before it is moved, and in many cases a series of exposures must be made to mark the various stages in the clearing. Many of these photographs will never be used, but you can never tell but that some question may arise, whereby a seemingly useless negative may become a record of the utmost value. Photography is absolutely essential on every side, and it is perhaps the most exacting of all the duties that an excavator has to face. On a particular piece of work I have taken and developed as many as fifty negatives in a single day.

Whenever possible, these particular branches of the work—surveying and photography—should be in the hands of separate experts. The man in charge will then have time to devote himself to what we may call the finer points of excavation. He will be able to play with his work, as a brother digger expressed it. In every excavation puzzles and problems constantly present themselves, and it is only by going constantly over the ground, looking at it from every point of view, and scrutinizing it in every kind of light, that you will be able to arrive at a solution of some of these problems. The meaning of a complex of walls, the evidence of reconstruction of a building, or of a change in plan on the part of the original architect, the significance of a change of level, where the remains of a later period have been superimposed upon those of an earlier one, the purport of some peculiarity in the surface debris, or in the stratification of a mound— these and a score of others are the questions that an excavator has to face, and it is upon his ability to answer them that he will stand or fall as an archaeologist.

Then, again, if he is freed from the labour of survey and photography, he will be able to devote more time and thought to the general organization of the work, and by that means to effect considerable economies both in time and money. Many a hundred pounds has been wasted by lack of system, and many an excavator has had to clear away his own dumps because he failed in the first instance to exercise a little forethought. The question of the distribution of the workmen is one that needs careful attention, and great wastage of labour can be avoided by moving men around from one place to another exactly when and where they are wanted, and never leaving more on a particular section of the work than are actually needed to keep it running smoothly. The number of labourers that an excavator can keep up with single-handed will depend naturally on the conditions of the work. On a big and more or less unproductive undertaking, such as pyramid clearing, he can look after an almost indefinite number. On rock-cut tombs he can perhaps keep pace with fifty; whereas on shallow graves—a pre-dynastic cemetery, for example— ten will keep him uncomfortably busy. The number of men who can be employed is also largely dependent on the type of site and formation of the locality of the excavation.

So much for the outdoor duties, the actual conduct of his excavations. There are plenty of other jobs to be done, and his off hours and evenings will be very fully occupied if he is to keep on terms with his work. His notes, his running plans, and the registration of the objects must be kept thoroughly up to date. There are the photographs to be developed, prints to be made, and a register kept, both of negatives and prints. There will be broken objects to be mended, objects in delicate condition to be treated, restorations to be considered, and bead-work to be re-threaded. Then comes the indoor photography, for each individual object must be photographed to scale, and in some cases from several points of view. The list could be extended almost indefinitely, and would include a number of jobs that would seem to have but a remote connexion with archaeology, such as account-keeping, doctoring the men, and settling their disputes. The workmen naturally have one day a week off, and the excavator will very likely begin the season with the idea that he too will take a weekly holiday. He will usually be obliged to abandon the idea after the first week, for he will find in this off day too good an opportunity to waste of catching up with the hundred and one jobs that have got ahead of him.

Such, in broad outline, is the life of the excavator. There are certain details of his work, more particularly those which have to do with note-taking and first-aid preservation of the different classes of objects, which we should like to dwell on at somewhat greater length. These are subjects which the ordinary reader will probably know little about, and they will be well illustrated in our description of the laboratory work of the past season.

Woodwork, for instance, is seldom in good condition and presents many problems. Damp and the white ant are its chief foes, and in unfavourable conditions nothing will be left of the wood but a heap of black dust, or a shell which crumbles at the touch. In the one case an entry in your notes to the effect that wood has been present is the most that you can do, but in the other there will generally be a certain amount of information to be gleaned. Measurements can certainly be secured; and the painted remains of an inscription, which may give you the name of the owner of the object, and which a single breath of wind or touch of the surface would be sufficient to efface, can be copied, if taken in hand without delay. Again, there will be cases in which the wooden frame or core of an object has decayed away, leaving scattered remains of the decoration—ivory, gold, faience, or what not—which originally covered its surface. By careful notes of the exact relative positions of this fallen decoration, supplemented by a subsequent fitting and piecing together, it will often be possible to work out the exact size and shape of the object. Then, by applying the original decoration to a new wooden core, you will have, instead of a miscellaneous collection of ivory, gold and faience fragments, useless for any purpose, an object which for all practical purposes is as good as new. Preservation of wood, unless it be in the very last stage of decay, is always possible by application of melted paraffin wax; by this means an object, which otherwise would have fallen to pieces, can be rendered perfectly solid and fit to handle.

The condition of wood naturally varies according to the site, and, fortunately for us, Luxor is in this respect perhaps the most favourable site in the whole of Egypt. We had trouble with the wood from the present tomb, but it arose, not from the condition in which we originally found it, but from subsequent shrinkage owing to change of atmosphere. This in an object of plain wood is not such a serious matter, but the Egyptians were extremely fond of applying a thin layer of gesso, on which prepared surface they painted scenes or made use of an overlay of gold foil. Naturally, as the wood shrank the gesso covering began to loosen up and buckle, and there was considerable danger that large parts of the surface might be lost. The problem is a difficult one. It is a perfectly easy matter to fix paint or gold foil to the gesso, but ordinary preservatives will not fix gesso to the wood. Here again, as we shall show, we had recourse eventually to paraffin wax.

The condition of textiles varies. Cloth in some cases is so strong that it might have come fresh from the loom, whereas in others it has been reduced by damp almost to the consistency of soot. In the present tomb the difficulty of handling it was considerably increased, both by the rough usage to which it had been subjected, and by the fact that so many of the garments were covered with a decoration of gold rosettes and bead-work.

Bead-work is in itself a complicated problem, and will perhaps tax an excavator's patience more than any other material with which he has to deal. There is so much of it. The Egyptians were passionately fond of beads, and it is by no means exceptional to find upon a single mummy an equipment consisting of a number of necklaces, two or three collars, a girdle or two, and a full set of bracelets and anklets. In such a case many thousands of beads will have been employed. Therein lies the test of patience, for in the recovery and restoration of this beadwork every single bead will have to be handled at least twice. Very careful work will be necessary to secure the original arrangement of the beads. The threads that held them together will all have rotted away, but nevertheless they will be lying for the most part in their correct relative positions, and by carefully blowing away the dust it may be possible to follow the whole length of necklace or collar, and secure the exact order of the beads. Re-threading may be done *in situ* as each section is laid bare—on a many-stringed girdle I once had twelve needles and thread going simultaneously—or, better still, the beads may be transferred one by one to a piece of cardboard on which a thin layer of plasticine has been spread. This has the advantage that gaps of the required length can be left for missing or doubtfully placed beads.

In very elaborate objects, where it is not possible to thread the beads as they are found, careful notes must be made, the re-stringing being done later, not in exact order, bead for bead, but in accordance with the original pattern and design. A tedious business this re-stringing will be, and a good deal of experimental work will probably be necessary before you arrive at the correct method of dealing with the particular problem. In a collar, for example, it may be necessary to

have three independent threading strings to every bead, if the rows are to lie smoothly in place. Restoration of missing or broken parts will sometimes be necessary if a reconstruction is to be effected. I once found a set of bracelets and anklets in which the rows of beads had been separated by perforated bars of wood covered with gold foil. The wood of which these separators was composed had entirely gone, leaving the gold foil shells; so I cut new pieces of wood to the shape, burnt out perforation holes with a red-hot needle, and covered the new bars with the original gold. Such restorations, based on actual evidence, are perfectly legitimate, and well worth the trouble. You will have secured for your museum, in place of a trayful of meaningless beads, or, worse still, a purely arbitrary and fanciful reconstruction, an object, attractive in itself, which has very considerable archaeological value.

Papyrus is frequently difficult to handle, and in its treatment more crimes have been committed than in any other branch of archaeology. If in fairly sound condition it should be wrapped in a damp cloth for a few hours, and then it can easily be straightened out under glass. Rolls that are torn and brittle, sure to separate into a number of small pieces during the process of unwrapping, should never be tackled unless you have plenty of time and space at your disposal. Careful and systematic work will ensure the correct spacing of almost all the fragments, whereas a desultory sorting, carried out in the intervals of other work, and perhaps by various hands, will never achieve a satisfactory result, and may end in the destruction of much valuable evidence. If only the Turin papyrus, for instance, had received careful treatment when it was first found, what a wealth of information it would have given us, and what heart-burnings we should have been saved!

Stone, as a rule, presents few difficulties in the field. Limestone will certainly contain salt, which must be soaked out of it, but this is a problem that can be taken in hand later in the museum, and need not detain us here. In the same way faience, pottery, and metal objects can usually be left for later treatment. We are only concerned here with work that must be carried out on the spot.

Detailed and copious notes should be taken at every stage of this preliminary work. It is difficult to take too many, for, though a thing may be perfectly clear to you at the moment, it by no means follows that it will be when the time comes for you to work over your material. In tomb-work as many notes as possible should be made while everything is still in position. Then, when you begin clearing, card and pencil should be kept handy, and every fresh item of evidence should be noted immediately you run across it. You are tempted so often to put off making the note until you have finished the actual piece of work on which you are engaged, but it is dangerous. Something will intervene, and as likely as not that particular note will never be made at all.

Now let us move to the laboratory, and put into practice some of the theories that we have been elaborating. It will be remembered that it was the tomb of Seti II (No. 15 in the Wilkinson catalogue of tomb numbers) that had been selected for us, and here we had established ourselves with our note-cards and our preservatives. The tomb was long and narrow, so that only the first bay could be used for practical work, the inner darker part being serviceable merely as storage space. As the objects were brought in they were deposited, still in their stretchers, in the middle section, and covered up until they should be wanted. Each in turn was brought up to the working bay for examination. There, after the surface dust had been cleared off, measurements, complete archaeological notes, and copies of inscriptions were entered on the filing cards. The necessary mending and preservative treatment followed after which it was taken just outside the entrance for scale photographs to be made. Finally, having passed through all these stages, the object was stored away in the innermost recesses of the tomb to await the final packing.

In the majority of cases no attempt at final treatment was made. It was manifestly impossible, for months, probably years, of reconstructive work are necessary if full use is to be made of the

Two pairs of earrings before reconstruction

material. All we could do here was to apply preliminary treatment, sufficient in any event to enable the object to support a journey in safety. Final restorations must be made in the museum, and they will need a far more fully equipped laboratory and a much larger staff of skilled helpers than we could ever hope to achieve in the Valley.

As the season advanced, and the laboratory grew more and more crowded, it became increasingly difficult to keep track of the work, and it was only by close attention to detail, and strict adherence to a very definite order of procedure, that we managed to keep clear of complications. As each object arrived its registration number was noted in an entry book, and in the same book a record was kept of the successive stages of its treatment. Each of the primary objects had been given its own registration number in the tomb, but as these were worked over in the laboratory an elaborate system of sub-numbering became necessary. A box, for instance, might contain fifty objects, any one of which must be clearly identifiable at all times, and these we distinguished by letters of the alphabet, or, where necessary, by a combination of letters. Constant care was necessary to keep these smaller objects from being separated from their identification tickets, especially in cases where protracted treatment was required. Not infrequently it happened that the component parts of a single object, scattered in the tomb, were entered under two or more numbers, and in this case cross-references in the notes were necessary. Note-cards, as completed, were filed away in cabinets, and in these filing cabinets we had, by the end of the season, a complete history of every object from the tomb, including:

1. Measurements, scale drawings, and archaeological notes.
2. Notes on the inscriptions by Dr. Alan Gardiner.
3. Notes by Mr. Lucas on the preservative treatment employed.
4. A photograph, showing the position of the object in the tomb.
5. A scale photograph, or series of photographs, of the object itself.
6. In the cases of boxes, a series of views, showing the different stages in the clearing.

So much for our system of work. Let us turn now to the individual treatment of a selected number of the antiquities. The first that required treatment in the laboratory was the wonderful painted casket (No. 21 in our register), and, if we had searched the whole tomb through, we should have been hard put to it to find a single object that presented a greater number of problems. For this reason it will be worth our while to give a detailed description of its treatment. Our first care was for the casket itself, which was coated with gesso, and covered from top to bottom with brilliantly painted scenes. With the exception of a slight widening of the joints owing to shrinkage, the wood was in perfect condition; the gesso had chipped a little at the corners and along the cracks, but was still in a reasonably firm state, and the paint, though a little discoloured in places, was perfectly fast and showed no signs of rubbing. It seemed as though but little treatment was necessary. The surface dust was removed, the discoloration of the painted surfaces was reduced with benzine, and the whole exterior of the casket was sprayed with a solution of celluloid in amylacetate to fix the gesso to the wood, particular attention being paid to tender places at the cracks. At the moment this seemed to be all that was required, but it was our first experience of the wood and gesso combination from the tomb, and we were to be disillusioned. Three or four weeks later we noticed that the joint cracks were getting wider, and that the gesso in other places was showing a tendency to buckle. It was clear enough what was happening. Owing to the change of temperature from the close, humid atmosphere of the tomb to the dry airiness of the laboratory, the wood had begun to shrink once more, and the gesso, not being able to follow it, was coming away from the wood altogether. The position was serious, for we were in danger of losing parts of the painted surface. Drastic measures were necessary, and after much discussion we decided on the use of melted paraffin wax. Courage was needed to take the step, but we were thoroughly justified by the result, for the wax penetrated the materials and held everything firm, and, so far from the colours being affected, as we had feared, it seemed to make them more brilliant than before. We used this process later on a number of other objects of wood and gesso, and found it extremely satisfactory. It is important that the surface should be heated, and that the wax should be brought as near to boiling-point as possible; otherwise it will chill and refuse to penetrate. Failing an oven we found the Egyptian sun quite hot enough for the purpose. Surplus wax can be removed by the application of heat, or by the use of benzine. There is another advantage in the process, in that blisters in the gesso can be pressed down into place again while the wax is still warm, and will hold quite firmly. In very bad cases it may be necessary to fill the blister in from behind by means of hot wax applied by a pipette.

So much for the outside of the casket. Now let us remove the lid and see what the inside has in store for us. This is an exciting moment, for there are beautiful things everywhere, and, thanks to the hurried re-packing carried out by the officials, there is nothing to forewarn one as to what the contents of any individual box may be. It will give the reader some idea of the difficulty of handling the material if I explain that it took me three weeks of hard work to get to the bottom of the box. The first thing we saw was on the right a pair of rush and papyrus sandals, in perfect condition; below them, just showing, a gilt head-rest, and, lower again, a confused mass of cloth, leather, and gold, of which we can make nothing as yet. On the left, crumpled into a bundle, there is a magnificent royal robe, and in the upper corner there are roughly shaped beads of dark resin. The robe it was that presented us with our first problem, a problem that was constantly to recur—how best to handle cloth that crumbled at the touch, and yet was covered with elaborate and heavy decoration. In this particular case the whole surface of the robe is covered with a network of faience beads, with a gold sequin filling in every alternate square in the net. These—beads and sequins—had originally been sewn to the cloth, but are now loose. A great many of them are upside down, the releasing of the tension when the thread snapped having evidently caused them to spring. At the borders of the robe there are bands of tiny glass beads of various colours, arranged in patterns. The upper layer of cloth was very deceptive in appearance. It looked reasonably solid, but if one tried to lift it, it fell to pieces in one's hand. Below, where it had been in contact with other things, the condition was much worse.

This question of cloth and its treatment was enormously complicated for us in the present tomb by the rough usage to which it had been subjected. Had it been spread out flat, or neatly folded, it would have been a comparatively simple matter to deal with it. We should, as a matter of fact, have had an easier task if it had been allowed to remain strewn about the floor of the chamber, as the plunderers had left it. Nothing could have been worse for our purposes than the treatment it had undergone in the tidying-up process, in which the various garments had been crushed, bundled and interfolded, and packed tightly into boxes with a mixture of other and, in some cases, most incongruous objects.

In the case of this present robe it would have been perfectly simple to solidify the whole of the upper layer and remove it in one piece, but this was a process to which there were serious objections. It involved, firstly, a certain amount of danger to whatever might lie beneath, for in the unpacking of these boxes we had to be continually on our guard lest, in our enthusiasm over the treatment or removal of an object, we might inflict damage on a still more valuable one which lay under it. Then, again, if we made the upper part of the robe solid, we should seriously have reduced the chances of extracting evidence as to size and shape, to say nothing of the details of ornamentation. In dealing with all these robes there were two alternatives before us. Something had to be sacrificed, and we had to make up our minds whether it should be the cloth or the decoration. It would have been quite possible, by the use of preservatives, to secure large pieces of the cloth, but, in the process, we should inevitably have disarranged and damaged the bead ornamentation that lay below. On the other hand, by sacrificing the cloth, picking it carefully away piece by piece, we could recover, as a rule, the whole scheme of decoration. This was the plan we usually adopted. Later, in the museum, it will be possible to make a new garment of the exact size, to which the original ornamentation—bead-work, gold sequins, or whatever it may be—can be applied. Restorations of this kind will be far more useful, and have a much greater archaeological value, than a few irregularly shaped pieces of preserved cloth and a collection of loose beads and sequins.

The size of the robe from this casket can be worked out with reasonable accuracy from the ornamentation. At the lower hem there was a band, composed of tiny beads arranged in a pattern, a pattern of which we were able to secure the exact details. From this band there hung, at equal intervals, a series of bead strings with a large pendant at the end of each string. We can thus calculate the circumference of the hem by multiplying the space between the strings by the number of pendants. That gives us the width of the robe. Now we can calculate the total area of decoration from the number of gold sequins employed, and, if we divide this total area by our known circumference at the bottom, we shall arrive at a fairly accurate approximation of the height. This naturally presupposes that our robe is the same width throughout, a method of cutting borne out by a number of undecorated garments of which we were able to secure the exact measurements.

This has been a long digression, but it was necessary, to show the nature of the problem with which we had to deal. We can return to the casket now, and really begin to explore its contents. First of all we removed the rush sandals, which were in beautifully firm condition, and presented no difficulties. Next came the gilt head-rest, and then, very carefully, we removed the robe. One large portion of its upper surface we managed to take out whole by the aid of a celluloid solution, and short lengths of the band decorations of small beads we preserved in wax for future reference. Then followed what we may call the second layer of the casket's contents. Here, to begin·with, were three pairs of sandals, or rather, to be accurate, two pairs of sandals and a pair of loose slippers. These were of leather, elaborately decorated with gold, and of wonderful workmanship. Unfortunately, their condition left much to be desired. They had suffered from their packing in the first place, but, worse than that, some of the leather had melted and run, gluing the sandals together and fastening them to other objects, making their extraction from the box a matter of extreme difficulty. So much of the leather had perished that the question of restoration became a serious problem. We secured the gold ornamentation that still remained in place with a solution of Canada balsam, and strengthened them generally as far as we could, but eventually it will probably be better to make new sandals and apply the old decoration to them.

Beneath the sandals there was a mass of decayed cloth, much of it of the consistency of soot, thickly spangled throughout with rosettes and sequins of gold and silver. This, sad to relate, represents a number of royal robes. The difficulty of trying to extract any intelligible record from it can be imagined, but a certain amount of assistance was given by the differences in the sizes and shapes of the sequins. There were at least seven distinct garments. One was an imitation leopard-skin cloak in cloth, with gilt head, and spots and claws of silver; while two of the others were head-dresses, made in the semblance of hawks with outstretched wings. Bundled in with the actual garments there were a number of other objects—two faience collarettes of beads and pendants, two caps or bags of tiny bead-work which had almost entirely fallen to pieces, a wooden tag inscribed in hieratic "Papyrus (?) sandals of His Majesty," a glove of plain linen, an archer's gauntlet, tapestry woven in coloured thread, a double necklace of large flat faience beads, and a number of linen belts or scarves. Below the garments there was a layer of rolls and pads of cloth, some of which were loin-cloths and others mere bandages; and below these again, resting on the bottom of the box, there were two boards, perforated at one end for hanging, whose purpose is still doubtful.

With very few exceptions—the rush sandals are a case in point—the garments it contained were those of a child. Our first idea was that the king might have kept stored away the clothes he wore as a boy; but later, on one of the belts, and on the sequins of one of the robes, we found the royal cartouche. He must, then, have worn them after he became king, from which it would seem to follow that he was quite a young boy when he succeeded to the throne. Another interesting piece of evidence in this connexion is supplied by the fact that on the lid of one of the other boxes there is a docket which reads, "The King's side-lock (?) as a boy." The question raises an interesting historical point, and we shall be eager to see, when the time comes, the evidence of age that the mummy will supply. Certainly, whenever the king appears upon the tomb furniture, he is represented as little more than a youth.

One other point with regard to the robes found in this and other boxes. Many of them are decorated with patterns in coloured linen threads. Some of these are examples of tapestry weaving, similar to the fragments found in the tomb of Thothmes IV,[1] but there were also undoubted cases of applied needlework. The material from this tomb will be of extreme importance to the history of textile art, and it needs very careful study.

We shall not have space here to describe the unpacking of the other boxes, but all were in the same jumbled state, and all had the same queer mixture of incongruous objects. Many of them contained from fifty to sixty individual pieces, each requiring its own registration card, and there was never any lack of excitement in the unpacking, for you never knew when you might not happen upon a magnificent gold scarab, a statuette, or a beautiful piece of jewellery. It was slow work, naturally, for hours at a time had to be spent working out with brush and bellows the exact order and arrangement of collar, necklace, or gold decoration, covered, as they ordinarily were, with the dust of decayed cloth. The collars were a frequent source of trouble. We found eight in all, of the Tell el Amarna leaf and flower type, and it needed great care and patience to work out the exact arrangement of the different types of pendants. They still need quite a lot of treatment to bring them back to their original colours, and there will have to be a certain amount of restoration of the broken and missing parts before they are ready for the final re-stringing. In one case we were lucky, for an elaborate three-string necklace, with a gilt pectoral at one end and a scarab-pendant at the other, lay flat upon the bottom of a box, so that we were able to remove it bead by bead, and re-string it on the spot in its exact original order.

The most elaborate piece of reconstruction that we had to do was in connexion with the corslet, which has been referred to more than once. This was a very elaborate affair, consisting of four separate parts—the corslet proper, inlaid with gold and carnelian, with border bands and braces of gold and coloured inlay; a collar with conventional imitation of beads in gold, carnelian, and green and blue faience; and two magnificent pectorals of openwork gold with coloured inlay, one for the chest, the other to hang behind as make-weight. Corslets of this type are depicted commonly enough on the monuments, and were evidently frequently worn, but we have never before been lucky enough to find a complete example. Unfortunately, the parts of it were sadly scattered, and there were points in the reconstruction of which we could not be absolutely certain. Most of it was found in Box 54, but, as we have already stated in Chapter 7, there were also parts of it in the small gold shrine and in Boxes 101 and 115, and single pieces from it were found scattered on the floor of the Antechamber, passage, and staircase. It was interesting working out the way in which it all fitted together.

The corslet proper lay in Box 54, resting upon a number of faience libation vases. This gave us the pattern and arrangement, with its upper and lower bands of inlaid gold plaques, and we were also able to recover from it its exact height in two or three separate places, and the fact that it was

The interior of box 54 showing the scattered parts of the corslet . . .

not the same height all the way round. It showed us, besides, that the upper row of the collar was joined on to the gold plaque brace bands, and that the gold bars fitted at the shoulders to the top of the brace bands. The exact order of the collar was recovered from the parts found in the gold shrine. The pectorals were also in the gold shrine, lying beside the collar sections, and that they actually fitted to the collar was proved by the curve of their upper edges. There were other gold bars in addition to those for the shoulders, and the perforated thread-holes in these, corresponding exactly with the holes in the scales, showed that they must have belonged to the corslet proper. These bars and the shoulder-bars alike were held together by sliding pins, to be

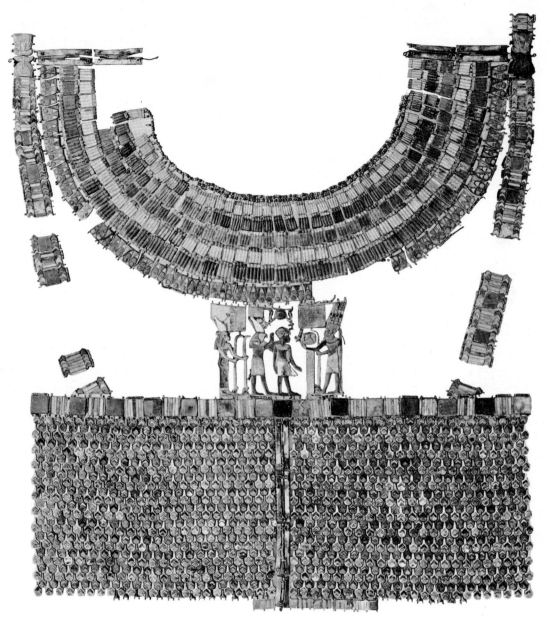

. . . and the corslet after reconstruction

adjusted after the corslet was in position. Our present reconstruction is purely a tentative one put together for photographic purposes, but the only really doubtful point in it is whether the gold bars fit to the front and back of the corslet, as they are here shown, or to its sides. The reason we have placed them in this position is that the bars are of different sizes, and by no combination is it possible to make the two equal lengths which the sides would require. The front and back of the corslet, on the other hand, we know were of different lengths. There are still a number of pieces missing, and these we hope may still turn up in the innermost chamber or in the Annexe.

The greater part of our winter's work in the laboratory was concerned with the boxes, working out and sorting over their confused jumble of contents. The single, larger, objects were much easier to deal with. Some were in very good condition, requiring nothing but surface cleaning and noting, but there were others which needed a certain amount of attention, if only minor repairs to make them fit for transport. In all our mending we had constant recourse to our box of floor-sweepings, fragments recovered by sweeping up and sifting the last layer of dust from the floor both of the Antechamber and entrance passage, and not infrequently we found there the piece of inlay, or whatever it might be, for which we were looking. The chariots we have not yet made any attempt to deal with. That must be done in Cairo later on, for they are in a great many sections, and their sorting and treatment will require very considerable working space—much more space than we can possibly arrange for in the Valley. As I explained earlier, the restoration and study of the material from this tomb will provide work for all of us for many years to come.

At the end of the season there came the question of packing, always an anxious business, but doubly so in this case owing to the enormous value of the material. Protection from dust as well as from actual damage was an important point, so every object was completely wrapped in cotton-wool or cloth, or both, before it was placed in its box. Delicate surfaces, such as the parts of the throne, the legs of the chairs and beds, or the bows and staves, were swathed in narrow bandages, in case anything should work loose in transit. Very fragile objects, like the funerary bouquets and the sandals, which would not bear ordinary packing, were laid in bran, Great care was taken to keep the antiquities in strictly classified groups, textiles all in one box, jewellery all in another, and so on. There may well be a delay of a year or two before some of the boxes are unpacked, and it will be a great saving of time and labour if all the objects of one type are in a single box. Eighty-nine boxes in all were packed, but to lessen the danger in transit these were enclosed within thirty-four heavy packing-cases.

Then came the question of transport. At the river bank a steam barge was waiting, sent by the Department of Antiquities, but between the laboratory and the river stretched a distance of five and a half miles of rough road, with awkward curves and dangerous gradients. Three possibilities of transport were open to us—camels, hand porterage and Décauville railway, and we decided on the third as least likely to jar the cases. They were loaded, accordingly, on a number of flat cars, and by the evening of 13 May they were ready to begin their journey down the Valley, the road by which they had passed, under such different circumstances, three thousand years before.

At daybreak on the following morning the cars began to move. Now, when we talk of railways the reader must not imagine that we had a line laid down for us all the way to the river, for a permanent way would take many months to construct. We had, on the contrary, to lay it as we went, carrying the rails round in a continuous chain as the cars moved forward. Fifty labourers were engaged in the work, and each had his particular job, pushing the cars, laying the rails, or bringing up the spare ones from behind. It sounds a tedious process, but it is wonderful how fast the ground can be covered. By ten o'clock on the morning of the 15th—fifteen hours of actual work—the whole distance had been accomplished, and the cases were safely stowed upon the barge. There were some anxious moments in the rough Valley road, but nothing untoward happened, and the fact that the whole operation was carried out in such short time, and without any kind of mishap, is a fine testimonial to the zeal of our workmen. I may add that the work was carried out under a scorching sun, with a shade temperature of considerably over a hundred, the metal rails under these conditions being almost too hot to touch.

On the river journey the cases were in charge of an escort of soldiers supplied by the Mudir of the Province, and after a seven-day journey all arrived safely in Cairo. There we unpacked a few of the more valuable objects, to be placed on immediate exhibition. The rest of the cases remain stored in the museum.

Detail from the painted wooden casket (see page 47)

11

The opening of the sealed door

B Y THE MIDDLE OF FEBRUARY our work in the Antechamber was finished. With the exception of the two sentinel statues, left for a special reason, all its contents had been removed to the laboratory, every inch of its floor had been swept and sifted for the last bead or fallen piece of inlay, and it now stood bare and empty. We were ready at last to penetrate the mystery of the sealed door.

Friday, the 17th, was the day appointed, and at two o'clock those who were to be privileged to witness the ceremony met by appointment above the tomb. They included Lord Carnarvon, Lady Evelyn Herbert, H.E. Abd el Halim Pasha Suleman, Minister of Public Works, M. Lacau, Director-General of the Service of Antiquities, Sir William Garstin, Sir Charles Cust, Mr. Lythgoe, Curator of the Egyptian Department of the Metropolitan Museum, New York, Professor Breasted, Dr. Alan Gardiner, Mr. Winlock, the Hon. Mervyn Herbert, the Hon. Richard Bethell, Mr. Engelbach, Chief Inspector of the Department of Antiquities, three Egyptian inspectors of the Department of Antiquities, the representative of the Government Press Bureau, and the members of the staff—about twenty persons in all. By a quarter past two the whole company had assembled, so we removed our coats and filed down the sloping passage into the tomb.

In the Antechamber everything was prepared and ready, and to those who had not visited it since the original opening of the tomb it must have presented a strange sight. We had screened the statues with boarding to protect them from possible damage, and between them we had erected a small platform, just high enough to enable us to reach the upper part of the doorway, having determined, as the safest plan, to work from the top downwards. A short distance back from the platform there was a barrier, and beyond, knowing that there might be hours of work ahead of us, we had provided chairs for the visitors. On either side standards had been set up for our lamps, their light shining full upon the doorway. Looking back, we realize what a strange, incongruous picture the chamber must have presented, but at the time I question whether such an idea even crossed our minds. One thought and one only was possible. There before us lay the sealed door, and with its opening we were to blot out the centuries and stand in the presence of a king who reigned three thousand years ago. My own feelings as I mounted the platform were a strange mixture, and it was with a trembling hand that I struck the first blow.

My first care was to locate the wooden lintel above the door: then very carefully I chipped away the plaster and picked out the small stones which formed the uppermost layer of the filling. The temptation to stop and peer inside at every moment was irresistible, and when, after about ten minutes' work, I had made a hole large enough to enable me to do so, I inserted

One of the sentinel statues

an electric torch. An astonishing sight its light revealed, for there, within a yard of the doorway, stretching as far as one could see and blocking the entrance to the chamber, stood what to all appearance was a solid wall of gold. For the moment there was no clue as to its meaning, so as quickly as I dared I set to work to widen the hole. This had now become an operation of considerable difficulty, for the stones of the masonry were not accurately squared blocks built regularly upon one another, but rough slabs of varying size, some so heavy that it took all one's strength to lift them: many of them, too, as the weight above was removed, were left so precariously balanced that the least false movement would have sent them sliding inwards to crash upon the contents of the chamber below. We were also endeavouring to preserve the seal-impressions upon the thick mortar of the outer face, and this added considerably to the difficulty of handling the stones. Mace and Callender were helping me by this time, and each stone was cleared on a regular system. With a crowbar I gently eased it up, Mace holding it to prevent it falling forwards; then he and I lifted it out and passed it back to Callender, who transferred it on to one of the foremen, and so, by a chain of workmen, up the passage and out of the tomb altogether.

With the removal of a very few stones the mystery of the golden wall was solved. We were at the entrance of the actual burial-chamber of the king, and that which barred our way was the side of an immense gilt shrine built to cover and protect the sarcophagus. It was visible now from the Antechamber by the light of the standard lamps, and as stone after stone was removed, and its gilded surface came gradually into view, we could, as though by electric current, feel the tingle of excitement which thrilled the spectators behind the barrier. We who were doing the work were probably less excited, for our whole energies were taken up with the task in hand—that of removing the blocking without an accident. The fall of a single stone might have done irreparable damage to the delicate surface of the shrine, so, directly the hole was large enough, we made an additional protection for it by inserting a mattress on the inner side of the door-blocking, suspending it from the wooden lintel of the doorway. Two hours of hard work it took us to clear away the blocking, or at least as much of it as was necessary for the moment; and at one point, when near the bottom, we had to delay operations for a space while we collected the scattered beads from a necklace brought by the plunderers from the chamber within and dropped upon the threshold. This last was a terrible trial to our patience, for it was a slow business, and we were all of us excited to see what might be within; but finally it was done, the last stones were removed, and the way to the innermost chamber lay open before us.

In clearing away the blocking of the doorway we had discovered that the level of the inner chamber was about four feet lower than that of the Antechamber, and this, combined with the fact that there was but a narrow space between door and shrine, made an entrance by no means easy to effect. Fortunately, there were no smaller antiquities at this end of the chamber, so I lowered myself down, and then, taking one of the portable lights, I edged cautiously to the corner of the shrine and looked beyond it. At the corner two beautiful alabaster vases blocked the way, but I could see that if these were removed we should have a clear path to the other end of the chamber; so, carefully marking the spot on which they stood, I picked them up— with the exception of the king's wishing-cup they were of finer quality and more graceful shape than any we had yet found—and passed them back to the Antechamber. Lord Carnarvon and M. Lacau now joined me, and, picking our way along the narrow passage between shrine and wall, paying out the wire of our light behind us, we investigated further.

It was, beyond any question, the sepulchral chamber in which we stood, for there, towering above us, was one of the great gilt shrines beneath which kings were laid. So enormous was this structure (17 feet by 11 feet, and 9 feet high, we found afterwards) that it filled within a little the entire area of the chamber, a space of some two feet only separating it from the walls

Lord Carnarvon (left) and Howard Carter opening the door to the sepulchral chamber

on all four sides, while its roof, with cornice top and torus moulding, reached almost to the ceiling. From top to bottom it was overlaid with gold, and upon its sides there were inlaid panels of brilliant blue faience, in which were represented, repeated over and over, the magic symbols which would ensure its strength and safety. Around the shrine, resting upon the ground, there were a number of funerary emblems, and, at the north end, the seven magic oars the king would need to ferry himself across the waters of the underworld. The walls of the chamber, unlike those of the Antechamber, were decorated with brightly painted scenes and inscriptions, brilliant in their colours, but evidently somewhat hastily executed.

These last details we must have noticed subsequently, for at the time our one thought was of the shrine and of its safety. Had the thieves penetrated within it and disturbed the royal burial? Here, on the eastern end, were the great folding doors, closed and bolted, but not sealed, that would answer the question for us. Eagerly we drew the bolts, swung back the doors, and there within was a second shrine with similar bolted doors, and upon the bolts a seal, intact. This seal we determined not to break, for our doubts were resolved, and we could not penetrate further without risk of serious damage to the monument. I think at the moment we did not even want to break the seal, for a feeling of intrusion had descended heavily upon us with the opening of the doors, heightened, probably, by the almost painful impressiveness of a linen pall, decorated with golden rosettes, which drooped above the inner shrine. We felt that we were in the presence of the dead king and must do him reverence, and in imagination could see the doors of the successive shrines open one after the other till the innermost disclosed the king himself. Carefully, and as silently as possible, we re-closed the great swing doors, and passed on to the farther end of the chamber.

Here a surprise awaited us, for a low door, eastwards from the sepulchral chamber, gave entrance to yet another chamber, smaller than the outer ones and not so lofty. This doorway, unlike the others, had not been closed and sealed. We were able, from where we stood, to get a clear view of the whole of the contents, and a single glance sufficed to tell us that here, within this little chamber, lay the greatest treasures of the tomb. Facing the doorway, on the farther side, stood the most beautiful monument that I have ever seen—so lovely that it made one gasp with wonder and admiration. The central portion of it consisted of a large shrine-shaped chest, completely overlaid with gold, and surmounted by a cornice of sacred cobras. Surrounding this, free-standing, were statues of the four tutelary goddesses of the dead—gracious figures with outstretched protective arms, so natural and lifelike in their pose, so pitiful and compassionate the expression upon their faces, that one felt it almost sacrilege to look at them. One guarded the shrine on each of its four sides, but whereas the figures at front and back kept their gaze firmly fixed upon their charge, an additional note of touching realism was imparted by the other two, for their heads were turned sideways, looking over their shoulders towards the entrance, as though to watch against surprise. There is a simple grandeur about this monument that made an irresistible appeal to the imagination, and I am not ashamed to confess that it brought a lump to my throat. It is undoubtedly the canopic chest and contains the jars which play such an important part in the ritual of mummification.

There were a number of other wonderful things in the chamber, but we found it hard to take them in at the time, so inevitably were one's eyes drawn back again and again to the lovely little goddess figures. Immediately in front of the entrance lay the figure of the jackal god Anubis, upon his shrine, swathed in linen cloth, and resting upon a portable sled, and behind this the head of a bull upon a stand—emblems, these, of the underworld. In the south side of the chamber lay an endless number of black shrines and chests, all closed and sealed save one, whose open doors revealed statues of Tutankhamen standing upon black leopards. On the farther wall were more shrine-shaped boxes and miniature coffins of gilded wood, these last

The oars placed between the outermost shrine and the wall of the Burial Chamber

undoubtedly containing funerary statuettes of the king. In the centre of the room, left of the Anubis and the bull, there was a row of magnificent caskets of ivory and wood, decorated and inlaid with gold and blue faience, one, whose lid we raised, containing a gorgeous ostrich-feather fan with ivory handle, fresh and strong to all appearance as when it left the maker's hand. There were also, distributed in different quarters of the chamber, a number of model boats with sails and rigging all complete, and, at the north side, yet another chariot.

Such, from a hurried survey, were the contents of this innermost chamber. We looked anxiously for evidence of plundering, but on the surface there was none. Unquestionably the thieves must have entered, but they cannot have done more than open two or three of the caskets. Most of the boxes, as has been said, have still their seals intact, and the whole contents of the chamber, in fortunate contrast to those of the Antechamber and the Annexe, still remain in position exactly as they were placed at the time of burial.

How much time we occupied in this first survey of the wonders of the tomb I cannot say, but it must have seemed endless to those anxiously waiting in the Antechamber. Not more than three at a time could be admitted with safety, so, when Lord Carnarvon and M. Lacau came out, the others came in pairs: first Lady Evelyn Herbert, the only woman present, with Sir William Garstin, and then the rest in turn. It was curious, as we stood in the Antechamber, to watch their faces as, one by one, they emerged from the door. Each had a dazed, bewildered look in his eyes, and each in turn, as he came out, threw up his hands before him, an unconscious gesture of impotence to describe in words the wonders that he had seen. They were indeed indescribable, and the emotions they had aroused in our minds were of too intimate a nature to communicate, even though we had the words at our command. It was an experience which, I am sure, none of us who were present is ever likely to forget, for in imagination—and not wholly in imagination either—we had been present at the funeral ceremonies of a king long dead and almost forgotten. At a quarter past two we had filed down into the tomb, and when, three hours later, hot, dusty, and dishevelled, we came out once more into the light of day, the very Valley seemed to have changed for us and taken on a more personal aspect. We had been given the Freedom.

17 February was a day set apart for an inspection of the tomb by Egyptologists, and fortunately most of those who were in the country were able to be present. On the following day the Queen of the Belgians and her son Prince Alexander, who had come to Egypt for that special purpose, honoured us with a visit, and were keenly interested in everything they saw. Lord and Lady Allenby and a number of other distinguished visitors were present on this occasion. A week later, for reasons stated in an earlier chapter, the tomb was closed and once again re-buried.

So ends our preliminary season's work on the tomb of King Tutankhamen. Now as to that which lies ahead of us. In the coming winter our first task, a difficult and anxious one, will be the dismantling of the shrines in the sepulchral chamber. It is probable, from evidence supplied by the Rameses IV papyrus, that there will be a succession of no fewer than five of these shrines, built one within the other, before we come to the stone sarcophagus in which the king is lying, and in the spaces between these shrines we may expect to find a number of beautiful objects. With the mummy—if, as we hope and believe, it remains untouched by plunderers—there should certainly lie the crowns and other regalia of a king of Egypt. How long this work in the sepulchral chamber will take we cannot tell at present, but it must be finished before we tackle the innermost chamber of all, and we shall count ourselves lucky if we can accomplish the clearing of both in a single season. A further season will surely be required for the Annexe with its confused jumble of contents.

Imagination falters at the thought of what the tomb may yet disclose, for the material dealt with so far represents but a quarter—and that probably the least important quarter—of the treasure which it contains. There are still many exciting moments in store for us before we complete our task, and we look forward eagerly to the work that lies ahead. One shadow must inevitably rest upon it, one regret, which all the world must share—the fact that Lord Carnarvon was not permitted to see the full fruition of his work[1]; and in the completion of that work we, who are to carry it out, would dedicate to his memory the best that in us lies.

Transporting objects from the tomb

12

Tutankhamen

WHENEVER AN ARCHAEOLOGICAL DISCOVERY lays bare traces of a remote age, and the vanished human lives it fostered, we turn at once instinctively to the facts revealed to us with which we are most in sympathy. And these are invariably human in their interests. A withered lotus flower, some emblem of affection, some simple domestic trait, will bring back the past for us, on its human side, far more vividly than the sentiment can be conveyed by austere records or pompous official inscriptions boasting how some dim "King of Kings" overwhelmed his enemies and trampled on their pride.

This is, to a certain extent, true of the discovery of the tomb of Tutankhamen. Of the young boy king we know very little, but as to his tastes and temperament we can now make some shrewd guesses. As the priestly vehicle through whom divine influence was transmitted to the Theban world, as the earthly representative of Re—the great Sun-god—the young king scarcely takes for us clear or realizable shape, but as a creature of ordinary human dispositions, a lover of the chase, as an eager sportsman, he becomes easily and amiably intelligible. We have here that "touch of nature which makes the whole world kin."

The religious aspects of most races become modified by time, circumstance and education. In some cases their feeling towards death and its mysteries is refined and spiritualized. With the growth of culture, love, pity, sorrow, affection, find tenderer modes of utterance and expression. Of this we have evidence in Greek epitaphs and Latin tomb inscriptions. But if the more delicate shades of sorrow be less obviously manifested by the ancient Egyptians, it is rather because the gentler human moods seem overwhelmed under the weight of their elaborate burial practices, than that these emotions are absent. Belief in the continuity of the human soul is the idea whence these practices were evolved. To strengthen this conviction and impress it on the world, no sacrifice was deemed too great. The afterlife seems in their eyes to have been more important than their worldly existence, and the most careless student of their customs may wonder at the lavish generosity with which this ancient people launched their dead on their last mysterious journey.

If, however, tradition and priestly practice governed ancient Egyptian burial ceremonial, as the contents of Tutankhamen's tomb suggest, their ritual left room for a personal side which confronted the grief of the mourners, whilst it aimed at encouraging the dead on their journey through the dangers of the Underworld. This human sentiment has not been concealed by the mysterious symbolism of a complex creed. It dawns on the observer gradually as he pursues his investigations. The impression of a personal sorrow is perhaps more distinctly conveyed to us from what we learn from the tomb of Tutankhamen than by most other discoveries. It meets us as an emotion which we are accustomed to deem comparatively modern in origin. The tiny

Tutankhamen. A detail from the golden shrine (see page 51)

wreath on the stately coffin, the beautiful alabaster wishing-cup with its touching inscription, the treasured reed with its suggestive memories—cut by the young king himself by the lake-side—these, and other objects, help to convey the message—the message of the living mourning the dead.

The sense of premature loss faintly haunts the tomb. The royal youth, obviously full of life and capable of enjoying it, had started, in very early manhood—who knows under what tragic circumstances?—on his last journey from the radiant Egyptian skies into the gloom of that tremendous Underworld. How could grief be best expressed? In his tomb we are conscious of this effort, and the emotion thus gently and gracefully exhibited is the expression of that human regret which knits our sympathies with a sorrow more than three thousand years old.

As has been already mentioned in earlier chapters, politically we gather that the king's brief reign and life must have been a singularly uneasy one. It may be that he was the tool of obscure political forces working behind the throne. This, at least from the sparse data that we have, is a reasonable conjecture. But however much Tutankhamen may have been the tool of political religious movements, whatever political influence the youthful king may have possessed, or whatever his own religious feelings, if any, may have been—and this must remain uncertain—we do gather not a little information as to his tastes and inclinations from the innumerable scenes on the furniture of his tomb. It is in these that we find the most vivid suggestions of Tutankhamen's affectionate domestic relations with the young queen, and that evidence of his love of sport, of the royal and youthful passion for the chase, which makes him so human to our sympathies after the lapse of so many dark centuries.

What, for instance, could be more charming than the tableau upon the throne, so touchingly represented? Such impressions, for the moment, seem to lift us across the gulf of years and destroy the sense of time. Ankhesenamen, the charming girlish wife, is seen adding a touch of perfume to the young king's collar, or putting the last touches to his toilet before he enters into some great function in the palace. Nor must we forget that little wreath of flowers, still retaining their tinge of colour, that farewell offering placed upon the brow of the young king's effigy as he lay within his quartzite sarcophagus.

Other incidents represented suggest even a touch of humour. Among episodes of the daily private life of the king and queen on a small golden *naos*, we find Tutankhamen accompanied by his lion-cub, shooting wild-duck with bow and arrow, whilst, at his feet, squats the girlish queen. With one hand she is handing him an arrow, while with the other she points out a fat duck. On the same *naos* the young spouse is represented offering to him sacred libations, flowers and collarettes, or tying a pendant around his neck. Here we have the young couple in various simple and engaging attitudes. The queen accompanies the king on another fowling expedition in a reed canoe. She is seen affectionately supporting his arm as though he were wearied by state affairs, and then again—and there is a suggestion of playfulness in these little glimpses of their private life—we find him pouring sweet perfume on her hand as they are resting in their cabinet. These are charming scenes and full of the kindliness which it pleases us to consider modern.

Upon a golden fan, found between the sepulchral shrines that covered and protected his sarcophagus, a fan, such as we see pictured in Roman times, and actually used today in the Vatican, is a beautifully embossed and chased picture of Tutankhamen, hunting ostriches for the plumes for that very flabellum. On its reverse side he is seen returning home triumphant, his attendants carrying his quarry—two dead ostriches—and the coveted feathers under his arm.

Scenes of the young sportsman's activities constantly confront us. Upon trappings of the chariot-harness he is shown practising archery. We gather, too, that, like some of our earlier kings, he was a lover of the bow. And, as proof of his proficiency in archery, there was treasured in his tomb, among boomerangs and similar missiles of the chase, a magnificent bow-of-honour,

A gold fan showing Tutankhamen hunting

covered with sheet-gold, decorated with fine filigree gold-work, and richly adorned with semi-precious stones and coloured glass. In a long box in the Antechamber of his tomb were a number of different kinds of bows decorated with ornamental barks and finely fashioned arrows, while lying nearest to him, under the golden shrines that shielded his sarcophagus, were other bows and arrows. The sheath of a handsome gold dagger, found girded to his waist within the wrappings of his mummy, has also wild animals embossed upon it. Even his cosmetic jar bears evidence of his pastime. On it are portrayed bulls, lions, hounds, gazelle and hare—the huntsman's favourite game. His slughi hounds are especially included in scenes suggesting fondness of field sport and of an open-air life.

There can be little doubt that in the Theban neighbourhood, in those days, the greater area of morass attracted and harboured large quantities of game. Game also abounded on its desert borders, and in the scrub of the desert wady. In the marshes the boy king shot all kinds of wild-fowl. In extensive preserves the desert afforded a varied field for the skill of the royal sportsman, who hunted in his chariot, while his courtiers followed in cars and his attendants coursed on foot. Within these preserves it would seem to have been the custom to collect every variety of game. When hunting, the young Tutankhamen shot with bow and arrow, his slughi hounds being loosed in turn on the game when sighted.

Of his interest in sport, as thus exhibited, we have striking evidence in a delightful and vigorous sketch found while nearing the entrance of his tomb, and possibly drawn by one of the artisans employed in making the sepulchre: it is on a flake of limestone and represents the young king, aided by his slughi hound, slaying a lion with a spear. When an ordinary artisan is capable of such vigorous work, we naturally expect art of extreme beauty from the highly-trained craftsmen employed by the rulers of Egypt, who seem to have been generally men of artistic discernment. The treasures in Tutankhamen's tomb showed how fully this expectation was justified.

One of the great artistic treasures is a painted wooden casket found in the Antechamber. Its outer face, completely covered with gesso, has, upon this prepared surface, a series of brilliantly coloured and exquisitely painted designs: hunting scenes upon its curved lid, battle scenes upon its sides, wherein Tutankhamen and his suite are most energetically engaged, whilst upon the ends of the box are representations of the king, in lion form, trampling upon his alien foes. The vigour, imagination, and dramatic force displayed in these scenes is extraordinary, and incomparable in Egyptian art. In the war scenes we see the youthful but all-conquering monarch trampling under foot, with great gusto, his African and Asiatic enemies. Fine as they are we must admit the braggart spirit is not absent. The mighty monarch, for the sake of effect no longer a slender youth, is shooting down his enemies from his chariot, panic is before him, the dead at his feet. Such pictures of Egyptian kings are, of course, traditional. They are probably, in this case, merely the customary homage of the court painter. That he took the field of war in person, especially at his age, is improbable, but of such polite fiction, kings and conquerors in the Oriental world have always been singularly tolerant. The paintings on the casket's lid are wonderfully spirited. Here we have hunting scenes full of the sense of speed and movement. Incident and action are manifold, and in them all Tutankhamen is accompanied by his slughi hounds. Even in the battle scenes his dogs are seen pulling and tearing at the defeated foe. The king in his chariot, drawn by prancing steeds, gorgeous in their trappings, is pursuing desert fauna. Before him flee antelope and ostrich, wild ass and hyena—all the denizens of the desert, including lions and lionesses. Seen between the flying figures of the animals and the feet of his followers, tufts of gay desert flora, forming the scrub of the wady, are charmingly suggested. Tutankhamen, with his slughi hounds around him—his followers at respectful distance—is thundering down the wady-bed, the panic-stricken quarry fleeing on all sides. The agonized beasts are rendered with the utmost realism. There are moments—in the group of hunted lions for example—when the artist reaches almost tragic force. The agonized, shaft-pierced beasts are portrayed with splendid power. One of them—the king beast—stricken to the heart—having sprung into the air in the final spasm of death, is falling headlong to the ground. Another clutches with his paw at a shaft which has entered his open mouth, and hangs broken in his jaws, meanwhile the half-grown cub is slinking away with tail between its legs, whilst wounded comrades lie in tortured postures of pathetic suffering. But if the historical accuracy of this beautiful work be doubted, there can be no two opinions as to its merits in interpreting the king's true passion and inclinations. These exquisite pictures in delicate miniature painting are, in fact, idealized hunting scenes wherein the young man's tastes and temperament, as well as the spirit of the chase, have been captured and interpreted.

Evidences of the kindlier affections are traits we scarcely expect to find among a Pharaoh's relics. His predecessors have left too few memories of the gentler feelings, still the messages of archaeology are not always those we most expect, and we are surprised, as well as touched, by the expression of simpler human feelings charmingly portrayed on Tutankhamen's funerary furniture. From them we gather that he was a gallant and amiable youth, loving horse and hound, sport and military display. But there is another side to the picture. The traditional ornament, worked in gold on the chariots, the beautiful carving of African and Asiatic prisoners bound to the king's walking-sticks, and on his furniture all suggest the formidable Pharaoh, bent, metaphorically at least, on "making his enemy his footstool", and typify the braggart spirit associated with the character of Egypt's ancient rulers, although as we have it here, it is less overwhelmingly expressed than in other tombs.

The silver trumpets dedicated to the legions or units of the Egyptian army, found in the Antechamber and Burial Chamber, appeal to the imagination. The military experience of Tutankhamen must have been small indeed, but we may nevertheless imagine him surrounded by his generals, state officials and courtiers, taking the salute whilst the massed legions in military pageant went by.

His mummy, like his statues, shows him to have been a slim youth with large head, presenting structural resemblance to the dreamer Ankhenaten, who in all probability was not only his father-in-law but also his father.

Thus step by step, the excavator's spade, in various departments of archaeology, is revealing to us the world of the past, and the more our knowledge extends, the greater grows our wonder —possibly our regret—that human nature should have so little changed during the few thousand years of which we have some historical knowledge. Especially our gaze is fixed on ancient Egypt which has given us such vivid glimpses of a wonderful past. On painted casket, decorated chair, on shrine, tomb chapel or temple wall, her ancient life passes in strange and moving pageant. In many points our sympathies meet, but it is chiefly by her art that we are brought nearest to her feeling, and that we recognize in the royal sportsman, the dog-lover, the young husband and the slender wife, creatures in human taste, emotion and affection, very like ourselves.

Thus we learn not to overvalue the present, and our modern perspective becomes less complacent and more philosophical. There are, we are tempted to believe, certain characteristics which became innate in man in those dim ages as yet but slightly touched by archaeological research. There are glimmering atavisms of which we are barely conscious, and it may be these that awaken in us sympathy for the youthful Tutankhamen, for his queen, and all the life suggested by his funerary furniture. It may be these instincts which make us yearn to unravel the mystery of those dim political intrigues by which we suspect he was beset, even whilst following his slughi hounds across marsh and desert, or shooting duck among the reeds with his smiling queen. The mystery of his life still eludes us—the shadows move but the dark is never quite uplifted.

African and Asiatic prisoners bound to one of the king's walking sticks

13

The Tomb and Burial Chamber

THE FEAR AND AWE associated with death were at least as deeply implanted in the minds of the ancient as in those of the modern world. These emotions have reached us through dim ancestral channels, colouring successive mythologies, moulding human conduct, nor have they left Christian theology untouched. At all times and in all races, death has loomed as the most tremendous mystery and the last inevitable necessity that man's obscure destiny must face—and pathetic have been his efforts to throw light on the darkness shrouding his future. His life and art were once mainly concerned with this insoluble problem. Human reason has always attempted to calm human fears; man's mind, yearning and active, has instinctively endeavoured to find in his beliefs solace for them—to call up some protection against the dangers that fill the dark gulf of the Unknown. But one touching glimmer of hope has always shone through the gloom. On the threshold of death he has sought comfort in the love and affection which he hoped would knit him to the living—a natural yearning revealed in ancient burial rituals. It is apparent in the expressed desire—as in Jacob's request to his son—that his bones should be laid amid his kin, and the beloved surroundings of his native land, and the evidence of scientific investigation suggests that the instinct was atavistic in its origin. But from the very earliest times the means of obtaining comfort in this great problem have been modified, whilst fundamental tradition has remained. In the Valley of the Nile a simple shallow grave developed into a great pyramid-tomb and mortuary chapel. From the most grandiose and impressive of all sepulchral efforts to guard the memory of the dead, change after change has moulded custom, until such simplicity has been attained that those vast ancient preparations have shrunk to a brief epitaph and a wreath of flowers. However, of those varied epoch-making transitions, we deal here with but one, that of the Egyptian New Empire.

Many of the funeral customs of the older Egyptian periods were widely practised in the Theban New Empire; where some of them disappear it was only to make room for more elaborate conceptions which were intended to be equally beneficial for the dead. One of the innovations was the increased amount of household furniture and personal effects that were placed in the tomb. Another, instead of the king's mortuary chapel and sepulchre being contiguous, in the New Empire the royal mummies were buried in elaborate hypogea excavated in the cliffs far away from their mortuary buildings. These were as sumptuous in decoration as their chapels. But in the Eighteenth Dynasty they began by decorating only the sepulchral chamber with texts deemed most necessary for the dead. Later, in the Nineteenth and Twentieth Dynasties, the preceding corridors, passages and antechambers, which led to the burial chamber—called "The-Golden-Hall"—were covered from end to end with elaborate texts and scenes taken

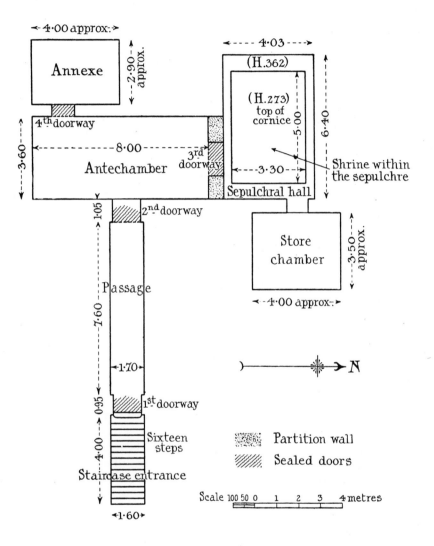

← 4·00 approx. →

Annexe

2·90 approx.

4·03

(H.362)

(H.273)
top of
cornice

5·00

6·40

4th doorway

3·60

8·00

3rd
doorway

Antechamber

Shrine within
the sepulchre

3·30

Sepulchral hall

1·05

2nd doorway

Store
chamber

3·50 approx.

Passage

7·60

← 4·00 approx. →

1·70

N

0·95

4·00

1st doorway

Sixteen
steps

Partition wall

Sealed doors

Staircase entrance

Scale 100 50 0   1   2   3   4 metres

← 1·60 →

Plan of Tutankhamen's tomb

principally from the sacred books concerning the realms of the dead, such as the books of "Amduat," "The Gates," "The Caverns," and "The Hymns to the Sun-god."

Most of these rock-cut hypogea were excavated in the desolate Valley of the Kings, actually some twenty-eight in number, while their mortuary chapels, many of them of the dimensions of great temples, were constructed on the desert plain bordering the arable land. It was in these buildings where ceremonies and offerings to the dead monarchs were celebrated, while "Osiris" rested in solitude, far away in the Valley, sealed within his "Silent Seat"—the tomb.

In the mortuary chapels upon the plain we find, as well as religious scenes, records of the individual reign to which they belong; but in the Valley tombs, or hypogea, texts concerning the realms of the dead and welcoming wishes of the gods of the West are alone found.

Commencing from the beginning of the Empire these rock-cut hypogea show stages of evolution, they gradually expand in importance, reaching their climax at the time of Thothmes IV, from which reign onwards, though we find certain additions, these additions disappear, and the tomb-plan gradually falls into decadence. It is only in the case of the tombs of the so-called heretic kings belonging to the "Aten" or monotheistic religion, that the orthodox pattern of the New Empire has not been adhered to. Hence, it is no surprise to find Tutankhamen's tomb unorthodox in type, though he reverted to the older religion—the worship of Amen. Contrary to Tutankhamen and King Ay, Horemheb, who usurped the throne and founded the Nineteenth Dynasty, in making his tomb in the Valley, reintroduced the orthodox plan in all its component parts. And in Horemheb's tomb one directly sees the transition from the Eighteenth Dynasty bent tomb to the straightened tomb form of his dynasty and of those which followed.

In the place of an elaborate series of corridors, sunken staircases, protective well and vestibule, further descending passages, antechamber, sepulchral hall, crypt and a series of four store-rooms, of the orthodox Theban plan, Tutankhamen's tomb merely comprises a sunken entrance-staircase, a descending passage, an antechamber with annexe, a burial chamber and one store-room, all small and of the simplest kind. In fact, it only conforms with the Theban pattern of the New Empire royal tomb in orientation, by having its burial chamber alone painted of a golden hue corresponding with "The-Golden-Hall," and by having in its walls niches for the magical figures of the four cardinal points.

The subjects painted upon the walls of this chamber, though resembling in many ways those of the tomb of his successor, King Ay, differ from those found in any of the other sepulchral chambers in the Valley. The style of painting is also not of Theban type, it shows distinct traits of El Amarna art. In contradistinction to this the decoration of Horemheb's tomb has distinct affinity with the art displayed in all the other royal tombs in the Valley, so much so that it led the late Sir Gaston Maspero into the supposition that it was the work of the same artists employed in Seti's tomb, constructed some twenty-five years later.

In orientation the Burial Chamber, as well as its nest of four shrines, sarcophagus, coffins and mummy, is east and west, accurate to within four degrees of magnetic north (November 1925). The doors of the shrines, in accordance with the guide-marks upon them, were intended to face west, but for reasons not altogether clear they were actually erected facing east: it may be that had the shrines been placed in their correct and intended orientation, access to their folding doors would have been most difficult, and their purpose constricted in that very small chamber, as it would have been wellnigh impossible to have introduced objects such as were found between the outermost and second shrines. In the following chapter other reasons for this incorrect orientation are suggested.

In shape the Burial Chamber is rectangular, having its long axis (east and west) at right angles to that of the Antechamber. With the exception of a difference in floor levels of about

Wall painting in the tomb showing Ay "opening the king's mouth"

four feet, the Antechamber and Burial Chamber were originally continuous, but were afterwards separated by a dry-masonry partition wall, in which was left a doorway guarded by the two sentinel statues of the king elsewhere described (on page 39).

The walls of the Burial Chamber were coated with a gypsum plaster, and were painted yellow with the exception of a dado which was coloured white. The rock ceiling was left plain in its rough and unfinished state. It is here interesting to note that traces of smoke, as from an oil lamp or torch, are visible upon the ceiling in the north-east corner.

The construction of the partition wall dividing the Antechamber from the Burial Chamber, and the plastering and decoration of the chamber itself, must have taken place after the burial of the king, the closing of the sarcophagus and the erection of the four shrines. This is proved by the following facts: the introduction of the sarcophagus, the burial, and the placing of the shrines, could not have been effected after the partition wall had been built, the doorway through it being insufficiently large. Again, the plastering and painting that covered the inner face of the partition wall was uniform with the rest of the decoration of the chamber. Thus the plastering and painting of the chamber must necessarily have been done after the erection of the shrines, under exceptionally difficult conditions and in a very confined space, which may account for the crudeness of the workmanship. The surfaces of the walls are covered with small brown fungus growths, the original germs of which were possibly introduced either with the plaster or the sizing of the paint, and were nourished by the enclosed humidity that exuded from the plaster after the chamber had been sealed up.

The subjects treated in the paintings upon the walls are of funerary and religious import. One scene is unprecedented, and that is the figure of the reigning King Ay presiding over the obsequies of his dead predecessor or co-regent.

Depicted on the east wall is a scene of the funeral procession wherein the deceased Tutankhamen upon a sledge is being drawn by courtiers to the tomb. The mummy is shown supported upon a lion-shaped bier, within a shrine on a boat, which rests upon the sledge. The bier painted here resembles that actually found in the sarcophagus under the coffins, while the shrine is of similar design to that which encloses the canopic chest and jars in the store-room of this tomb. Over the dead king are festoons of garlands; on the boat in front of the shrine is a sphinx rampant; before and behind the shrine are the mourning goddesses Nephthys and Isis respectively; and attached to the prow and stern of the boat, as well as on both sides of the shrine, are red and white pennants. The courtiers and high officials forming the cortège are divided up in the following order: a group of five nobles, then two groups of two nobles each, two officials wearing garments such as distinguish the viziers, and lastly a courtier. Each personage wears upon his wig or bare shaven head, as the case may be, a white linen fillet such as is usually found in funeral processions illustrated in private tomb chapels, and like those still used by the modern Egyptian on such occasions to distinguish relatives and retainers of the deceased's household. A legend above this procession tells us: "The Courtiers of the Royal Household going in procession with the Osiris King Tutankhamen to the West. They 'voice': O King! Come in peace! O God! Protector of the Land."

The wish calls to mind the not uncommon custom still in vogue in the Nile Valley, the deceased being often carried around the grave by the bearers to ensure approval, and the scene vividly calls to mind (Genesis, ch. 50, vv. 4–7) Joseph's burial of his father Jacob: "And when the days of his mourning were past, Joseph spake unto the house of Pharaoh, saying, If now I have found grace in your eyes, speak, I pray you, in the ears of Pharaoh saying, My father made me swear, saying, Lo, I die: in my grave which I have digged for me in the land of Canaan, there shalt thou bury me. Now therefore let me go up, I pray thee, and bury my father, and I will come again. And Pharaoh said, Go up, and bury thy father, according as he made thee

A detail of the sarcophagus showing one of the goddesses

swear. And Joseph went up to bury his father: and with him went up all the servants of Pharaoh, the elders of his house, and all the elders of the land of Egypt."

On the north wall, east corner, we find the scene of historical importance of Ay as king with royal insignia, clad in a leopard's skin of the *Sem* priest. Here King Ay officiates at the funeral ceremony of "The Opening of the Mouth" of the dead Tutankhamen represented as Osiris. Between the living and the dead monarchs are the objects connected with the ceremonial laid out upon a table, which are the adze, a human finger, the hind limb of an ox, the fan of a single ostrich feather, and a double plume-like object: these are surmounted by a row of five gold and silver cups containing what may be balls of incense such as we found in the Antechamber.

In the centre of the north wall Tutankhamen, wearing a wig, fillet and white kilt, stands before the goddess Nut, "Lady of Heaven, Mistress of the Gods," who gives "health and life to his nostril."

The third scene, at the west end of the wall, refers to the king's spiritual rather than his bodily form: it shows Tutankhamen followed by his "Ka" (spirit) embracing Osiris.

On the west wall are vignettes selected from certain chapters of the Book concerning Amduat (that which is within the Underworld), which are repeated among the mural decorations in the tomb of King Ay in the Wadyein: the outstanding features here being the assembly of the sacred cynocephalus apes, the "Kheper-boat-of-Re" and a procession of deities named: Maa, Nebtuba, Heru, Kashu and Nehes.

The south wall, wherein was the sealed doorway to the chamber, was composed partly of the built partition wall and the bed-rock itself. Depicted upon it are scenes of the king before certain divinities. At the west end, King Tutankhamen is figured between Anubis and Isis. He wears the *Khat* head-dress. The goddess Isis repeats here the same wishes as those of Nut upon the north wall, the words of which I have already given. Behind Anubis, the goddess Isis is again figured and she holds in both her hands symbols of water. She is accompanied by three "Great Gods, Lords of Duat" (i.e. of the Underworld).

These paintings, rough, conventional and severely simple as they are, have not the same austere character of the more elaborate texts and vignettes in the other Theban royal tombs; neither in their rendering do they show that affinity common to the art of those tombs. In fact, they might be described as almost transitional—between El Amarna and Theban style—the subjects themselves being curtailed in the greatest possible degree. These artistic traits are equally noticeable in the art displayed by the funerary furniture found in the tomb.

The rest of the tomb, i.e. the Antechamber, Annexe and Store-room, is quite simple and, like the descending passage, their well-cut rock surfaces are left unsmoothed.

We now turn to the contents of the Burial Chamber. When we entered it we found, lying beside a small hole made by the robbers through the masonry of the door which had been subsequently reclosed by the ancient Egyptian officials, portions of two necklaces dropped by a thief. Around the four sides of the great shrine which occupied almost the entire area of the chamber, were divers objects and emblems. A brief examination of the shrine and the objects surrounding it, showed that little damage had been done in this chamber by the predatory intruders, except that the folding doors of the great shrine had been opened for the purpose of peering in, and that the sealings of the wine-jars, placed between the shrine and the walls of the chamber, had been broken. But although the Burial Chamber had suffered little from the activities of the thieves, many objects had been stolen from the small Store-room beyond. Standing in the south-east corner was a lamp resting upon a trellis-work pedestal, carved out of pure translucent calcite. This lamp of chalice form, flanked with fretwork-ornament symbolizing "Unity" and "Eternity," ranks among the most interesting objects we had so far discovered. Its chalice-like cup, which held the oil and a floating wick, was neither decorated on its exterior nor interior surfaces, yet when the lamp was lit the king and queen were seen in brilliant colours within the thickness of its translucent stone. We, at first, were puzzled to know how this ingenious effect was accomplished. The explanation would seem to be that there were two cups turned and fitted, one within the other, and that on the outer wall of the inner cup a picture had been painted in semi-transparent colours, visible only through the translucent calcite when the lamp was lit.

Beneath this unique lamp, wrapped in reeds, was a silver trumpet, which, though tarnished with age, were it blown would still fill the Valley with a resounding blast. Neatly engraved upon it is a whorl of calices and sepals, the prenomen and nomen of Tutankhamen, and representations of the gods Re, Amen and Ptah. It is not unlikely that these gods may have had some connexion with the division of the field army into three corps or units, each legion under the special patronage of one of these deities—army divisions such as we well know existed in the reign of Rameses the Great. At the Dog River in Phoenicia are three military stelae of that reign, one to each of these gods, which were probably erected by the respective corps of the army. On a stelé recently discovered in Beisan in Palestine the same divisions or corps occur. We may assume, therefore, that this silver trumpet with its gold mountings is of military significance, and that the creation of those three legions patronized by Re, Amen and Ptah, of the Imperial army organization, existed in the Eighteenth Dynasty and probably before Tutankhamen's reign.

At the eastern end of the shrine were two massive folding doors, closed with ebony bolts shot into copper staples, their panels decorated with strange figures—headless demon guardians of the caverns of the Underworld. Before these doors stood an exquisite triple-lamp of floral-form, carved out of a single block of translucent calcite, in shape three lotiform cups, with stems and leaves springing from a single circular base, strangely suggestive as symbolizing the Theban Triad and resembling the *Tricerion* or three-branched candlestick that typifies the Holy Trinity of the Christian era. In front, standing along the east wall, was Amen's sacred goose (*Chenalopex Aegyptiacus*, Linn.) of wood, varnished black, and swathed in linen; beside it were two rush-work baskets collapsed with age, and a wine-jar bearing the legend: "Year 5, wine of the house of (?) Tutankhamen, from the Western river Chief of the Vintners, Kha."

Resting upon the ground, between the shrine and the north wall, were magic oars to ferry the king's barque across the waters of the Nether World, and with them, one at each end, curious devices in varnished black wood: one representing a *hes* vase between *propylae*, the other having "Feathers of Truth" between two kiosks, which contained faience cups filled respectively with natron and resin. At the western end of the chamber, in the northern and southern corners, were austere golden emblems of Anubis hung on lotiform poles, erect, standing some five or six feet in height, in alabaster pots, placed upon reed mats. They may belong to the dark world under the earth, where the sun sinks, and where also the dead sleep: emblems it may be to guide the dead through this domain, for was not Anubis—the Jackal—a prowler of the dusk, and did not Re send him forth to bury Osiris? But, in truth, their meaning is obscure and probably nearly as remote from Tutankhamen as his day from ours. With these emblems were four gilt wooden objects which may signify the swathing linen of the dead; on the other hand, these curious symbols of gilt wood, according to Dr. Alan Gardiner, have given rise to the phonetic hieroglyph "to awake," thus one might infer that they may have some connexion with the awakening of the dead. On the floor, beside these curious symbols, were four small rough clay troughs, in which they may have stood. Resting against the south-west corner was an immense funerary bouquet composed of twigs and branches of the persea (*Mimasops Schimperi*) and olive (*Olea Europa*).

When we drew back those ebony bolts of the great shrine, the doors swung back as if only

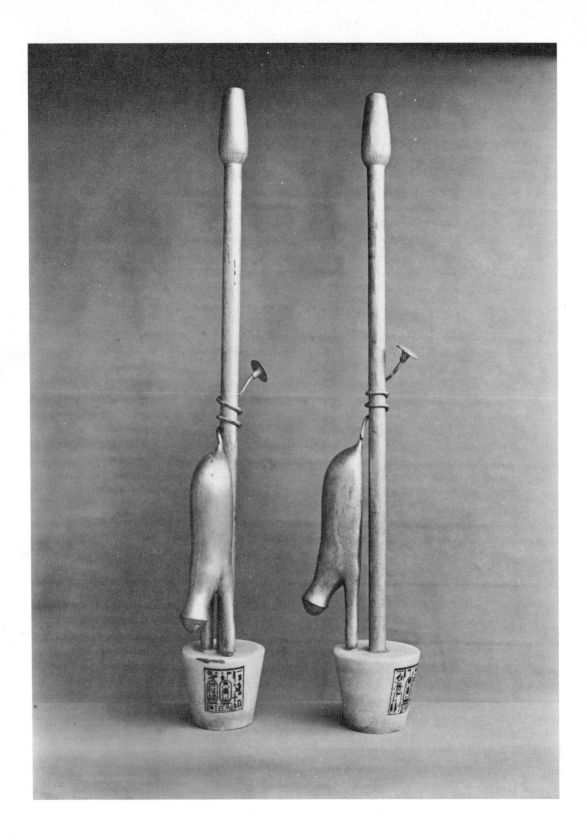

closed yesterday, and revealed within yet another shrine, in type like the first, save for the blue inlay. It has similar bolted doors, but upon them was a seal intact, bearing the name of Tutankhamen and a recumbent jackal over Egypt's nine foes. Above the shrine drooped a linen pall. This bespangled linen pall brown with age, still hanging on its curious wooden supports, was rent by the weight of the gilt bronze marguerites sewn to its fabric. The shrine, dazzling from the brilliance of its gold, was decorated with scenes wrought, in beautiful incised-relief, from the book "Of that which is in the Underworld"—that guide to the Hereafter, which points out to the deceased the road he should take, and explains to him the various malefic powers he must meet during his subterranean journey. According to this book two routes led him to the land of the blessed, one by water, the other by land, and it further shows that there were by-ways leading to seething rivers of fire by which he must not travel.

The pall made us realize that we were in the presence of a dead king of past ages. The unbroken seal upon the closed doors of the second shrine gave us the data we were seeking. Had the tomb-robbers, who had entered the Antechamber, its Annexe, the Burial Chamber and its Store-room by any chance reached the king? The shrine was intact, its doors bore their original seal uninjured, indicating that the robbers had not reached him. Henceforth, we knew that, within the shrine, we should be treading where no one had entered, and that we should be dealing with material untouched and unharmed since the boy king was laid to rest nearly three thousand three hundred years ago. We had at last found what we never dreamed of attaining—an absolute insight into the funerary customs followed in the burial of an ancient Pharaoh. Ten years of toil had not been wasted and our hopes were to be realized with a result far exceeding our expectations.

In front of the shrine's doors stood the king and queen's perfume vase carved of pure semi-translucent alabaster (calcite), a rare masterpiece of intricate stone-carving embellished with gold and ivory. It would seem that the royal lapidary delighted in intricate design typifying the "Union of the Two Countries," Upper and Lower Egypt, symbolized by a knot of stems of conventional papyrus and lotus flowers, but here he has even surpassed himself by adding to his favourite theme two charming epicene figures of Hapi. They represent the Upper and Lower Nile, and they embrace not only the flanking floral ornament, but also slender sceptres encircled by uraei bearing the red and white crowns of the "Two Kingdoms." The lip of the vase itself the artist has surmounted with a vulture with wide spreading wings. Unhappily, so delicate was the workmanship, the intumescence of the sacred material it held had burst the vase asunder. In front of this beautiful object, partially covered by fallen portions of the pall, stood another powerful piece of conventional art embodying, in this case, certain characteristics of the eastern Mediterranean. This was a cosmetic jar of various kinds of carved calcite which still contained its cosmetic, plastic and fragrant. This jar is remarkable for its unique design; it is cylindrical in shape, rests on four prisoners of African and Mediterranean type, it has a *Bes* column on either side, a delightful recumbent lion with long protruding red tongue on the lid, and upon its sides are scenes among desert flora, incised and filled in with pigment, of lions attacking bulls, hounds chasing antelope, gazelle and hare.

On either side, between the two shrines, stacked in the right and left corners, were numerous ceremonial maces, sticks, staves and bows, some carefully wrapped in linen. Perhaps the choicest of them all are the gold and silver sticks, made of two thin tubular shafts supporting tiny statuettes of the youthful monarch, cast and chased in their respective metals. It would be almost impossible to describe the refinement of these graceful figures of sedate but youthful bearing. Chubby little figures are here represented very subtly modelled. Their crowns and skirts are chased. The gesture of their hands is of youthful simplicity. Both are exactly alike save for their metals. They are clearly the production of a master hand. These gold and silver

The two curious Anubis emblems

sticks were in all probability intended for ceremonial and processional purposes.

A series of curved batons, most elaborately decorated with minute marquetry of variegated barks, iridescent elytra of beetles, and broad bands of burnished gold with scroll-pattern borders, next claimed our admiration. One of these was completely veneered with intricate ivory and ebony patterns, divided by bands of floral decoration, and had carved hunting devices on its ivory tips. Among other sticks of perhaps more personal nature, was a simple plain gold stick with lapis lazuli glass top, inscribed "Take for thyself the wand of gold in order that thou mayest follow thy beloved father Amen, most beloved of gods;" another was encrusted with exquisite glass inlay intermingled with gold filigree work on the handle, called "The beautiful stick of His Majesty;" the third was a plain reed mounted with broad gold and electrum ferrules and plaited gold wire. We wondered why such an ordinary and plain reed should have been so richly mounted, but the legend written upon it gave the touching solution: "A reed which His Majesty cut with his own hand." The remainder of this remarkable collection of royal appurtenances was of a more ceremonial and religious kind, such as maces, *Uas* sceptres, crooked and forked sticks, made of wood covered with gesso and gilt.

Such were the appointments of the Burial Chamber, mostly of a religious character, some of them almost austere, but all of them in some way conveying an insight into the past, and expressing a fine art in the service of superstition. One could not but be deeply impressed by this superb example of solicitude for the well-being of the dead, animated as it was by extreme felicity. In fact, the whole chamber and its appointments beautifully represented the mentality of those ancients. Mingled with a fear of the very gods and demons of their own creation, one is conscious of sincere feeling and affection for the dead. From its very severity it might be the actual burial of the god himself, instead of his representative on earth who, in passing from this earthly life, became one of the "Lords of the West." Its appointments, like those of the Antechamber, may almost be divided into two categories: the personal and the religious— the personal objects reflecting the tastes of the young king, the religious objects reflecting the superstitions of the past. The former were placed there in tender thought for the deceased, the latter for his protection in the Underworld—for even when the great Sun-god himself entered on his nocturnal journey, his path through those regions was beset by all kinds of snares.

But the problems here suggested are difficult. The meaning of some of the emblems placed in the tomb, giving rise, as they do, to much conjecture today, may have been almost as obscure to the ancient Thebans as to ourselves. It is doubtful whether they could have given us a reason for placing many of them in the tomb. The true significance of the symbols might well have been lost years before the age of Tutankhamen and tradition may have held them to be necessary for the welfare of the dead long after the reason for their use had been forgotten.

Beside this traditional paraphernalia necessary to meet and vanquish the dark powers of the Nether World, there were magical figures placed in small recesses in the walls, facing north, south, east and west, covered with plaster, conforming with the ritual laid down in "the Book of the Dead," for the defence of the tomb and its owner. Associated with these magical figures are incantations "to repel the enemy of Osiris [the deceased], in whatsoever form he may come." Magic for once seems to have prevailed. For of twenty-seven monarchs of the Imperial Age of Egypt buried in this valley, who have suffered every kind of depredation, Tutankhamen, alone has lain unscathed, even though predatory hands violated his tomb—or may we believe, as those ancient Thebans might readily claim, that Tutankhamen's long security is due to Amenre's protection of his convert who, in acknowledging that Theban god's triumph over the religious revolution of Akhenaten, reconstructed his sanctuaries and re-endowed his temples?

The top of a gold stick showing the king aged about twelve

14

Clearing the Burial Chamber and opening the sarcophagus

THE SECOND SEASON'S WORK actually began in the laboratory, under Mr. Mace, who dealt with the magnificent chariots and the ceremonial couches that were left over from the first season. While he was carrying out this work of preservation and packing, with the aid of Mr. Callender, I began by removing the two guardian statues that stood before the doorway of the Burial Chamber, and then, as it was necessary, demolished the partition wall dividing it from the Antechamber.

Without first demolishing that partition wall, it would have been impossible to have dealt with the great shrines within the Burial Chamber, or to remove many of the funereal paraphernalia therein. Even then our great difficulty was due to the confined space in which we had to carry out the most difficult task of dismantling those shrines, which proved to be four in number, nested one within the other.

Beyond the very limited space and high temperature which prevailed, our difficulties were further increased by the great weight of the various sections and panels of which those complex shrines were constructed. These were made of $2\frac{1}{4}$-inch oak[1] planking, and overlaid with superbly delicate gold-work upon gesso. The wood-planking, though perfectly sound, had shrunk in the course of three thousand three hundred years in that very dry atmosphere, the gold-work upon the gesso had, if at all, slightly expanded; the result in any case was a space between the basic wood-planking and the ornamented gold surface which, when touched, tended to crush and fall away. Thus our problem was how to deal in that very limited space with those sections of the shrines, weighing from a quarter to three-quarters of a ton, when taking them apart and removing them, without causing them undue damage.

Other complications arose during this undertaking, and one of them was due to the fact that those sections were held together by means of secret wooden tongues let into the thickness of the wood-planking of the panels, roof sections, cornice pieces and "styles." It was only by slightly forcing open the cracks between those different sections, and by that means discovering the positions of the tongues that held them together, inserting a fine saw and severing them, that we were able to free them and take them apart. No sooner had we discovered the method of overcoming this complication, had dealt with the various sections of the great outermost shrine, and become proud of ourselves, anticipating that we had learnt how to treat the next shrine or shrines, than we found that, in the very next shrine, although held together in a similar manner, many of the hidden tongues were of solid bronze, inscribed with the names of Tutankhamen. These could not of course be sawn through as in the first case. We had therefore to find other methods. In fact, contrary to our expectations, the farther we proceeded, although the space in which we could work had been increased, new and unforeseen obstacles continually occurred.

For instance, after our scaffolding and hoisting tackle had been introduced it occupied practically all the available space, leaving little for ourselves in which to work. When some of the parts were freed, there was insufficient room to remove them from the chamber. We bumped our heads, nipped our fingers, we had to squeeze in and out like weàsels, and work in all kinds of embarrassing positions. I think I remember that one of the eminent chemists assisting us in the preservation work, when taking records of various phenomena in the tomb, found that he had also recorded a certain percentage of profanity! Nevertheless, I am glad to say that in the conflict we did more harm to ourselves than to the shrines.

Such was our task during the second season's work in the Burial Chamber. First we had to remove those strange guardian figures in the Antechamber bearing the impressive legend: "The Good God of whom one be proud, the Sovereign of whom one boasts, the Royal Ka of Harakhte, Osiris, the King Lord of the Lands, Nebkheperure;" next to demolish the partition wall that divides the Antechamber from the Burial Chamber, built as it was of dry masonry, bonded with heavy logs of wood, and covered on both sides with a coat of hard plaster; finally to dismantle the great shrines within the chamber; and, in so doing, to unmask the magnificent yellow quartzite sarcophagus containing the mortal remains of the king shielded in their centre. The undertaking took us eighty-four days of real manual labour. It will give some idea of the magnitude of that operation when it is mentioned that the outermost of those golden shrines, occupying nearly the whole of the Burial Chamber, measured some 17 feet in length, 11 feet in width, and over 9 feet in height, and that the four shrines comprised in all some eighty sections, each section or part having to be dealt with by a method different from the last, and every section needing first to be temporarily treated so as to allow it to be handled with the least risk of damage.

The demolition of the partition wall gave a clear view of the great outermost shrine, and we were able, for the first time, to realize its grandeur, especially its admirable gold-work and blue faience inlay, overlaid with gilt protective emblems—*Ded* and *Thet* alternately.

Having got this far, the next procedure was to remove and transport to the laboratory all the portable funerary equipment that had been placed around the chamber, between the walls and the sides of the outermost shrine, and then to construct, and introduce the necessary scaffolding and hoisting tackle preparatory to dismantling the outermost shrine. Our gear, necessarily of primitive kind, being placed in position, we began by first unhanging the very heavy folding doors of the outermost shrine, which were hinged on copper pivots inserted in corresponding sockets in the lintel and in the threshold. This was a very tedious and hazardous task, as the front part of the entablature of the shrine, had to be slightly raised to free the upper and lower pivot-hinges fixed on the back rails of the doors. We then hoisted and removed the three roof sections that were tongued to the entablature. After that, we took apart the entablature which comprised four sections of cornice moulding and frieze, tongued to their corresponding panels, and held together, at the four corners, by means of heavy copper S-shaped dowels, each bearing inscriptions such as north-east, south-west, etc., to show their correct orientation.

Having removed the entablature, the panels of the shrine had to be dealt with. They now stood unsupported save for our temporary struts and the four corner uprights to which they were tongued. The panels were comparatively easy to free, but there being insufficient room to permit of their egress, we had to lean them against the corresponding walls of the chamber and leave them there, pending some future time when they could be passed out—in other words until after the dismantling and removal of the inner shrines, which, at that time, prevented their exit. The removal of the corner pieces completed our primary task—the dismantling of the first (outermost) shrine.

The next and very delicate problem was the linen pall that completely covered the second shrine. Its tissue was much decayed and in very fragile state; its drooping edges were badly torn from the weight of its own material, and by the metal marguerites that were sewn to it. Happily, as a result of Dr. Alexander Scott's experiments, duroprene (a chlorinated rubber compound dissolved in an organic solvent such as zylene) proved most efficacious in reinforcing the deteriorated fabric. It strengthened the tissues sufficiently to enable us to roll it on to a wooden roller, expressly made for the purpose, and transport it to the laboratory where eventually the fabric could be finally treated and relined.

The linen pall and the wooden framework forming its curious supports being disposed of, we were able to study the question of the second shrine—a beautiful gilt construction almost exactly similar to the first, save for the absence of the blue faience inlay. The doors of this second shrine were bolted top and bottom, and carefully fastened with cord tied to metal staples and sealed. The clay seal upon this cord was intact. It bore impressions of two distinct seals, one bearing Tutankhamen's prenomen, Kheperunebre, surmounting "A Jackal over nine Foes," the second bore the device of the royal necropolis seal, "The Jackal over nine Foes," without other distinguishing mark or royal insignia. Here was a great piece of luck, as manifestly behind those two seals we should be dealing with material unharmed since the burial of the king. It was with great care that the cords were severed, those folding doors opened, which, when swung back, revealed yet a third shrine, also sealed and intact—the seal impressions upon this third shrine being identical to those on the second.

At this point of our undertaking we realized that it would now be possible, by opening those further doors, to solve the secret the shrines had so jealously guarded throughout the centuries. I therefore decided before any other procedure to make the experiment. It was an exciting moment in our arduous task that cannot easily be forgotten. We were to witness a spectacle as no other man in our times has been privileged to see. With suppressed excitement I carefully cut the cord, removed that precious seal, drew back the bolts, and opened the doors, when a fourth shrine was revealed, similar in design and even more brilliant in workmanship than the last. The decisive moment was at hand! An indescribable moment for an archaeologist! What was beneath and what did that fourth shrine contain? With intense excitement I drew back the bolts of the last and unsealed doors; they slowly swung open, and there, filling the entire area within, effectually barring any further progress, stood an immense yellow quartzite sarcophagus, intact, with the lid still firmly fixed in its place, just as the pious hands had left it. It was certainly a thrilling moment, as we gazed upon the spectacle enhanced by the striking contrast—the glitter of metal—of the golden shrines shielding it. Especially striking were the outstretched hand and wing of a goddess sculptured on the end of the sarcophagus, as if to ward off an intruder. It symbolized an idea beautiful in conception, and, indeed, seemed an eloquent illustration of the perfect faith and tender solicitude for the well-being of their loved one, that animated the people who dwelt in that land over thirty centuries ago.

We were now able to profit by the experience we had acquired and had a much clearer conception of the operation immediately before us: the three remaining shrines would have to be taken to pieces and removed before the problem of the sarcophagus could be contemplated. And thus it was that we laboured for another month, first dismantling the second shrine, then the third, until the fourth (innermost) shrine, the last and smallest, was completely freed. When this was achieved we saw that this last shrine had all the appearance of a golden tabernacle. Upon its folding doors and west end, were winged figures of the tutelary goddesses of the dead, in fine bas-relief, majestic in their protective significance, whilst the walls of the shrine were covered with religious texts.

Howard Carter opening the doors of the second shrine

We found between the third and fourth (innermost) shrines ceremonial bows and arrows, and with them, a pair of the gorgeous flabella—the insignia of princes, fans so prominent in scenes where kings are depicted, carried by inferior officers behind their chief. Beautiful specimens they were—one lying at the head, the other along the south side of the innermost shrine. The one at the head, wrought in sheet-gold, bears a charming and historical scene of the young King Tutankhamen in his chariot, followed by his favourite hound, hunting ostrich for feathers for the fan, as the inscription upon the handle says in "the Eastern desert of Heliopolis;" on the reverse side of the fan, also finely embossed and chased, the young "Lord of Valour" is depicted returning triumphant, his quarry, two ostriches, borne on the shoulders of two attendants who precede him, the plumes under his arm. The second fan, larger and perhaps more resplendent, was of ebony, overlaid with sheet-gold and encrusted with turquoise, lapis lazuli, and carnelian-coloured glass, as well as translucent calcite: the palm of the fan being emblazoned with the titulary of Tutankhamen. Unfortunately, only the debris remained of the actual feathers of these two flabella. Although these had suffered from the havoc of insects, enough still remained to show us that they once had been alternate white and brown plumes—forty-two on each fan.

The roof and cornice of the fourth (innermost) shrine, contrary to our expectations, was of different form, and was made in one piece, instead of in several sections as in the case of the roofs of the preceding shrines. It was thus very heavy, and the question was how to raise it and turn it in that very narrow space. It was one of our most difficult problems, and it took several laborious days before it could be lifted, gradually turned, and hauled into the Antechamber where it now rests. Taking apart the sides, ends and doors of this innermost shrine was a much easier undertaking. It enclosed and, as it proved, exactly fitted the sarcophagus. It was the last of those complex problems involved in the dismantling of the four shrines, hallowed as they were by ancient memories. Our task of over eighty days was thus ended.

During the process of our work it became clear that the ancient Egyptian staff of undertakers must have had extreme difficulty in erecting the shrines within that limited space. Their task, however, was perhaps easier than ours, as in their case, the wood was new and pliable, the gold ornamentation firm and strong. In that narrow area it must have been neccessary for them to have placed the parts of the four shrines in correct order around the four walls of the chamber: the various parts and panels of the outermost shrine being introduced first, and those of the innermost shrine last. The next logical step in that operation must have been first to erect the innermost shrine and lastly the outermost. And that was what apparently occurred. The carpentry and joinery of those constructions exhibited great skill, and each section was carefully numbered and oriented to show not only how they fitted, but also their correct orientation. Hence the constructors of those shrines were manifestly past-masters in their work, but on the other hand there was evidence that the obsequies had been hurriedly performed, and that the workmen in charge of those last rites were anything but careful men. They had, with little doubt, placed those parts around the sarcophagus, but in their carelessness had reversed their order in regard to the four cardinal points. They had leant them against the four walls around the sarcophagus they were to shield, contrary to the instructions written upon the different parts, with a result that, when they were erected, the doors of the shrines faced east instead of west, the foot ends west instead of east, and the side panels were likewise transposed. This may have been a pardonable fault, the chamber being too small for correct orientation, although there were other signs of slovenliness. Sections had obviously been banged together, regardless of the risk of damage to their gilt ornamentation. Deep dents from blows from a heavy hammer-like implement are visible to the present day on the gold-work, parts of the surfaces in some cases had been actually knocked off, and the workmen's refuse, such as chips of wood, had never been cleared away.

The raising of the roof of the last shrine bared the lid of the sarcophagus, the removal of the three sides and doors of that shrine freed that great stone monument. We were more than repaid. For there, free standing from all surrounding structure, stood, as if in state, a magnificent sarcophagus of wonderful workmanship, carved out of a solid block of finest yellow quartzite, measuring 9 feet in length, 4 feet 10 inches in width, and 4 feet 10 inches high.

It was on 3 February that we first had a clear view of this sepulchral masterpiece, ranking as it does among the finest specimens of its kind the world possesses. It has a rich entablature consisting of a cavetto-cornice, taurus moulding and frieze of inscription. But the outstanding features of the sarcophagus are the guardian goddesses Isis, Nephthys, Neith and Selkit, carved in high relief on each of the four corners, so placed that their full spread wings and outstretched arms encircle it with their protective embrace. Round the base is a dado of protective symbols *Ded* and *Thet*. The corners of the casket rested upon alabaster slabs. Between the last shrine and the sarcophagus there were no objects, save for a *Ded*-symbol placed on the south side for "Strength" and possibly "Protection" of the owner.

As our light fell on the noble quartzite monument, it illuminated, in repeated detail, that last solemn appeal to gods and men, and made us feel that, in the young king's case, a dignity had been added even to death. With the profound silence that reigned the emotion deepened, the past and present seemed to meet—time to stand and wait, and one asked oneself, was it not yesterday that, with pomp and ceremony, they had laid the young king in that casket?—so fresh, so seemingly recent, were those touching claims on our pity that, the more we gazed on them, the more the illusion gathered strength. It made one wish that his journey through those grim tunnels of the Underworld might be unperturbed until he attained complete felicity!—as those four goddesses, sculptured in high relief at the corners, seemed to plead as they shielded their charge. For in them had we not a perfect Egyptian elegy in stone?

The lid made of rose granite tinted to match the quartzite sarcophagus, was cracked in the middle and firmly embedded in the rebated top edges. The cracks had been carefully cemented and painted over to match the rest, in such a way as to leave no doubt that it had not been tampered with. Undoubtedly the original intention must have been to provide a quartzite lid in keeping with the sarcophagus itself; it would therefore appear that some accident had occurred. It may be that the intended lid was not ready in time for the burial of the king, and that this crudely made granite slab was substituted in its place.

The crack greatly complicated our final effort, the raising of this lid, for had it been intact the operation would have been far easier. The difficulty, however, was overcome by passing angle irons along and closely fitting the sides of the slab, which permitted it to be raised by differential pulleys as one piece. At this last ceremony many were present: the Governor of the Keneh Province and Mohamed Zaglul Pasha (Under-Secretary of State for Public Works), Mr. E. S. Harkness (Chairman of the Board of Trustees of the Metropolitan Museum of Art, New York), Dr. Breasted (Professor of Egyptology and Oriental History in the University of Chicago), the Chief Inspector of Antiquities, Upper Egypt; Mr. A. M. Lythgoe (Curator of the Egyptian Department of the Metropolitan Museum of Art, New York), Professor Newberry (Honorary Reader of Egyptian Art at the Liverpool University), Dr. Alan Gardiner, the well-known philologist; Mr. H. E. Winlock (Director of the Egyptian Expedition of the Metropolitan Museum of Art, New York), Mr. Norman de Garies Davies (of the same museum), Dr. Douglas Derry (Professor of Anatomy at the Kasr-el-Aini School of Medicine, Cairo), Mr. Robert Mond, M. Foucart (Directeur de l'Institut Français d'Archéologie), M. Bruyère (Directeur de l'Expedition Française), Major the Hon. J. J. Astor, Messrs. Mace, Callender, Lucas, Burton and Bethell and the Assistant Curator of the Cairo Museum.

Many strange scenes must have happened in the Valley of the Tombs of the Kings since it became the royal burial ground of the Theban New Empire, but one may be pardoned for

Overleaf: the golden effigy of the boy king in the sarcophagus

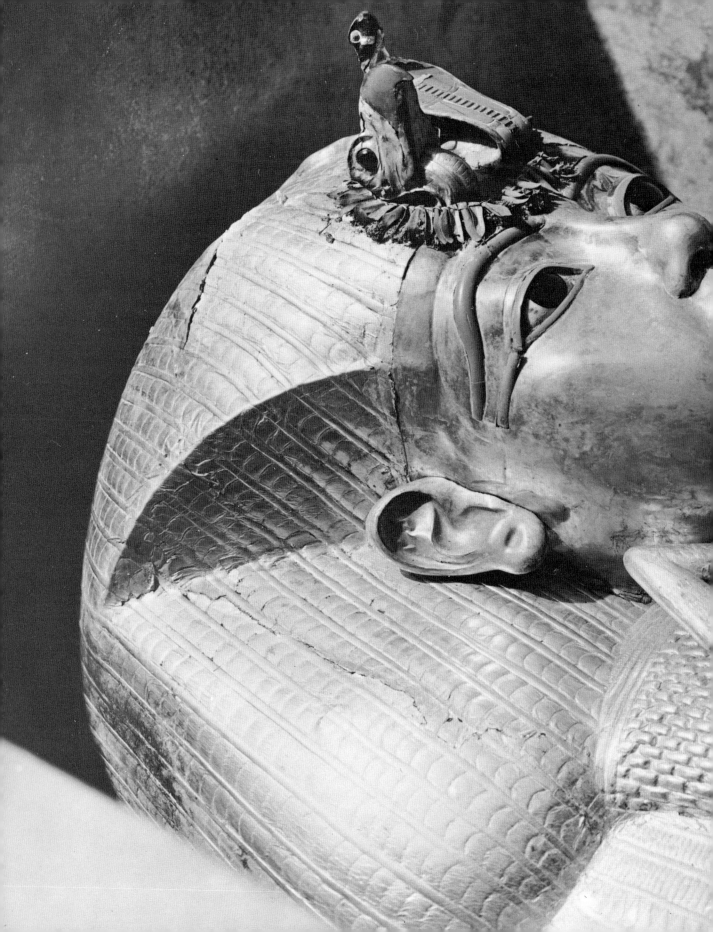

thinking that the present scene was not the least interesting or dramatic. For ourselves it was the one supreme and culminating moment—a moment looked forward to ever since it became evident that the chambers discovered, in November 1922, must be the tomb of Tutankhamen, and not a cache of his furniture as had been claimed. None of us but felt the solemnity of the occasion, none of us but was affected by the prospect of what we were about to see—the burial custom of a king of ancient Egypt of thirty-three centuries ago. How would the king be found? Such were the anticipatory speculations running in our minds during the silence maintained.

The tackle for raising the lid was in position. I gave the word. Amid intense silence the huge slab, broken in two, weighing over a ton and a quarter, rose from its bed. The light shone into the sarcophagus. A sight met our eyes that at first puzzled us. It was a little disappointing. The contents were completely covered by fine linen shrouds. The lid being suspended in mid-air, we rolled back those covering shrouds, one by one, and as the last was removed a gasp of wonderment escaped our lips, so gorgeous was the sight that met our eyes: a golden effigy of the young boy king, of most magnificent workmanship, filled the whole of the interior of the sarcophagus. This was the lid of a wonderful anthropoid coffin, some 7 feet in length, resting upon a low bier in the form of a lion, and no doubt the outermost coffin of a series of coffins, nested one within the other, enclosing the mortal remains of the king. Enclasping the body of this magnificent monument are two winged goddesses, Isis and Neith, wrought in rich gold-work upon gesso, as brilliant as the day the coffin was made. To it an additional charm was added, by the fact that, while this decoration was rendered in fine low bas-relief, the head and hands of the king were in the round, in massive gold of the finest sculpture, surpassing anything we could have imagined. The hands, crossed over the breast, held the royal emblems—the Crook and the Flail—encrusted with deep blue faience. The face and features were wonderfully wrought in sheet-gold. The eyes were of aragonite and obsidian, the eyebrows and eyelids inlaid with lapis lazuli glass. There was a touch of realism, for while the rest of this anthropoid coffin, covered with feathered ornament, was of brilliant gold, that of the bare face and hands seemed different, the gold of the flesh being of different alloy, thus conveying an impression of the greyness of death. Upon the forehead of this recumbent figure of the young boy king were two emblems delicately worked in brilliant inlay—the Cobra and the Vulture—symbols of Upper and Lower Egypt, but perhaps the most touching by its human simplicity was the tiny wreath of flowers around these symbols, as it pleased us to think, the last farewell offering of the widowed girl queen to her husband, the youthful representative of the "Two Kingdoms."

Among all that regal splendour, that royal magnificence—everywhere the glint of gold—there was nothing so beautiful as those few withered flowers, still retaining their tinge of colour. They told us what a short period three thousand three hundred years really was—but Yesterday and the Morrow. In fact, that touch of nature made that ancient and our modern civilization kin.

Thus from stairway, steep descending passage, Antechamber and Burial Chamber, from those golden shrines and from that noble sarcophagus, our eyes were now turned to its contents—a gold encased coffin, in form a recumbent figure of the young king, symbolizing Osiris or, it would seem, by its fearless gaze, man's ancient trust in immortality. Many and disturbing were our emotions awakened by that Osiride form. Most of them voiceless. But, in that silence, to listen—you could almost hear the ghostly footsteps of the departing mourners.

Our lights were lowered, once more we mounted those sixteen steps, once more we beheld the blue vault of the heavens, where the Sun is Lord, but our inner thoughts still lingered over the splendour of that vanished Pharaoh, with his last appeal upon his coffin written upon our minds: "Oh Mother Nut! spread thy wings over me as the Imperishable Stars."

15

The state chariots

E VERY ADDITION to our knowledge of the subject tends to increase our admiration for the
technical skill displayed by the ancient Egyptian craftsmen when they were dealing with
the relatively limited means at their disposal.

That they were adepts in vehicular structure has already been established by the paintings
upon the walls of their tomb chapels, and also by the beautiful specimens of their chariots
discovered in Egypt during the nineteenth and twentieth centuries.

A specimen exhibited in the Egyptian collection at Florence, another in the Cairo Museum
discovered by Mr. Theodore M. Davis in the Tomb of Yuaa and Tuaa, are striking examples
of their proficiency. They are well constructed, strong and at the same time exceedingly light.
They consist of a bent-wood framework, strengthened, and in one case ornamented, with
leather, but though well made and having beautiful lines, these are of a type such as were used
by the Theban notables, and might be described as curricles since they have none of the magnificence of the state chariots, of which the "body" discovered in the tomb of Thothmes IV
was our first example. This last, also discovered by Mr. Davis and in the Cairo Museum, had
unfortunately been broken up by the early plunderers of that tomb. Its wheels, axle and pole
had been destroyed, but the "body," the only portion that was left of the chariot, was not only a
wonderful example of vehicular construction, but must have been a masterpiece of artistic
workmanship. It was covered on both outside and inside with battle scenes and traditional
ornament modelled in low relief upon an extraordinary light panelled bent-wood framework,
the surfaces of which were prepared with canvas and gesso, no doubt, once overlaid with gold,
but the full extent of its splendour was never realized until the more complete specimens were
discovered in the Antechamber of this tomb.

We found them here heaped together in confusion, and they, too, had unfortunately suffered,
the thieves having very roughly handled them in their endeavours to tear off the more valuable
portions of the gold decoration. But the confusion in which we found these state chariots was
not merely due to those plunderers. The entrance passage of the tomb was too narrow to admit
of their ingress in their complete form, so they had been taken to pieces, and even their axles
sawn in two to get them in the chamber, where their dismembered parts had been heaped one
upon the other. However, with the exception of some minor details of the ornamentation that
had been wrenched away, and of the leather-work melted from humid heat to a viscid mass,
they are otherwise complete, even to the remains of their rugs, and can, when time allows, be
put together again. Their admirable design and gorgeousness will justify any amount of time
and work bestowed upon them. Covered from top to bottom with gold, every inch of which is

decorated with embossed patterns and traditional scenes, they have upon their borders and framework elaborate ornament of semi-precious stones and polychrome glass encrusted upon the gold casing.

Like all the other examples, the bodies of these chariots are not provided with a seat. The royal charioteer always stood, and rarely if ever sat while driving. They are entirely open at the back, so that the driver might readily leap to the ground and up again as might be necessary. The floor consisted of a mesh of interlaced leathern thongs which were covered either with an animal skin or a linen rug of very long pile, in order, by its elasticity, to render the motion of the carriage more easy. This elastic bottom to the body was the early form of spring—the true, or more efficacious spring, such as we use to-day, was not applied to wheel carriages in Europe until the seventeenth century. Before that period the bodies of carriages were suspended by long leather straps from pillars erected upon the under-carriage. With the Egyptian chariots additional ease was provided by placing the wheels and axle-tree as far back as possible, and thus utilizing as much of the springiness of the pole as was practical.

The carriage proper of these chariots comprises an axle-tree and (two) wheels. This, for reasons already stated, was set under the extreme back of the body, but as the body rested partly on the pole, and the pole was permanently fixed to the axle-tree, the pole also formed part of the under-carriage or carriage proper. Thus as the body of the chariot rested on the axle-tree and pole, the pole was especially bent at that extremity so that the floor of the body would, when harnessed to the horses, be approximately horizontal. The weight of the body and charioteer was therefore taken partly by the wheels and partly by the horses, but as the charioteer stood well back in the body, the carriage proper received the greater part of this weight. The body was bound by leathern thongs both to the axle-tree and the pole, and it was also stayed by means of thick leathern straps attached to its upper front rim and the shaft of the pole. Hence, it will be seen that the pole acted not only as the means of yoking the horses, but also partly as the under-carriage or carriage proper.

The wheels, of six spokes or radial bars, show in their construction a special mechanical knowledge on which we have made little advance. They, in the lightest manner possible, are constructed so as to be the strongest and most durable form for a nave and radial bars for a wooden wheel.

As some of these specimens are encased with sheet-gold, and their uniqueness forbids their being taken to pieces for proper examination, I shall use as an example the fragments of a wheel discovered during Lord Carnarvon's researches in the tomb of Amenhetep III, in Wadyein—a branch valley of the Valley of the Tombs of the Kings. They are, no doubt, from the same royal workshops and are not more than (at most) twenty-five years earlier. With these fragments of a wheel were found a few parts of the framework of the body of the chariot, and also a few fragments of the harness saddles, all of which have every appearance of being of similar construction to that of the more perfect specimens found in Tutankhamen's tomb. The fragments of the wheel are from the nave, the lower parts of the radial bars, and portions of the inner and outer flanges of the nave, to which a good deal of their leather bindings still adhere. The structure consists of: six V-shaped parts made of bent-wood, each so devised as to comprise a segment of the nave and half-section of two radial bars or spokes of the wheel. These V-shaped parts when put together, form a nave or hub and six complete radial bars. In the hub portion of each of these six V-shaped sections are two mortice halvings so devised that, when united, they form six mortice slots in the nave, designed to receive corresponding dovetail tenons upon the rims of the two cylindrical flanges, which were fitted to the inner and outer sides of the nave of the wheel. Thus these long cylindrical flanges, contrived to keep the wheel upright during any lateral movement, served also a very important constructive purpose—their tenons, when

The chariots as they were found in the Antechamber

fitted into the mortice slots of the nave, interlocked all the parts and formed a perfect hub. The flanges, hub, and radial bar sections, when assembled, were bound with raw hide which, when it dried, shrunk and held them tight.

If I have made myself clear, it will be seen that this ingenious form of chariot wheel possesses not only all elements of lightness, but it tends to neutralize risk of splitting, and to combine even greater solidity when under any reasonable weight. So excellent is the joinery that in portions of the specimen under discussion, even though it has suffered very rough handling, the joints are hardly visible to the naked eye. The radial bars appear to have been morticed to the felloe or outer rim of the wheel, and the splitting element eliminated by having shoulders to the tenons. The tyres were of leather.

The industry of carriage-making depends, to a great extent, upon the selection of the materials. The ancient Egyptians selected, as we now do, suitable woods for the different parts. The woods were artificially (mechanically) bent. Carriage-making necessitates a combination of crafts rarely united in one trade, embracing as it does such divers materials. In the ancient Egyptian mural paintings and sculptures, the Egyptian artists have not failed to point out what parts were the peculiar province of the carpenter, wheelwright, currier and other craftsmen.

The draught gear, such as the yoke, fixed to the end of the pole and attached to the harness saddles upon the withers of the horses, sufficed for all purposes of draught, as well as for backing the chariot; it also kept the horses at the same distance and in the same relative position. Spur-like goads were fixed to the breast harness and the bridle in such a manner as to prevent the horses from breaking from the line of draught—as there were two of these spur-like goads to each chariot found in this tomb, it would appear that only one was attached to each horse, and that on the outside.

From various paintings of the king in his chariot, we know that the horses were decked with sumptuous housings, neck coverings, and that a crest of ostrich feathers was fastened to the head-stall and bridle. Of these trappings there were no traces whatever in the tomb. The actual harness of leather, evidently of breast type, had unfortunately perished, but as the greater part of its decoration—embossed sheet-gold—was there, with careful study and time the bulk of it can be reconstructed. As yet we do not know what kind of bit was employed for command over the horses—the robbers took all the heavy metal they could carry away and, no doubt, also the metal bits. From the gait and general demeanour of the horses portrayed upon the painted casket in this tomb, one would expect to find that the bits were of a heavy "curb" type. The reins were evidently passed through rings attached to the breast harness, and were long enough to be tied round the royal waist, so that the king's arms would be free to defend himself—for the king always drove alone in his chariot. Blinkers were used—several pairs were preserved in the tomb —and the chariots were richly mounted with quivers full of arrows, the bow being the principal arm of attack. One of the predominant features peculiar to the royal chariots was a golden-solar-hawk, fixed upon the end of the pole. It was the cockade, so to speak, of the royal house, which like the crests of ostrich feathers upon the heads of the horses, were only used by the king and princes of the household.

The four chariots discovered in the Antechamber (there are others in the Store-room of the Burial Chamber not yet touched) can be divided into two categories: state chariots and curricles. Of these, the latter were more open, of lighter construction probably for hunting or exercising purposes.

The gold encased state chariots, with their sumptuous housings and harness trappings, must have produced a magnificent effect in the royal pageants, especially when it is remembered how the burnished metal must have reflected the brilliant Eastern sun—a fact emphasized by the following quotation from a tablet of Akhenaten, demarcating the limits of his city: "His Majesty

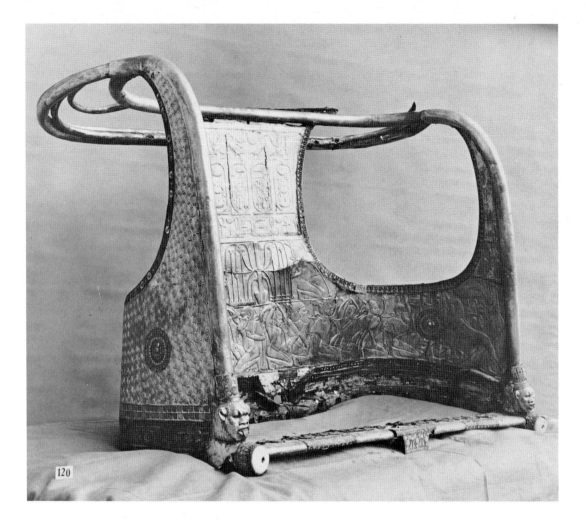

The body of one of the chariots

ascended a great chariot of electrum, like Aten when he rises from his horizon and filling the land with his love . . .''

From the following somewhat brief description, but more especially from the selection of illustrations of the chariots and their parts, it is hoped that some idea may be gathered of their gorgeousness. Their effect when in motion under Egyptian skies must have been one of dazzling splendour, with the jewelled trappings flashing back the light, the horses' plumes waving, in a pageant of brightness, colour, gleam and richness, probably rarely surpassed at any other period, or by any other splendour-loving race. Some such impression as this we gather, not only from the monuments, but from what time and circumstance have left us in this tomb.

The "bodies" of the state chariots are not only quite open at the back, but they have lozenge-shaped openings at the sides. Attached to the bent-wood upper rim of the body is a secondary rim which forms a shelf-like projection, the space between these two rims being filled in with an openwork design consisting, in the centre, of the traditional device of "Unity of the Two Kingdoms," and on either side the captive foes of Egypt. The gold casing on the front of the

A pair of fly whisks

A pair of blinkers

bodies is embossed and encrusted with traditional ornament: in one case with elaborate coil-pattern, in the other with feather, scroll, and ox-eye ornament, and in each case with a panel bearing the titulary of the king. Similarly on the inside of the body of the chariots is the king's titulary supported by the symbolical "Union" of the "Two Countries," to which, on one example, are tied Northern and Southern prisoners, and below that a wonderful frieze of conquered foes, with their arms lashed behind them, kneeling before Tutankhamen triumphant as a human-headed lion crushing Egypt's alien enemies. Traditional ornament of this kind, wherein the conquered races are typified by separate figures conventional in attitude, but individual in character and detail, was regarded by general consent as naturally symbolizing the power of the monarch. This desire to humiliate the foe, the absence of magnanimity in conquerors, are but the spirit of unbridled imagination rendered pictorially in those Pharaonic battle scenes, wherein the vigour and variety of the mêlées are of incomparable intensity. On the other example, the interior, like the outside, is decorated with a simple feather, scroll and ox-eye pattern. Added to this decoration are encrusted medallions of silver and gold, fixed on the lower part of the panels.

On both of the chariots, the lozenge-shaped openings in the sides of the bodies have margins of floral design, encrusted with semi-precious stones, glass and faience. At the juncture where the body rests on the axle, are highly ornamented bosses of stone, in one instance surmounted by a grotesque gold head of the god Bes. Their wooden axles have at intervals, collars of gold richly encrusted with glass and semi-precious stones, worked in floral devices, and the names of enemy countries. Each pair of wheels has its spokes, hub and rims covered with thin sheet-gold; the tyres being of leather. The wooden poles are left plain save for a gold cap at the end, whereon the royal golden-solar-hawk was fixed. Embossed, and completely filling the field of the disk upon the head of the solar-hawk, is a device incorporating the king's prenomen. As the Pharaohs were looked upon as the Sun-god's earthly representatives, would it be a too daring hypothesis to suggest that this device symbolized his supposed solar origin? The bent-wood yokes, which were joined to the pole, were overlaid with gold and, in one case, have alien captives forming the curved ends.

The ends of the harness saddles to which the yokes were fixed, are decorated with heads of the household god Bes. Through the god's widely-opened mouth passed the girth straps. This combined scheme of ornament and strap fastening, may possibly have been inspired by the fact that this god is represented throughout the tomb furniture with long protruding tongue—the straps here issuing from the mouth convey that idea. Surmounting the back of the harness saddles are centre-pieces with reels of aragonite decorated with fine red-gold filigree-work. With each chariot a pair of spur-like goads, already mentioned, were found; and also the ever necessary horsehair fly-whisks. There were also quaintly ornamented blinkers from the bridles of the horses.

These highly ornate chariots may well be said to have taken in Egyptian ceremonial the place of the state coach in modern pageant.

16

The opening of the three coffins

PAST EXPERIENCE had taught us that it would be well to resume our work on the tomb of Tutankhamen as soon as the decline of the great heat rendered it practicable, our aim being to carry it out with due scientific procedure, with the least possible interruption and to be able to open the tomb to the public as early as possible during the tourist season. Our anticipations were fully justified, for, between 1 January and 15 March, 1926, there were over 12,000 visitors to the tomb, and during the same period I received 278 applications for permission to inspect the objects and the work in the laboratory.

After having purchased necessary materials for the campaign, I left London on 23 September and arrived in Cairo on the 28th. There was as usual not a little to be done in Cairo before I could leave for Luxor. In work of this sort in Egypt, delays may be anticipated and must be patiently accepted. Monsieur Lacau, the Director-General of the Department of Antiquities, was absent in Europe. On 1 October I saw Mr. Edgar, acting for Monsieur Lacau at the Museum, when I arranged with him that the electric light in the Valley of the Tombs of the Kings should be in readiness to start from 11 October, and at the same time I took the opportunity to discuss with him the general programme for the season's work.

The first task obviously would be to raise the nest of coffins from the sarcophagus, to open and examine them one by one; secondly to examine the king's mummy, with the aid of Dr. Douglas Derry, Professor of Anatomy in the Medical School at Kasr-el-Aini, and Dr. Saleh Bey Hamdi, formerly Director of the same school; lastly, if time allowed, to investigate, clear and record the contents of the Store-room leading out of the Burial Chamber—undertakings which, as every object would need preserving and packing for transport to Cairo, would more than provide ample occupation for the season. However, the last part of the programme—that of the Store-room—proved impossible of realization on account of the state of the mass of material found on the king's mummy. Even raising and opening the nest of three coffins, as it proved to be, took far longer than was anticipated.

It was also arranged that Mr. A. Lucas should go with me to Luxor on 6 October and resume his duties as chemist in the work of preservation.

The question arose as to whether M. Lacau, who was on leave in Europe, would wish to be present during the actual unwrapping of the mummy. Upon finding that he would not be back in Egypt before November, I suggested, in order to avoid any possible delay, that a cable should be sent to ascertain the date of his return, and in the event of its being deferred, to ask whether he would object to Mr. Edgar representing him during the examination.

On the following day a reply was received from Monsieur Lacau saying that he desired to be present at the examination of the royal mummy and that he trusted that the delay might not inconvenience me. To meet his wishes upon the matter, I arranged with Drs. Derry and Saleh Bey to defer their coming to Luxor until 10 November.

With archaeological work the reverse of what is anticipated almost always occurs. As events turned out the work of dealing with the actual coffins fully occupied the intervening period, and we were only just ready for the examination of the mummy when M. Lacau and the doctors arrived.

On 3 October I inspected the Tutankhamen exhibits in the Cairo Museum with Mr. Lucas, in order to study them from the point of view of preservation, a problem of extreme interest and importance in dealing with antiquities, especially of a fragile nature. The throne had undoubtedly darkened since it had been exhibited in the museum, and it was decided that this discoloration could be removed by hot wax treatment, a protective measure which we proposed to carry out during the spring. There was little doubt that the objects which allowed of the paraffin wax treatment had been improved by it, and were consequently in better condition; it was therefore agreed that this method was permanently the most effective and generally the best.

The Press is a great and necessary force in modern civilization, but it is occasionally eager for more news than actually exists. It is, too, exceedingly competitive. Research of all kinds owes much to intelligent publicity and it was hoped that the machinery organized by the Egyptian Government for distributing the news would prove adequate, but soon after my arrival, I was a little disappointed to discover that the correspondents, both local and foreign, were imperfectly satisfied.

Before I left Cairo I had an agreeable interview with H. E. Abdel Hamid Pasha Bedawi, Conseiller Royal to the Public Works Ministry, to whom I explained our plans. They met his complete approval, and on the following evening, accompanied by Mr. Lucas, I started for Luxor, whence, on the following day, after an interview with the Bey, the Marmour of Luxor, and Tewfik Effendi Boulos, the Chief Inspector for the Department of Antiquities of Upper Egypt, we crossed over to the village of Gurna—Western Thebes.

In spite of the heat it was pleasant to be back in those familiar but ever impressive surroundings, still unawakened from the silence of their summer sleep. A brief inspection soon showed us that the tomb, the magazine and the laboratory were all in good order. It was a relief to see how well the men had carried out their various duties, for on resuming work after a lapse of some months, one is always haunted by a faint sense of apprehension lest something should have miscarried.

I at once instructed my *Reises* to enrol the necessary labour—some twenty-five men and seventy-five boys—and to set to work to uncover the entrance of the tomb next morning.

To begin a new season's work is a less simple task than is perhaps generally imagined. There is always much to be done. The first few days are usually employed in getting ready—in putting in order and testing the various instruments and gear. To begin work, under conditions so different from those prevailing in Europe, in a country where many simple appliances and facilities are not easily obtainable, needs much prearrangement and forethought. The problem, especially in the desert, consists mainly in the simplification of one's requirements or the adapting of the material available. Even with that especially ordered from England, or elsewhere, it may happen, on examination on the spot, that it proves slightly too large or too small, and needs to be fitted to the requirements, whilst the men in charge have to be taught its uses. Thus several tedious days may be spent in preparation brightened, however, by the broad smiles on the *Reises'* faces when they first realize the advantages of some new gadget as a practical help in their forthcoming labours.

It was on 10 October at 6.30 a.m. that the uncovering of the entrance of the tomb commenced. The men and boys set to work with a will to remove the mass of rubbish heaped over the entrance staircase for protective purposes at the end of the previous season's work. They laboured like ants, and although the temperature in the Valley was ranging from 97° to 105° Fahrenheit, and the air grey with dust, their swing and go suggested an enthusiasm for their task. It was a pleasure to see them as they worked.

With the help of an extra number of boys for carrying the rubbish, the clearance of the entrance to the tomb was finished on the following day, when we were able to connect up our electrical installation with that of the Royal Tombs, and make an inspection of the interior.

First we removed the watertight timber-blocking before the entrance doorway, composed of Turkish oak beams interlaced with soft deal boards, by which the wooden portcullis door of the passage entrance had been screened; then the wooden portcullis of the passage was unlocked; at the farther end of the descending passage, we removed the sheet screening the securely locked steel gate, and once more entered the Antechamber and Burial Chamber.

Familiarity can never entirely dissipate the feeling of mystery—the sense of vanished but haunting forces that cling to the tomb. The conviction of the unity of past and present is constantly impressed upon the archaeological adventurer, even when absorbed in the mechanical details of his work. These are varied enough. For instance, it was encouraging to find that, save for a few grains of disintegrated plaster fallen from the ceiling on the black modern pall with which I had covered the sarcophagus, hardly a trace of dust had settled in the tomb since it was closed down the previous year.

It was interesting to note the effect, on the invading forms of minute insect life, of the various insecticides with which I had then sprinkled the tomb. It is true that a few traces of those fish-like insects usually found in dark places, were still left, but the insecticides, on the whole, had acted effectively, for these pests had been almost entirely destroyed.

And now once more our powerful electric lamps lit up the great quartzite sarcophagus. Under the plate-glass screen which I had placed over it, was revealed the gold-encased coffin that seems to gather power of appealing to the emotions the more it is seen. With the shadows of the ancient gods there can be no vulgar intimacy.

The inspection over, and everything having been found in satisfactory condition, the tomb was reclosed. We then made our way to the laboratory, of which the entrance, for the summer months, had been protected by a heavy wooden screen. Here everything was free from dust and insects and, like the magazine, was in good order.

Thus our season had begun. The Valley, awakened from its summer sleep for the last two days by bawling workmen and screaming boys, was at peace again, and quiet will possess it until the winter migrants and their followers invade its golden silence.

The Antechamber freed of its beautiful furniture, the Burial Chamber denuded of its golden shrines, leaves the now open stone sarcophagus in the centre with its coffins within alone retaining their secret. The task before us now was to raise the lid of the first outermost coffin, as it rested in the sarcophagus.

This great gilded wooden coffin, 7 feet 4 inches in length, anthropoid in shape, wearing the *Khat* head-dress, with face and hands in heavier sheet-gold, is of *Rishi* type—a term applied when the main decoration consists of a feather design, a fashion common to coffins of the preceding Intermediate and Seventeenth Dynasty Theban periods. During the New Empire, in the case of burials of high officials and commoners, the style of decoration of coffins completely changes at the beginning of the Eighteenth Dynasty; but in the case of the royal coffin, as we now see, the older fashion still survived, with only very slight modification, such as the addition of figures of certain tutelary goddesses. This is a complete inversion of the usual order of things—fashion generally changing more rapidly with the upper than with the lower stations in life. May not this connote some religious idea in connexion with a king? There may be tradition behind it. The goddess Isis once protected the dead body of Osiris by taking him within her wings, thus she protects this new Osiris as represented by the effigy.

After careful study of the coffin it was decided that the original silver handles—two on each side—manifestly made for the purpose, were sufficiently well preserved still to support the weight of the lid, and could be used without danger in raising it. The lid was fixed to the shell by means of ten solid silver tongues, fitted into corresponding sockets in the thickness of the shell (four on each side, one at the head-, and one at the foot-end) where they were held in place by substantial gold-headed silver pins. Could we remove the silver pins by which the lid was fixed to the shell of the coffin without disturbing the coffin in the sarcophagus? As the coffin filled up nearly the whole of the interior of the sarcophagus, leaving only the smallest space, especially at the head- and foot-ends, it was by no means easy to extract the pins. By careful manipulation, however, it was found possible to withdraw them, with the exception of the pin at the head-end where there was only space enough to pull it half out. It had therefore to be filed through before the inner half could be withdrawn.

The next step was to place in position the hoisting tackle necessary for lifting the lid. This tackle consisted of two sets of three sheaf pulley-blocks provided with automatic brakes, fixed to an overhead scaffold, the pulleys being slung so as to come immediately above the centre of the lid opposite each pair of handles. The tackle was attached to the handles of the lid of the coffin by means of slings, and thus a correct centralization of its weight was assured, otherwise there would have been a danger of the lid bumping against the sides of the sarcophagus the moment it became free and pendent.

It was a moment as anxious as exciting. The lid came up fairly readily, revealing a second magnificent anthropoid coffin, covered with a thin gossamer linen sheet, darkened and much decayed. Upon this linen shroud were lying floral garlands, composed of olive and willow leaves, petals of the blue lotus and cornflower, whilst a small wreath of similar kind had been placed, also over the shroud, on the emblems of the forehead. Underneath this covering, in places, glimpses could be obtained of rich multi-coloured glass decoration encrusted upon the fine gold-work of the coffin.

Some time was spent in the previous summer working out the methods to be followed in this undertaking, and in providing the necessary appliances, thus it was completed in one morning when otherwise it would have occupied several days at least. The tomb was closed, everything being left undisturbed to await Mr. Harry Burton's photographic records.

Thus far our progress had been fairly satisfactory, but we now became conscious of a rather ominous feature. The second coffin which, so far as visible through the linen covering, had every appearance of being a wonderful piece of workmanship, showed distinct signs of the effect of some form of dampness and, here and there, tendency for its beautiful inlay to fall away. This was, I must admit, disconcerting, suggesting as it did the existence of former humidity of some kind within the nest of coffins. Should this prove the case, the preservation of the royal mummy would be less satisfactory than we had hoped.

On 15 October Mr. Burton arrived, and on the 17th, early in the morning, he successfully completed the photographic records of the shroud and floral garlands that covered the second coffin, as it rested within the shell of the first, in the sarcophagus.

These records complete, we had now to consider how best to deal with the second coffin, as well as the shell of the first. Manifestly, our difficulties were increased on account of the depth of the sarcophagus, and it was evident that the outer shell and the second coffin, neither of which was in a condition to bear much handling, must be raised together. This was eventually accomplished by means of pulleys as before, attachment being attained by means of steel pins

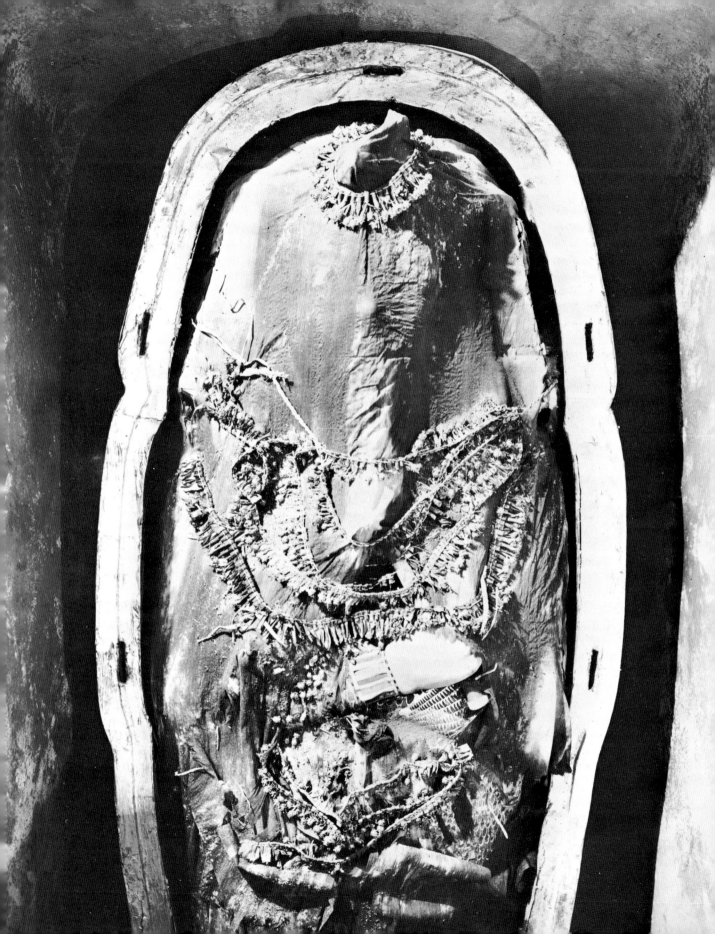

passed through the tongue-sockets of the first outermost shell. In this way hoisting was possible with the minimum of handling.

In spite of the great weight of the coffins—far heavier than at first seemed possible—they were successfully raised to just above the level of the top of the sarcophagus, when wooden planks were passed under them. In the confined space, and with the restricted head-room available, the task proved one of no little difficulty. It was much increased by the necessity of avoiding damage to the fragile gesso-gilt surfaces of the outermost coffin.

Further records having been taken, I was then able to remove the chaplet and garlands, and roll back the covering shroud. It was one more exciting moment. We could now gaze, with admiring eyes, upon the finest example of the ancient coffin-maker's art ever yet seen—Osiride, again in form, but most delicate in conception, and very beautiful in line. As it now lay in the outer shell which rested upon the modern improvised trestles, it presented a wonderful picture of Majesty lying in State.

The chaplet and garlands placed upon the shroud in memory of "the wreaths given to Osiris on his triumphant exit from the Judgement-hall of Heliopolis," which, as Dr. Gardiner remarks, reminds us of the "crown of righteousness" (2 Tim. iv. 8), were but illustration of Pliny's description of ancient Egyptian wreaths. When the care and precision with which these are fashioned is recognized, there is strong reason for the belief that this particular occupation with the ancient Egyptians, as in later days, must have been a specialized trade.

This second coffin, 6 feet 8 inches in length, sumptuously inlaid on thick gold-foil with cut and engraved opaque glass, simulating red jasper, lapis lazuli and turquoise respectively, is similar in form and design to the first. It symbolizes Osiris, it is *Rishi* in ornament, but it differs in certain detail. In this case the king wears the *Nemes* head-dress, and in place of the protective figures of Isis and Nephthys, the body is embraced with the wings of the vulture Nekhebet and of the serpent Buto. The arresting feature is the delicacy and superiority of the conception, which confer upon it at once the position of a masterpiece.

We were now faced by a complicated problem, not unlike the one we had to solve two seasons before when the covering shrines were dismantled. It was again a case of the unexpected happening. Conclusions drawn from former evidence or example are not to be trusted. For some unknown reason the reverse too often proves to be the case. On seeing that there were handles on the outer coffin for lowering or raising it, we were led to expect similar metal handles on the second coffin. There was none, and their absence placed us in a dilemma. The second coffin proved exceedingly heavy; its decorated surface very fragile; it fitted the outer shell so closely that it was not possible to pass one's little finger between the two. Its lid was fixed, as in the case of the outer coffin, with gold-headed silver pins which, as the coffin lay in the outer shell, could not be extracted. It was evident that it would have to be lifted in its entirety from the outer shell before anything further could be done. Thus the problem which confronted us was to discover a method of doing this with the minimum risk of damage to its delicate inlay, that had already suffered from some kind of humidity, the origin of which was then unknown.

It may be, under the strain of such operations as these, that one is too conscious of the risk of irreparable damage to the rare and beautiful object one desires to preserve intact. Much in the early days of Egyptian archaeological research has undoubtedly been lost to us by too eager or careless handling, more still from want of necessary appliances at the right moment; but against ill luck, even when every possible precaution has been taken, no man is secure. Everything may seem to be going well until suddenly, in the crisis of the process, you hear a crack—little pieces of surface ornament fall. Your nerves are at an almost painful tension. What is happening? All available room in the narrow space is crowded by your men. What action is needed to avert a catastrophe? There is, too, another danger. As the lid is being raised, the excitement of seeing

The wreath, garlands of flowers and linen shroud covering the second coffin

some new and beautiful object may attract the workmen's attention; for a moment their duty is forgotten and irreparable damage in consequence may be done.

Such are often the anxious impressions uppermost in the archaeologist's memory when his friends inquire what his emotions in these thrilling moments may have been. Only those who have had to handle heavy yet fragile antiquities in circumstances of similar difficulty, can realize how exacting and nerve-racking the strain and responsibility may become. Moreover, in the case before us, we could not be sure that the wood of the coffin was sufficiently well preserved to bear its own weight. However, after long consultations, and having studied the problem for nearly two days, we devised a plan. To remove the second coffin from the shell of the first, some points of attachment were necessary. There were, it will be remembered, no handles, so it was judged best to make use of the metal pins which fastened down the lid.

Inspection showed, however, that although the space between the shell of the outer coffin and the second coffin was insufficient to enable us to withdraw these pins entirely, they could still be pulled out about a quarter of an inch, so as to permit stout copper wire attachments to be fixed to them and to the overhead scaffold. This we did successfully. Strong metal eyelets were then screwed into the thickness of the top edge of the shell of the outer coffin, so as to enable it to be lowered from the second coffin by means of ropes working on the pulleys.

On the following day, after these preparations, we were able to proceed with the next stage. It proved to be one of the most important moments in the dismantling of the tomb. The process adopted was the reverse of that which might at first appear to be the natural order of things. We lowered the outer shell from the second coffin, instead of lifting the second coffin out of the first. The reason for this was that the head-room was insufficient, and the weight being stationary, there would be less risk of undue stress upon those ancient silver pins. The operation proved successful. The shell of the outer coffin was lowered once more into the sarcophagus, leaving, for a moment, the second coffin suspended in mid-air by means of the ten stout wire attachments. A wooden tray sufficiently large to span the opening of the sarcophagus was then passed under it, and thus the second coffin strongly supported, stood before us free and accessible. The wire attachments having been severed, the overhead gear removed, Mr. Burton made his records, and we were able to turn our energies to the raising of its lid.

The entire inlaid surface was indeed, as already mentioned, in a very fragile condition, and any handling, so far as possible, had to be avoided. In order therefore to lift the lid without causing injury, metal eyelets, to serve as handles, were screwed into it·at four points where there would be no danger of permanent disfigurement. To these eyelets our hoisting tackle was fixed, the gold-headed silver nails were extracted and the lid was slowly raised.

There was at first some slight tendency for the lid to stick, but gradually it rose from its bed and, when high enough to clear the contents of the coffin, it was lowered on to a wooden tray placed at the side to receive it.

This revealed a third coffin which, like its predecessors, was Osiride in form, but the main details of the workmanship were hidden by a close-fitting reddish-coloured linen shroud. The burnished gold face was bare; placed over the neck and breast was an elaborate bead and floral collarette, sewn upon a backing of papyrus, and tucked immediately above the *Nemes* head-dress was a linen napkin.

Mr. Burton at once made his photographic records. I then removed the floral collarette and linen coverings. An astounding fact was disclosed. This third coffin, 6 feet $1\frac{3}{4}$ of an inch in length, was made of solid gold! The mystery of the enormous weight, which hitherto had puzzled us, was now clear. It explained also why the weight had diminished so slightly after the first coffin, and the lid of the second coffin, had been removed. Its weight was still as much as eight strong men could lift.

The third coffin

The face of this gold coffin was again that of the king, but the features though conventional, by symbolizing Osiris, were even more youthful than those on the other coffins. In actual design it reverted to that of the outermost coffin, inasmuch as it was *Rishi*, and had engraved upon it figures of Isis and Nephthys, but auxiliary to this design were winged figures of Nekhebet and Buto. These latter protective figures, emblematic of Upper and Lower Egypt, were the prominent feature, for they are superimposed in gorgeous and massive cloisonné work over the richly engraved ornament of the coffin—their inlay being natural semi-precious stones. In addition to this decoration, over the conventional collarette of "the Hawk"—again in auxiliary cloisonné work—was a double detachable necklace of large disk-shaped beads of red and yellow gold and blue faience, which enhanced the richness of the whole effect. But the ultimate details of the ornamentation were hidden by a black lustrous coating due to liquid unguents that had evidently been profusely poured over the coffin. As a result this unparalleled monument was not only disfigured—as it afterwards proved, only temporarily—but was stuck fast to the interior of the second coffin, the consolidated liquid filling up the space between the second and third coffins almost to the level of the lid of the third.

These consecration unguents, which had obviously been used in great quantity, were doubtless the cause of the disintegration observed when dealing with the outer coffins which, as they were in a practically hermetically sealed quartzite sarcophagus, cannot have been affected by outside influences. As a further result it may be mentioned that the covering shroud and floral collarette mingled with blue faience beads had suffered, and although these at first appeared to be in good condition, they proved so brittle that the material broke the very instant it was touched.

We raised the third coffin contained in the shell of the second, which now rested on the top of the sarcophagus, and moved them into the Antechamber where they were more accessible, both for examination and manipulation. It was then that the wonder and magnitude of our last discovery more completely dawned upon us. This unique and wonderful monument— a coffin over 6 feet in length, of the finest art, wrought in solid gold of $2\frac{1}{2}$ to $3\frac{1}{2}$ millimetres in thickness—represented an enormous mass of pure bullion.

How great must have been the wealth buried with those ancient Pharaohs! What riches that Valley must have once concealed! Of the twenty-seven monarchs buried there, Tutankhamen was probably of the least importance. How great must have been the temptation to the greed and rapacity of the audacious contemporary tomb robbers! What stronger incentive can be imagined than those vast treasures of gold! The plundering of royal tombs, recorded in the reign of Rameses IX, becomes easily intelligible when the incentive to these crimes is measured by this gold coffin of Tutankhamen. It must have represented fabulous wealth to the stone-cutters, artisans, water-carriers and peasants—to contemporary workers generally, such as the men implicated in the tomb robberies. These plunderings occurred in the reigns of the later Ramessides (1200–1000 B.C.) and are recorded in legal documents now known as the Abbott, Amherst, Turin and Mayer papyri, discovered in Thebes about the beginning of last century. Probably the thieves, who made their practically ineffectual raid on Tutankhamen's tomb, were aware of the mass of bullion covering the remains of the young Pharaoh under its protective shrines, sarcophagus and nested coffins.

Our first object now was to protect from injury and, so far as was possible for the moment, to conserve the delicate inlay on the shell of the second coffin. The process used we knew to be effective. It was, therefore, lightly brushed to remove loose dust, sponged with warm water and ammonia, and when dry, the whole surface covered with a thick coating of paraffin wax applied hot with a long brush. This wax as it cooled and solidified held the inlay securely in position so that the coffin could be handled with impunity. The great advantage of this system is that the wax coating may be removed by heat at any time should further restoration be considered necessary,

A detail of an unguent vase

and the mere reheating of the wax has also a cleansing quality.

The next problem for consideration, requiring a certain amount of experimental work, was to ascertain the most satisfactory, and at the same time the most expeditious manner, of dealing with those ancient consolidated consecration unguents, that not only covered the body of the coffin but completely filled the space between the two, thus sticking them fast and for the moment preventing further progress in investigation. Mr. Lucas made a preliminary analysis of this substance. In appearance it was black, and resembled pitch; in those places where the layer was thin, as on the lid of the coffin, the material was hard and brittle, but where a thicker layer had accumulated, as was the case under and between the coffins, the interior of the material was soft and plastic. Its smell when warm was penetrating, somewhat fragrant, not unpleasant, and suggestive of wood-pitch. Naturally a complete chemical analysis was not then possible, but, as a result of a preliminary examination, it was found to contain fatty matter and resin. There was no mineral pitch or bitumen present, and even the presence of wood-pitch, which was suggested by the smell, could not then be proved. There can be little doubt from the manner in which this material had run down the sides of the third coffin and collected underneath, that it was in a liquid or semi-liquid condition when employed.

On account of its nature, it follows that this substance could be melted by heat and dissolved by certain solvents, but neither of these methods in the existing circumstances was practicable. So we decided to raise the lid and examine the contents before any further procedure, and before applying any drastic measures. Luckily the line of junction between the lid and the coffin was visible and, with difficulty, accessible, except at the extreme foot-end where the second and third coffins practically touched.

The lid was fastened to the shell by means of eight gold tenons (four on each side), which were held in their corresponding sockets by nails. Thus, if the nails could be extracted the lid could be raised. In the narrow space between the two coffins ordinary implements for extracting metal pins were useless, and others had to be devised. With long screwdrivers converted to meet the conditions, the nails or pins of solid gold, that unfortunately had to be sacrificed, were removed piecemeal. The lid was raised by its golden handles and the mummy of the king disclosed.

At such moments the emotions evade verbal expression, complex and stirring as they are. Three thousand years and more had elapsed since men's eyes had gazed into that golden coffin. Time, measured by the brevity of human life, seemed to lose its common perspectives before a spectacle so vividly recalling the solemn religious rites of a vanished civilization. But it is useless to dwell on such sentiments, based as they are on feelings of awe and human pity. The emotional side is no part of archaeological research. Here at last lay all that was left of the youthful Pharaoh, hitherto little more to us than the shadow of a name.

Before us, occupying the whole of the interior of the golden coffin, was an impressive, neat and carefully made mummy, over which had been poured anointing unguents as in the case of the outside of its coffin—again in great quantity—consolidated and blackened by age. In contradistinction to the general dark and sombre effect, due to these unguents, was a brilliant, one might say magnificent, burnished gold mask or similitude of the king, covering his head and shoulders, which, like the feet, had been intentionally avoided when using the unguents. The mummy was fashioned to symbolize Osiris. The beaten gold mask, a beautiful and unique specimen of ancient portraiture, bears a sad but calm expression suggestive of youth overtaken prematurely by death. Upon its forehead, wrought in massive gold, were the royal insignia —the Nekhebet vulture and Buto serpent—emblems of the Two Kingdoms over which he had reigned. To the chin was attached the conventional Osiride beard, wrought in gold and lapis-lazuli-coloured glass; around the throat was a triple necklace of yellow and red gold and blue faience disk-shaped beads; pendent from the neck by flexible gold inlaid straps was a large black resin scarab that rested between the hands and bore the *Bennu* ritual. The burnished gold hands,

The gold mask

crossed over the breast, separate from the mask, were sewn to the material of the linen wrappings, and grasped the Flagellum and Crozier—the emblems of Osiris. Immediately below these was the simple outermost linen covering, adorned with richly inlaid gold trappings pendent from a large pectoral-like figure of the *Ba* bird or soul, of gold cloisonné work, its full-spread wings stretched over the body. As these gorgeous trappings had been subjected to the consecration unguents, their detail and brilliance were hardly visible, and to this must be attributed the disastrous deterioration which we discovered to have taken place in the case of many of the objects.

But through this obstruction it could be faintly seen that these trappings, made of heavy gold plaques held together by threads of beads, bore welcoming speeches of the gods—for example, on the longitudinal bands down the centre, the goddess of the sky, Nut, the Divine Mother, says:—"I reckon thy beauties, O Osiris, King Kheperunebre; thy soul livest: thy veins are firm. Thou smellest the air and goest out as a god, going out as Atum, O Osiris, Tutankhamen. Thou goest out and thou enterest with Ra . . ." The god of the earth, the prince of the gods, Geb, says:—"My beloved son, inheritor of the throne of Osiris, the King Kheperunebre; thy nobility is perfect: Thy Royal Palace is powerful; Thy name is in the mouth of the Rekhyt, thy stability is in the mouth of the living, O Osiris, King Tutankhamen, Thy heart is in thy body eternally. He is before the spirits of the living, like Re he rests in heaven." While the texts upon the transverse bands open with words, such as "Honoured before Anubis, Hapy, Kebehsenuef, Duamutef," and "Justified before Osiris."

Accompanying these bands along the sides of the mummy, from the shoulders to the feet, were festoons of even more ornate straps attached to the transverse bands, and made up of elaborate small inlaid gold plaques also threaded together with beads. The devices on these side straps were of geometrical patterns, *Ded* and *Thet* symbols, solar uraei, and cartouches of the king. These, when cleaned, seemed to have been made up in part of a residue from Smenkhkare's burial, for some of the cloisonné plaques bore on the back texts from the "Chapter of the Heart" wherein Smenkhkare's names were introduced, and had, in most cases, been afterwards purposely defaced.

When these trappings were cleaned it became clear that the jeweller had made the main part of these trappings (texts and festoons) to measure, that the finished mummy proved larger than was originally expected, and that pieces were cut, others added, to make them fit.

Though the attributes upon this mummy are those of the gods, the likeness is certainly that of Tutankhamen, comely and placid, with the features recognizable on all his statues and coffins. From certain aspects the face here recalls his father-in-law Akhenaten, in others, especially in profile, perhaps an even stronger likeness to the great Queen Tyi, Akhenaten's mother, or, in other words, as those features gazed at you, there was an incipient gleam of affinity to both of those predecessors.

Those liquid unguents so lavishly used would seem to have been applied as part of the burial ritual for the consecration of the dead king, before his entrance into the presence of the great god Osiris of the Underworld. It was particularly noticeable that, both on the third coffin and the king's mummy itself, the head and feet had been carefully avoided, although some of the same liquid had been poured on the feet (only) of the first outermost coffin. One's thoughts turned, as one mused on the nature of that last ceremony and its intention, to that touching scene "in the house of the leper," when "there came a woman having an alabaster box of ointment of spikenard very precious" and to Christ's words: "she is come aforehand to anoint my body to the burying" (Mark xiv. 8).

When the detailed photographic records were made by Mr. Burton, we were better able to make a closer examination of the actual state of things, and the preservation of the mummy. The

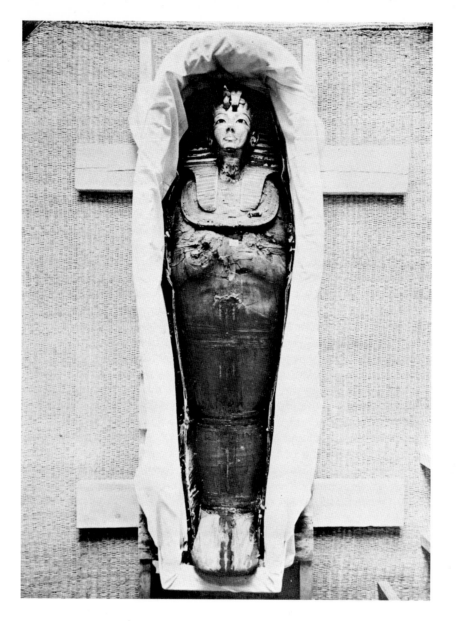

The royal mummy within its coffin

greater part of the flagellum and crozier was completely decomposed, and had already fallen to dust; the threads that once held the hands and trappings in place upon the outer linen covering, were decayed, and in consequence the various sections fell apart at the slightest touch; the black resin scarab was covered by minute fissures, probably the result of contraction; consequently, these external trappings and ornaments had to be removed, piece by piece, and placed in corresponding order and position upon a tray for future cleaning and remounting. The farther we proceeded the more evident it became that the covering wrappings and the mummy were both in a parlous state. They were completely carbonized by the action that had been set up by the fatty acids of the unguents with which they had been saturated.

But, alas! both the mask and the mummy were stuck fast to the bottom of the coffin by the consolidated residue of the unguents, and no amount of legitimate force could move them. What was to be done?

Since it was known that this adhesive material could be softened by heat, it was hoped that an exposure to the midday sun would melt it sufficiently to allow the mummy to be raised. A trial therefore was made for several hours in sun temperature reaching as high as 149° Fahrenheit (65° C.) without any success and, as other means were not practicable, it became evident that we should have to make all further examination of the king's remains in the coffins.

As a matter of fact, after the scientific examination of the king's mummy *in situ*, and its final removal from the gold coffin, that very difficult question of removing the gold mask and extricating the gold coffin from the shell of the second coffin, had to be solved.

Originally something like two bucketsful of the liquid unguents had been poured over the golden coffin, and a similar amount over the body inside. As heat was the only practical means of melting this material and rendering it amenable, in order to apply a temperature sufficiently high for the purpose, without causing damage to those wonderful specimens of ancient Egyptian arts and crafts, the interior of the golden coffin had to be completely lined with thick plates of zinc, which would not melt under a temperature of 968° Fahrenheit (520° C.). The coffins were then reversed upon trestles, the outside one being protected against undue heat and fire by several blankets saturated and kept wet with water. Our next procedure was to place under the hollow of the gold coffin several Primus paraffin lamps burning at full blast. The heat from the lamps had to be regulated so as to keep the temperature well within the melting-point of zinc. It should be noted here that the coating of wax upon the surface of the second coffin acted as a pyrometer— while it remained unmelted under the wet blanketing there was manifestly no fear of injury.

Although the temperature arrived at was some 932° Fahrenheit (500° C.), it took several hours before any real effect was noticeable. The moment signs of movement became apparent, the lamps were turned out, and the coffins left suspended upon the trestles, when, after an hour, they began to fall apart. The movement at first was almost imperceptible owing to the tenacity of the material, but we were able to separate them by lifting up the wooden shell of the second coffin, thus leaving the shell of the gold coffin resting upon the trestles. Its very nature was hardly recognizable, and all we could see was a dripping mass of viscous pitch-like material which proved very difficult to remove, even with quantities of solvents—the principal of which was acetone.

In the same manner that the outside of the golden coffin was covered with a viscid mass, so was the interior, to which still adhered the gold mask. This mask had also been protected by being bound with a folded wet blanket continually fed with water, its face padded with wet wadding. As it had necessarily been subjected to the full power of the heat collected in the interior of the coffin, it was freed and lifted away with comparative ease, though to its back, as in the case of the coffin, there adhered a great mass of viscous unguents, which had eventually to be removed with the aid of a blast lamp and cleaning solvents.

We have now, in the natural sequence of our work, to return to the first coffin that had still to be raised out of the sarcophagus. This was successfully achieved, as in previous operations, by means of our hoisting tackle attached to the overhead scaffolding. After it had been lifted sufficiently high to clear the top of the sarcophagus, a wooden tray was passed beneath it, and it was thus carried up to the laboratory where its lid was already under treatment. It proved to be of great weight, and like the shrines, was probably of an oak wood. It had unfortunately suffered from humidity evaporated from those liquid unguents, which had caused the gesso-gilt surfaces to blister and buckle to such an extent that, in many places, this overlaying decoration had become detached from the basic wood. Fortunately this injury need not be permanent. By patiently filling in the interstices with hot paraffin wax, in time, with patience and care it can be repaired, and the decorated surfaces once more be made good and firm.

The only remaining object in the sarcophagus was the gilt bed-shaped bier with lion's head and feet. It stood on the bottom and served as a support to the first (outermost) coffin. It was made of a stout and heavy wood covered with gesso-gilt; but the astonishing fact was that, after supporting the weight of those three great coffins—more than a ton and a quarter—for over thirty centuries, it was still intact. Strips of broad webbing were passed under it, and this splendid example of ancient Egyptian construction was raised out of the sarcophagus. It stands about 12 inches in height, 7 feet 6 inches in length, and is curved so as to receive and to fit the base of the outermost coffin. The central panel is designed in low relief to represent a cord-mesh—like the string mesh of the Sudanese *Angaribes* (bedsteads) of today. The joints of the framework are hardly sprung, thus bearing witness to the quality of the wood and the excellence of the joinery.

Lying on the bottom of the sarcophagus beneath this bier were a number of wooden chips bearing traces of gesso-gilt ornamentation. These were at first puzzling, but their presence was accounted for upon further examination. The design on the gesso-gilt surface was identical with that on the edge of the first (outermost) coffin, from which pieces had been crudely hacked away by some sharp instrument like a carpenter's adze. The obvious explanation is that the foot-end of the coffin, as it rested on the bier, was too high to allow the lid of the sarcophagus to be lowered in place, and it was therefore cut down by those whose duty it was to close the sarcophagus. This is evidence of want of forethought on the part of the workmen. This mutilation of the coffin had not been noticed before, owing to its having been hidden by the anointing un-guents, the presence of which, in this case only on the feet, might have been an endeavour to cover the disfiguring scar, and thus may not be of religious significance.

Besides these chips were some rags, a stout wooden lever, portions of floral garlands fallen from the burial, and the transcending example of religious handicraft—the highly ornamented gold and silver receptacle for sacred unguents.

The Burial Chamber and sarcophagus were now empty and we were able, for the first time, to consider more closely the funerary customs followed in the burial of a Pharaoh, as revealed to us by Tutankhamen's tomb, and something, I venture to think, has been added to our knowledge.

The more one considers it the more deeply one is impressed by the extreme care and enormous costliness lavished by this ancient people on the enshrinement of their dead. Barrier after barrier was raised to guard their remains from the predatory hands against which, in death, these great kings too ineffectually sought protection. The process was as elaborate as it was costly.

First we have the golden shrines profusely decorated and of magnificent workmanship. They were sealed and nested one in the other over an immense and superbly sculptured monolithic quartzite sarcophagus. The sarcophagus, in its turn, contained three great anthropoid coffins of wood and gold which bear the likeness of the king with repeated *Rishi* and Osiride symbolism.

Everywhere there was evidence of the accomplished artist and skilful craftsman, intent on the mysteries of a vanished religion, and the problems of death. Finally we reach the monarch him-self, profusely anointed with sacred unguents and covered with numberless amulets and emblems for his betterment, as well as personal ornaments for his glory.

The modern observer indeed is astounded at the enormous labour and expense bestowed on these royal burials, even when the titanic excavations of their rock-cut tombs is disregarded. Consider the carving and gilding of the elaborate shrines; the hewing and transport of that quartzite sarcophagus; the moulding, carving, inlaying of the magnificent coffins, the costly and intricate goldsmith's work expended upon them, the crowd of craftsmen employed, the precious metal and material so generously devoted to the princely dead. But we do not know all, there are the contents of two more chambers yet to be seen!

17

Points of interest in Egyptian burial customs

UNDOUBTEDLY THE GREATEST CEREMONY which awaited every Egyptian, in due proportion to his rank, was his funeral.

With the ancient Egyptian in all stations of life, from the Pharaoh to the peasant, there was a profound yearning for a good burial. To secure this wish he made, in accordance with his rank, elaborate preparations and it was naturally his desire that his survivors would see that they were carried out. The general attitude of mind of the ancient Egyptians towards the benefits of a good burial is expressed, with simple dignity, in the story of a certain Sinuhe which has come down to us from the Middle Kingdom, some forty centuries ago, and is translated by Dr. Alan Gardiner:

> "Remember then the day of burial, the passing into beatitude; when the night shall be devoted to thee with oils and with bandages, the handiwork of Tayt [i.e. the goddess of weaving]. There is a procession to be made for thee on the day thou art reunited with the earth: thy mummy-case of gold, with head of lapis lazuli, a heaven [i.e. shrine] above thee—the while that thou art placed upon the hearse, and oxen drag thee. Then shall musicians await thy coming, and the dance of the *Muu* be performed at the door of thy tomb. The words of offering shall be pronounced on thy behalf, and victims slaughtered at the door of thy stele."[1]

This may be regarded as a general expression of optimism prevailing among those ancient people, but pessimists have existed in all ages, and we have an Egyptian poet lamenting in the following lines the uselessness of fine sepulchres: "He who built there in granite, who constructed a hall in a pyramid; who supplied there what was beautiful in fine work . . . his altar shall be as empty as those of the weary, who die on the canal embankment without leaving any survivors."[2]

These quotations convey to us both the sanguine and dissenting views held on this subject, but although the latter is of rare occurrence, we have some idea of what was the practice. Actual cliff-tombs were commenced during the lifetime of the deceased: for example, Queen Hatshepsut prepared for herself a cliff-tomb on the western side of the mountain of Thebes, when she was consort to Thothmes II, and another, and later one, in the Valley of the Tombs of the Kings, when she actually reigned as a monarch. In a similar way Horemheb had two tombs, one as general of the army, the other as king after he had usurped the throne. But perhaps the most striking instance of all is that of King Akhenaten, who as early as the sixth year of his reign, when he was about eighteen years of age, when setting up tablets demarcating the limits of his city Akhetaten (El Amarna), decrees:

> "There shall be made for me a sepulchre in the Orient Mountain; my burial shall be (made) therein in the multitude of jubilees which Aten my father hath ordained for me, and the burial of the chief wife of the king, Nefertiti, shall be made therein in that multitude of years . . . (and the burial of) the king's daughter Mertaten shall be made in it in that multitude of years."[3]

Further, Akhenaten decrees that, should he, his queen, Nefertiti, or his eldest daughter, Mertaten, die "in any town" outside the limits of his city, that they shall be brought to, and buried in, the sepulchre prepared by him "in the Orient Mountain" of his city. There are other examples of this kind which need not be quoted.

Not only was the cliff-tomb commenced during life, but also the stone sarcophagus was prepared, as in the case of Queen Hatshepsut; and, if the Turin papyrus relating to the tomb of Rameses IV be accepted as a project, as I think it really was, so were the covering gilt wooden shrines, and some of the essentially religious funerary objects. But the results of archaeological research suggest also that the greater part of the burial equipment was made after death, though no doubt the deceased had made preliminary provisions. This point is strongly indicated by the fact, that, on practically all funerary furniture, the names, titles, and rank, are those of the deceased at the time of death. The objects which obviously belonged to his lifetime are the exception.

In the case of Tutankhamen's tomb there is sufficient evidence to show that at least most of the funerary appurtenances were made after death, during the period of mummification, and the subsequent period, whatever it may have been, necessary for the carrying out of the customs prior to burial. This point is confirmed by the fact that the funerary statues, statuettes, coffins and mask show a certain hurried workmanship, and depict Tutankhamen at the age of his death, as is proved by his mummy. While, in contradistinction, an obvious piece of El Amarna palace furniture, such as the throne, bears his early and original *Aten* name, and the ceremonial gold and silver sticks which depict him about the age he became king.

It therefore becomes clear that a great part of the funerary appurtenances which could not be made during the lifetime of the deceased depended largely on the fidelity of his successor.

Herodotus, writing some nine centuries after the death of Tutankhamen, gives a short account of the way in which the Egyptians conducted their mournings, and also of the method of mummification employed in his day: "On the death in any house of a man of consequence, forthwith the women of the family beplaster their heads, and sometimes even their faces, with mud; and then, leaving the body indoors, sally forth and wander through the city, with their dress fastened by a band, and their bosoms bare, beating themselves as they walk. All the female relations join them and do the same. The men too, similarly begirt, beat their breasts separately. When the ceremonies are over, the body is carried away to be embalmed."

"There are," he wrote, "a set of men in Egypt who practice the art of embalming, and make it their proper business. These persons, when a body is brought to them, show the bearers various models of corpses, made of wood, and painted so as to resemble nature. The most perfect is said to be after the manner of him whom I do not think it religious to name in connexion with such a matter;[4] the second sort is inferior to the first, and less costly; the third is the cheapest of all. All this the embalmers explain, and then ask in which way it is wished that the corpse should be prepared. The bearers tell them, and having concluded their bargain, take their departure, while the embalmers, left to themselves, proceed to their task." Referring to "the most perfect process," as he terms it, Herodotus, after telling us how the brain and softer parts of the body are treated, proceeds: "Then the body is placed in natrum for seventy days, and covered entirely over. After the expiration of that space of time, which must not be exceeded,[5] the body is washed, and wrapped round, from head to foot, with bandages of fine linen cloth, smeared over with gum, which is used generally by the Egyptians in place of glue, and in this state is given back to the relatives, who enclose it in a wooden case which they have had made for the purpose, shaped in the figure of a man. Then fastening the case, they place it in a sepulchral chamber, upright against the wall."

Although the method of embalming described by the great Greek historian refers to a much later date, the process, as archaeological research has shown, was very similar to that employed in earlier times.

In ordinary cases the practice was certainly one likely to lead to abuses, and we may be sure that the neighbourhood of the burial grounds was peopled by hungry professional embalmers, and the meaner priests, eager to prey upon the relations. In the case of a royal and sacred personage, no doubt, the operation would be carried out within the palace or its adjuncts in pomp and ceremony and under special supervision.

The length of time for mummification given by Herodotus is confirmed by a Theban stele of a noble of the reign of Thothmes III, ably translated and published by Dr. Alan Gardiner.[6] The stele also throws valuable light upon the burial rites about a century before Tutankhamen.

"A goodly burial arrives in peace, thy seventy days having been fulfilled in thy place of embalming. Thou art placed on the bier . . . and art drawn by bulls without blemish, thy road being besprinkled with milk until thou reachest the door of thy tomb. The children of thy children, united of one accord, weep with loving hearts. Opened is thy mouth by the lector, and thy purification is made by the *Sem* priest. Horus adjusts for thee thy mouth, and opens for thee thy eyes and ears, thy flesh and thy bones being perfect in all that appertains to thee. There are recited for thee spells and glorifications. There is made for thee an offering-which-the-King-gives, thy own true heart being with thee. . . . Thou comest in thy former shape, even as on the day wherein thou wast born. There is brought to thee the son thou lovest, the courtiers making obeisance. Thou enterest into the land given of the King, into the sepulchre of the West. There are performed rites for thee as for those of yore. . . ."

But upon the subject of the period for mummification, and for the mourning of the dead, I should also refer the reader to the well-known passage in Genesis (chapter 50, vv. 2 & 3), wherein "Joseph commanded his servants the physicians to embalm his father: and the physicians embalmed Israel. And forty days were fulfilled for him: for so are fulfilled the days of those which are embalmed: and the Egyptians mourned for him three score and ten days."

Some evidence of the obsequies of Tutankhamen is afforded by the material found in a cache of large pottery jars, discovered by Mr. Theodore M. Davis (1907–8) in the Valley, a little distance from the king's tomb. Their contents proved to be accessories used during the funeral ceremonies of the young king, and afterwards gathered together and packed away within jars —which seems to have been the custom in Egyptian burials. Among the material there were clay seals of Tutankhamen and of the royal necropolis, and floral collars of a kind represented as worn by mourners in burial scenes. The floral collars, sewn upon sheets of papyrus, are the counterparts of that found on the gold coffin; the pottery vases are also similar to specimens in the tomb. This discovery indicates that pottery vases were broken as well as that the seals on certain objects were removed, and that linen head-shawls and floral collars were worn during the royal funerary ritual; but the material throws no light upon the ministrations of the "divine servants" and lectors who must have officiated at the burial. However, that King Ay, Tutankhamen's successor, was present, and that he acted as the *Sem* priest, is clear from the scene depicted on the north wall of the Burial Chamber of the tomb. Also the scene on the east wall of the same chamber shows that the king's mummy, on its sledge, was dragged to the tomb, at least for some distance, by courtiers and high officials, instead of by oxen which were used in non-royal funerals.

It is manifest, after the actual burial ceremonies, that the tomb must have remained open and have been in the hands of workmen for a long time, for it is obvious that the nest of shrines, covering the sarcophagus, could only have been erected after the great coffins were placed in position, and the sarcophagus closed. In the same way the partition wall, dividing the Antechamber from the Burial Chamber, must have been built after the erection of the shrines, and the furniture filling both chambers subsequently introduced.

These last facts open up an interesting question: where were all the valuable and delicate objects that eventually filled those rooms, while these lengthy operations—the erection of the shrines and the building of the partition wall—were being carried out? As we have no evidence that any store-room existed in the Valley, although there might have been temporary constructions serving for that purpose, does it mean that the funerary furniture was brought from the royal workshop only when their place was ready? If these objects were not brought to the tomb simultaneously, the obsequies would be of a different character from that generally supposed. It has been usually imagined that all the furniture was carried behind the coffin in the funeral procession, thus forming a gorgeous pageant. But, as we have just seen, it would appear that many of the funerary objects must have been transported to the tomb after the actual burial of the king, when the chambers were ready to receive them.

When the tomb was eventually closed and sealed, the seals of the dead king were used instead of those of his successor.

To return to Tutankhamen: his mummy and his coffins were all scrupulously fashioned to represent and symbolize the one great god of the dead, Osiris. For this we seem to have an impressive reason. The close association in funeral custom with that deity, was in all probability due to the belief that Osiris was in many ways nearer than any other deity to man. For on this earth he suffered the pangs of death, was buried, and rose again from mortal death to immortal life. The mummy itself was carefully orientated east and west and, as it will be seen in the succeeding chapter, the insignia were so placed on it as to agree in position with the Two Kingdoms, Upper and Lower Egypt. The amulets and ornaments of religious import were conscientiously disposed within its wrappings, in accordance with the ritual of the Book of the Dead.

As will have been already gathered from the preceding chapter, we found, to our dismay, that the mummy of Tutankhamen was in poor condition, due, as is now clear, to the profuse anointing to which it had been subjected. It was, however, evident that this anointing formed an essential part of the king's burial.

There was the amplest evidence that the body had been carefully mummified, wrapped and adorned with all the accessories, before the liquids had been poured over it. In all probability those once liquid unguents were merely of pious significance, and had been applied for a sacred purpose either before or during the burial rites, to consecrate or purify the dead king, or to help him towards initiation on his journey through the mysteries of the shadowy Underworld. Egyptian ritual was full of symbolism. The anointing by the gods of the body of Osiris would give the ceremony all the weight of religious tradition.

That there had been method in the pouring of these liquids was also evident. Apparently they had not been dispensed without design. Both on the effigy on the (innermost) coffin of gold, and over the wrappings of the mummy itself, the liquid had been poured over the body and legs only. The face and feet had been avoided, except in the case of the first (outermost) coffin, whereon a small amount had been definitely poured on the feet only, though, as already suggested in the previous chapter, this may possibly have been for quite another purpose.

But whatever the sacred intention, the result, so far as archaeology is concerned, has been unfortunate. There can be little doubt that the use of the liquids within the wood and metal coffins was the main cause of the extremely bad condition of their contents. The action of the composite liquid employed has been threefold: first, the decomposition of the fatty matter, by producing fatty acids, has acted destructively upon certain qualities of the glass inlay and cement of the objects; secondly, the oxidation of the resin has given rise to a kind of slow spontaneous combustion, resulting in the carbonization of the linen fabric and, in a less degree, of the tissues and even of the bones of the mummy; thirdly, the quantity of liquid poured both over the innermost coffin and mummy itself was sufficient to form a pitch-like cement which consolidated the contents.

The result is disappointing to this extent. Time and mischance, aided by the chemical decomposition suggested, have robbed archaeology of part at least of what might have been a great opportunity—the scientific examination, the systematic unwrapping of the mummy, for which we had hoped, were consequently rendered nearly impossible.

Naturally a question here arises as to whether all the other royal mummies of the Egyptian New Empire were subjected to similar treatment in respect to anointing? I believe, although those remains show but slight traces of similar resinous matter, such a ceremony was common to all.

It must be remembered in the case of the royal mummies discovered both in the cache of Deir el Bahari and in the tomb of Amenhetep II that not one of them had either their original wrappings or coffins, rough coffins having been substituted by the priests in the Twentieth and Twenty-first Dynasties. Thus, by having been denuded of their original coverings and coffins, those royal mummies at an early date were freed from the destructive elements from which Tutankhamen's mummy suffered. In other words, the royal tomb-robberies occurred before there had been sufficient time for the unguents to penetrate far into the voluminous wrappings, or set up much decomposition.

The alabaster jars belonging to Rameses II and Merenptah containing those very unguents, discovered by Lord Carnarvon and myself in the Valley in 1920, are evidence of the constant use of those materials. The hieratic inscriptions upon the jars mention, "Oil of the first quality from Libya"; "oil of the first quality of divine things," and "fat of *Tauat*."

But for the anointing oils, I believe that the wrappings, and all accessories of Tutankhamen's mummy in the solid gold coffin, would have been found practically as perfect as when first placed in the coffin.

We might now with advantage reconsider some impressions gathered from our investigation of the burial rites of the ancient Egyptians, so far as the discovery of this tomb has added to our knowledge. In the first place, former documentary evidence makes it clear that it was a constant belief in the religion of the ancient Egyptians that the solicitude of the living ensured the welfare of the dead: also that the rare dissenting traces of pessimistic philosophy which have come down to us, throwing doubts on the utility of constructing vast mortuary temples, chapels and tombs in their honour, could obviously have had but little influence on the strength and intensity of this cult.

We gather from this tomb that in the case of a royal burial, the succeeding king acts as the *Sem* priest in the ritual of "the opening of the mouth," and that courtiers and high officials replaced oxen in dragging the bier.

Our knowledge gathered from other sources for the period of mummification, shows that it was at least seventy days, or possibly more, but whether the period of mourning was contemporaneous with it is still uncertain, though it seems clear that the funeral took place immediately after the completion of mummification. However this may be, it is now evident that, between a royal burial and the closing of the tomb, some time must have elapsed for the various intricate preparations before the chambers were ready to receive their full equipment, and that consequently it does not seem probable that the whole of the funerary furniture could have been carried in the procession of the mummy. It is difficult to conceive that the great quantity of delicate and extremely valuable articles, not to mention boxes of jewellery and gold vessels, etc., such as filled the Burial Chamber and its adjacent rooms, could have been stacked there, while the workmen and tackle necessary for closing the sarcophagus, erecting the shrines and building the thick masonry partition wall, were present. Further, it would have been wellnigh impossible for the workmen to have carried out their task, had those chambers been encumbered with furniture as we found them. I might here note that upon the outermost shrine there were distinct splashes of plaster, whereas the funerary furniture bore no such evidence.

In the case of royal burials we may also infer that it was the custom to bury the late king behind necropolis seals bearing his own name. If then each Pharaoh was buried behind his own seals, a question arises as to when the seal of the successor came into force and that of the late king became obsolete. To this no clear answer can yet be given. When the tomb of Tutankhamen was reclosed after the depredations of the tomb-thieves, which probably occurred not long after his burial, the seals then used were those of the royal necropolis which bore no royal names; and this was also the case when King Horemheb ordered the tomb of Thothmes IV to be restored after its violation by robbers.

Whether the whole of the tomb equipment was made before or after the king's death, is a question of interest upon which some evidence has been gathered. In some instances there is little doubt. Some objects bear a distinct clue; in the case of others, deduction evades us. Thus we gather that some objects were made during his lifetime—even at an early age—and that others were made immediately following or soon after his death.

Another important and interesting fact borne on the mind, is the tenacity of the Osiris cult throughout the history of ancient Egypt. The mummy and its coffin were consistently made in the form of the deity, whose mortal experiences brought him nearer than any other god of the Egyptian pantheon to human sympathies, and it is the mysterious influence of this divinity that shines through the cults of more than one later creed.

There remains but one other fact to be noted. The discovery of Tutankhamen's tomb has brought to light a custom hitherto little known—that of profusely anointing the royal mummy—which, in the case of the young king, has worked such deplorable havoc from an archaeological point of view. We had expected to find the mummy in better condition than most of those that have come down to us, torn as they had been from their coffins by profane hands in dynastic times. But alas! we were disappointed, and here we have a grim example of the irony which may sometimes await research. The tomb robbers who dragged the remains of the Pharaohs from their coverings for plunder, or the pious priests who hid them to save them from further violations, at least protected those royal remains against the chemical action of the sacred unguents before there was time for corrosion.

18

The examination of the royal mummy

To MOST INVESTIGATORS, and especially to those absorbed in archaeological research, there are moments when their work becomes of transcending interest, and it was now our good fortune to pass through one of these rare and wonderful periods. The time that immediately followed we shall ever recall with the profoundest satisfaction. After years of toil—of excavating, conserving and recording—we were to see, with the eye of reality, that which we had hitherto beheld only in imagination. The investigation for us had been one of the greatest interest, nor will it, I venture to hope, be entirely without importance to archaeology. Something at least has been added to confirm or extend our knowledge of the funeral rituals of the Pharaohs in relation to their ancient myths and traditions.

On 11 November, at 9.45 a.m., the examination of the royal mummy was commenced. There were present H.E. Saleh Enan Pasha, Under-Secretary of State to the Ministry of Public Works; H.E. Sayed Fuad Bey el Kholi, Governor of the Province of Keneh; Monsieur Pierre Lacau, the Director-General of the Department of Antiquities; Dr. Douglas Derry, Professor of Anatomy in the Faculty of Medicine, Egyptian University; Dr. Saleh Bey Hamdi, Director of the Sanitary Services, Alexandria; Mr. A. Lucas, Government chemist, Department of Antiquities; Mr. Harry Burton of the Metropolitan Museum of Art, New York; Tewfik Effendi Boulos, Chief Inspector of the Department of Antiquities, Upper Egypt; and Mohamed Shaaban Effendi, Assistant Curator, Cairo Museum.

The external ornaments and inlaid gold trappings described having been removed, the king's mummy lay bare with its simple outer coverings and gold mask. It occupied the whole of the interior of the gold coffin, measuring in total length 6 feet 1 inch.

The outer wrappings consisted of one large linen sheet, held in position by three longitudinal (one down the centre and one at each side) and four transverse bands of the same material, corresponding in position to the flexible inlaid gold trappings already mentioned. These linen bands had evidently been fastened to the linen covering by some such adhesive as Herodotus has described. They were doubled, and varied from $2\frac{3}{4}$ to $3\frac{1}{2}$ inches in width. The central longitudinal band, beginning in the middle of the abdomen (in reality thorax), was passed under the lower layer of each of the three transverse bands, over the feet, under the soles, and doubled back below the second layer of transverse bands. At each side of the feet the linen wrappings had been rubbed, the result probably of friction against the sides of the metal coffin during transport to the tomb. The mummy lay at a slight angle, suggesting that it had been subjected to some shock when lowered into the sarcophagus. There was also similar evidence to imply that the unguents had been poured over the mummy and coffin before they were lowered into the sarcophagus—the liquid being at different levels on the two sides, suggesting the tilting of the coffin.

In consequence of the fragile and carbonized condition of the linen swathing, the whole of the exposed surface was painted over with melted paraffin wax of such a temperature that when congealed it formed a thin coating on the surface, with minimum penetration of the decayed wrappings beneath. When the wax had cooled, Dr. Derry made a longitudinal incision down the centre of the outer binding to the depth penetrated by the wax, thus enabling the consolidated layer to be removed in large pieces. Nor did our troubles end here. The very voluminous under-wrappings were found to be in even worse condition of carbonization and decay. We had hoped, by removing a thin outer layer of bandage from the mummy, to free it at the points of adhesion to the coffin so that it might be removed, but in this we were again disappointed. It was found that the linen beneath the mummy and the body itself had been so saturated by the unguents which formed a pitch-like mass at the bottom of the coffin and held it embedded so firmly, that it was impossible to raise it except at risk of great damage. Even after the greater part of the bandages had been carefully removed, the consolidated material had to be chiselled away from beneath the limbs and trunk before it was possible to raise the king's remains.

The bandages that actually enveloped the head were in a better state of preservation than those on the rest of the body, inasmuch as they had not been saturated by the unguents, and consequently had only suffered from indirect oxidation. This was also the case to a large extent with the wrappings on the feet.

The general system of bandaging so far as could be discovered was of normal character: it comprised a series of bandages, sheets and pads of linen, where the latter were required to complete the anthropoid form, the whole showing evidence of considerable care. The linen was evidently of a very fine cambric-like nature. The numerous objects found upon the mummy were enclosed in alternate layers of the voluminous wrappings, and literally covered the king from head to foot; some of the larger objects were caught up in many different layers of bindings which were wound crosswise and transversely.

Although the actual examination had necessarily to be carried out beginning from the feet upwards, for the sake of clarity, in the following description, I will describe it from the head downwards, enumerating each object and point of interest in proper sequence.

Upon the top of the head was a large pad of conic form, composed of wads of linen, wrapped in the manner of a modern surgical head-bandage, and in shape suggestive of the *Atef* crown of Osiris, without such accessories as the horns and feather. The purpose of this pad is obscure; from its shape it might be thought to be a crown, but, on the other hand, it could well be merely a tall pad to support and fill the empty space within the hollow of the *Nemes* head-dress of the gold mask, especially in view of the fact that the mask is an integral part of the external equipment of the mummy, making it coincide with the effigies upon the coffins.

Beneath this crown-like pad, lying on the back of the mask, was a small amuletic *Urs* pillow, or headrest, made of iron, which, according to Chapter CLXVI of the "Book of the Dead," has the following significance: "Rise up from non-existence, O prostrate one . . . overthrowest thou thy enemies, triumphest thou over what they do against thee." Such amulets are usually made of haematite, but in this case pure iron has taken the place of that ore, a fact that gives us a very important milestone in the development and growth of the history of civilization—of this more anon.

Next to the pad and encircling the top of the head, was a double tie (the Arabic *aqal*), not unlike that of the Bedouin head-dress, made of fibre tightly bound with cord and having loops at the ends to which were doubtless attached tapes for tying at the back of the head. Its use is unknown, its like or parallel never before having been found. It suggests a relief to the head

The skull cap on the mummy's head

from the pressure of a crown.

The removal of a few layers of wrappings revealed a magnificent diadem completely encircling the king's head—an object of extreme beauty and of simple fillet type. In design it comprises a richly ornamented gold ribbon of contiguous circles of carnelian, having minute gold bosses affixed to their centres, with, at the back, a floral and disk-shaped bow, from which hang two ribbon-like gold appendages similarly decorated. On both sides of the fillet are appendages of a like but broader kind, and having a massive pendent uraeus attached to their front margins. The insignia of northern and southern sovereignty of this diadem, I should here mention, were found lower down, separate, and on the right and left thighs respectively, and as the king lay within the sarcophagus, east and west—his head towards the west—the uraeus of Buto being on the left side, and the vulture of Nekhebet on the right, the insignia took their correct geographical position, as did also those emblems on the coffins. Both of these golden emblems of royalty

The head of the king's mummy as first revealed

have grooved fastenings on the back, into which fit corresponding T-shaped tongues upon the diadem. They are thus movable and could be fitted on to whatever crown the king might have worn.

The golden Nekhebet with obsidian eyes is a remarkable example of fine metal-work. The shape of the head, occiput covered with wrinkles, and at the back of the neck a partial collar of short stiff feathers, make it quite clear that the bird, representing the Upper Egyptian goddess, was *Vultur auricularis*, Daud.—the sociable vulture. This particular species is to-day plentiful in Nubia, not uncommon in the middle and southern provinces of Egypt, but seldom if ever seen in Lower Egypt.

This diadem must have had a very early origin, inasmuch as it seems to have derived its name *Seshnen* and form from the circlet-ribbon worn on the head by men and women of all classes, as far back as the Old Kingdom, some 1,500 years before the New Empire. Moreover, there is evidence enough to show that we may consider it to be among ancient Egyptian funerary

144

appurtenances, since it is to be found mentioned among the coffin texts of the Middle Kingdom, and diadems of this kind are known to have been found thrice in connexion with royal burials: once analogous, but not identical, at Lahun, among the jewellery discovered by Professor Sir William Flinders Petrie, of a Princess Sathathoriunut of the Middle Kingdom; and twice in the royal Theban pyramid-tombs of the Seventeenth Dynasty—one upon a burial of an Antef, the other mentioned in connexion with the ancient Egyptian plunderers of the burial of Sebekemsaf. In both the latter cases, curiously enough, they were found by professional tomb-thieves: that of Sebekemsaf is mentioned in the records of the famous royal tomb robberies which occurred during the reign of Rameses IX, when the king's diadem and the rest of the treasure found, was divided up among the thieves as metal. The discovery of the third diadem, that of an Antef king, was made less than a century ago by predatory Arabs, when it passed from hand to hand until finally it found its way to the Leyden Museum.

More than often when this type of diadem is depicted upon the monuments, the king is represented wearing it around a wig in conjunction with, and surmounted by, the *Atef* crown of Osiris.

Around the forehead, underneath a few more layers of linen, was a broad temple-band of burnished gold terminating behind and above the ears. At its extremities are slots through which linen tapes were passed and tied in a bow at the back of the head. This band held in place, over the brow and temples, a fine cambric-like linen *Khat* head-dress, unfortunately reduced by decay to such an irreparable condition that it was only recognizable from a portion of the kind of pigtail at the back common to this head-dress. Sewn to this *Khat* head-dress were the royal insignia, being a second set found upon the king. The uraeus, with body and tail in flexible sections of gold-work threaded together, and bordered with minute beads, was passed over the axis of the crown of the head as far back as the *lambda*, whilst the Nekhebet vulture (in this case with open wings, and with characteristics identical with those already described) covered the top of the head-dress, its body being parallel with the uraeus. In order that the soft linen of this head-dress should take its conventional shape, pads of linen had been placed under it and above the temples.

Beneath the *Khat* head-dress were further layers of bandaging that covered a skull-cap of fine linen fabric, fitting tightly over the shaven head of the king, and embroidered with an elaborate device of uraei in minute gold and faience beads. The cap was kept in place by a gold temple-band similar to that just described. Each uraeus of the device bears in its centre the *Aten* cartouche of the Sun. The fabric of the cap was unfortunately much carbonized and decayed, but the bead-work had suffered far less, the device being practically perfect, since it adhered to the head of the king. To have attempted to remove this exquisite piece of work would have been disastrous, so it was treated with a thin coating of wax and left as it was found.

The removal of the final wrappings that protected the face of the king needed the utmost care, as owing to the carbonized state of the head there was always the risk of injury to the very fragile features. We realized the peculiar importance and responsibility attached to our task. At the touch of a sable brush the last few fragments of decayed fabric fell away, revealing a serene and placid countenance, that of a young man. The face was refined and cultured, the features well formed, especially the clearly marked lips, and I think I may here record, without wishing to encroach on the province of Drs. Derry and Saleh Bey Hamdi, the first and most striking impression to all present: namely, the remarkable structural resemblance to his father-in-law, Akhenaten—an affinity that has been visible on the monuments.

This strong likeness—for it is too evident to be set down to mere accident—presents the historian of this period with an entirely new and unexpected fact, and one which may throw some light on the ephemeral Smenkhkare, as well as on Tutankhamen, both of whom acquired the throne by marrying Akhenaten's daughters. The obscurity of their parentage becomes

A pair of Tutankhamen's earrings (see page 72)

intelligible if these two kings were the offspring of an unofficial marriage—an hypothesis by no means improbable since there are precedents for it in the royal family of the Eighteenth Dynasty. Thothmes I, son of Amenhetep I, by an unofficial wife, Sensenb, became king by his marriage to the Crown Princess Ahmes. Hatshepsut was married to her half-brother, Thothmes II. In fact, when the royal wife had no male issue or surviving son, such marriages were generally the rule.

The further the problem suggested by this structural affinity visibly existing between Akhenaten and Tutankhamen is studied, the more interesting grows the light thrown on contemporary history and ancient sociology.

This affinity may have been derived either directly through Akhenaten or indirectly through Queen Tyi. The peculiar physical traits exhibited both in Akhenaten and Tutankhamen are not to be found in the preceding Amenhetep and Thothmes family, but they are noticeable in certain more intimate, as distinguished from more conventional, portraits of Queen Tyi, from whom Akhenaten seems to have inherited his physical peculiarities. It is possible therefore that Tutankhamen may also have inherited them from the same source, and may even have been a grandson of Queen Tyi through some other offspring. But on this point of apparent blood-relationship of the two kings, the following letter from among the cuneiform correspondence found at El Amarna, seems to throw considerable light:

From Dushratta (King of Mittanni, Upper Mesopotamia) to Napkhuria (Akhenaten, King of Egypt).

"To Napkhuria, the King of Egypt, my brother, my son-in-law, who loves me and whom I love, has spoken thus Dushratta, the King of Mittanni, thy father-in-law, who loves thee, thy brother: I am in health. Mayst thou be in health! To thy houses, (to) Teie, thy mother, the mistress of Egypt, (to) Tatukhepa, my daughter, thy wife, to thy other wives, to thy children, to thy great ones, to thy chariots, to thy horses, to thy warriors, to thy land and to everything, that belongs to thee, may there be health in a very high degree."[1]

Throughout Egyptian history, with rare exception, such as the offspring of Rameses II, the recognized children are generally confined to the issue of the chief wife—called "The Great Royal Wife"—who in the case of Akhenaten would be the children of The Great Royal Wife, Nefertiti. For this reason only Nefertiti's children—all daughters—are recorded on the monuments, and the reference to Akhenaten's "other wives," in the letter quoted, has hitherto been assumed to be merely a conventional presumption on King Dushratta's part.

Judging from the precedent of other Egyptian monarchs, there is every reason to believe that Akhenaten had other wives, and that the phrase "Thy other wives," is something more definite than a conventional presumption. Further, in these circumstances one cannot but feel that, unless there be evidence to the contrary—negative evidence being no proof—this view must be accepted, especially as we know that the Mesopotamian king in question had been closely allied by marriage for several generations with the Egyptian royal house.

Thus, since Queen Nefertiti had no son, it is not improbable that a son by a less important marriage may have been selected as co-regent and successor, and his marriage to the eldest living official daughter would follow as a matter of course.

That either Tutankhamen was a son of Akhenaten or grandson of Queen Tyi from other issue seems to be, for the moment, the only possible explanation of this very perceptible affinity between the two men.

There is one point more of great interest: the king's head shows that, through the convention

The "Birth of the Sun" pectoral ornament

of the period, the finer contemporary representations of the king upon the monuments, beyond all doubt, are accurate portraits of Tutankhamen.

Upon the king's neck there were two kinds of symbolical collars and twenty amulets grouped in six layers, and between each of these layers were numerous linen bandages. A "Collar of Horus" in chased sheet-gold covered the neck and formed the uppermost layer. It was attached to the neck by means of beaten gold wire, having a tag or counterbalance at the back. Among the Egyptian forms of personal ornament, such collars or collarettes were perhaps the most prevalent and certainly predominant. But that they also had a much deeper significance than mere personal adornment becomes manifest from the important part they play in this royal burial, as well as in burial ceremonial generally. As will be seen from this and many other examples to come, they had attached to them a sort of tag acting as a kind of counterbalance at the back, which was called *mankhet*. According to instructions in the Pyramid texts, the coffin texts of the Middle Kingdom, and in the rubric of the "Book of the Dead" of the New Empire, these collars with their tags were to be placed upon the deceased's neck or on his breast. They were to be of many kinds of different materials and of different workmanship—a custom thoroughly illustrated in this burial.

The second layer or group of objects comprised four amulets, held round the neck by gold wires and placed over the throat in the following order, commencing from right to left: a red jasper *Thet*, an inscribed gold *Ded*, a green felspar *Uaz* sceptre, and a second gold *Ded* inlaid with faience. Immediately beneath this group and forming the third layer were three amulets: on the right and left side of the neck, two curious palm-leaf-like symbols in gold, and between them, tied on the same cord, a serpent *Zt* of thin chased sheet-gold. An amulet of *Thoth* in green felspar, a serpent's head in red carnelian, Horus in lapis lazuli, Anubis in green felspar, and an *Uaz* sceptre also in green felspar, formed the fourth layer. Each amulet of this group was bound to the neck by gold wire. The amulets of the fifth layer were all made of sheet-gold and chased. They were eight in number and fastened around the neck-bandages by strings. Among these eight symbols there were four distinct types: one human-headed winged serpent, one uraeus, one double uraeus, and five vultures, which were distributed over the throat, one partly covering the other, the human-headed winged serpent on the extreme right, the uraeus and Nekhebet vulture on the left side. The texts found upon coffins dating before the New Empire give different names for each of these symbols where it is stated they should be placed "at his head." Two of the vultures seem to be of the Mut type (*gyps fulvus*, Gm., the griffin vulture), the other three of Nekhebet. Their frailness shows that they were not intended for actual use in lifetime, but designed purely for sepulchral purposes. Below these symbols, tied round the last few bandages and forming the sixth layer, was a small sort of dog-collar formed of four rows of beads.

This profusion of amulets and sacred symbols placed on the neck of the king are of extreme significance, suggesting as they do how greatly the dangers of the Underworld were feared for the dead. No doubt they were intended to protect him against injury on his journey through the hereafter. The quality and quantity of these protective symbols would naturally depend on his high rank and wealth, as well as upon the affection of his survivors. The actual meaning of many of them is not clear, nor do we know the exact nomenclature, nor the powers ascribed to them. However, we do know that they were placed there for the help and guidance of the dead, and made as beautiful and costly as possible.

In accordance with the rubric of the "Book of the Dead," whoever wears the *Ded*—the emblem of Osiris—may "enter into the realms of the dead, eat the food of Osiris, and be justified." The symbol seems to represent "Firmness," "Stability," "Preservation" and "Protection." The sacred book also states that it should be of gold and placed on the neck of him whom it is supposed to protect, and thus enable him "to enter in through the gates of Amduat . . . rise up as a perfect soul in the Underworld." He on whom the *Thet* symbol—the girdle of Isis—is hung, will be guarded by Isis and Horus, and be welcomed with joy into the Kingdom of Osiris. The book further instructs that it must be "of red jasper," that "it is the blood, incantations and power of Isis"—a charm "for the protection of this mighty one, protecting him from doing of what to him is hateful." The *Uaz* sceptre, of green felspar, seems to represent "Verdure," "Fertility" and "Eternal Youth," to which it was hoped the deceased might attain in the Underworld. The serpent's head in carnelian may have been a talisman for protection against obnoxious reptiles, with which the tunnels of Amduat were supposed to abound.

We learn also from the "Book of the Dead" that, when these mystic emblems were placed on the deceased, the magic spells associated with them were to be uttered "in solemn voice." In the case of the amulets and symbols found upon the king, there were traces of a small papyrus that bore a ritual, written in white linear hieroglyphs, but too decayed and disintegrated to allow of practical conservation, though here and there names of gods, such as Osiris and Isis, were with difficulty decipherable. I am therefore of the belief that this diminutive document, disintegrated beyond recovery, possibly pertained to such spells.

Symbols of certain divinities were duplicated, and often two were combined, especially those of Nekhebet and Buto—were they thus rendered more effective?

These ornaments of a mystic and personal nature upon the king, are so numerous that a full description of each in detail would far exceed the limits of this volume. I shall, however, endeavour to convey briefly the principal facts and point out their more striking features. As we have already seen, they all have a particular meaning, being seldom, if ever, placed upon the mummy for the sake of mere beauty and effect. In them will be found great ingenuity. The principles of ornamental art and symbolism have been combined with a result that they have both meaning and effect. Their details, when studied, are not mere crude imitation of nature, but natural objects, selected by symbolism and fashioned by symmetry into ornaments, with only here and there objects of purely geometrical type.

Those of the head and neck have been mentioned and we next come to the objects found upon the body and arms.

Covering the thorax—that is from the neck down to the abdomen—were thirty-five objects, disposed in seventeen groups which formed thirteen layers, included in a complicated series of bandaging that enveloped the whole of the body.

The first of these groups was a series of four gold collars extending well below the clavicles, covering the shoulders but pendent from the neck by means of wire, and having the usual *mankhet* at the back. Each collar was placed so as only partially to cover the other. The uppermost, on the right, takes the form of the Nekhebet vulture, with open wings; the second, over the left side, combines both the winged serpent Buto and the vulture Nekhebet; the third, still farther over the left shoulder, is of the serpent Buto alone, but with full-spread wings; the fourth and outermost, slightly right of the centre of the chest, takes the form of the collar of "The Hawk," which represents an ordinary collarette of tubular beads, with heads of "The Hawk" for shoulder pieces. Below these different collars, dependent from a long gold wire, reaching as far down as the umbilicus, was a large black resin scarab, mounted upon a gold *funda* and having inlaid upon its wing-cases, in coloured glass, a *Bennu* bird. Inscribed upon the base of the scarab is the *Bennu* text.

The *Bennu* is a bird of the heron family *Ardeidoe* and, from the numerous existing vignettes in colour, probably *Ardea cinerea*, Linn., the common heron. This bird, which is often identified with the heart, is one of the many forms the deceased takes when he "comes forth as a soul living after death;" it is also connected with the Sun-god. From certain corrupt representations it might be mistaken for one of the night species of herons, but as the "Book of the Dead" (Chapter XIII) mentions: "I enter as a Hawk and come forth as a Bennu at Dawn," there can be little doubt that the common heron, one of the earliest of risers among all birds, is intended.

Next to this rather meagre substitute for the well-known heart scarab, came a large pectoral-hawk-collar in chased sheet-gold; its body covering the whole of the lower part of the thorax, its wings extending upwards under the armpits. In the texts of the world beyond the grave it is called "The Collar of Horus," but whatever may be its powers, from the aesthetic point of view it is far surpassed by a magnificent collar of similar form, found immediately underneath and almost exactly similarly placed—a pectoral-collar of Horus entirely made up of inlaid gold plaques fashioned in the manner of cloisonné work. This beautiful specimen of jeweller's craft forms the first of a series of three similar collars, and as the other two follow but a few layers down, I will in due course describe them together. Over this collar of cloisonné work was placed a plain sheet of papyrus paper, and under it, over the middle of the thorax, another collar of "The Hawk", of chased sheet-gold, like that in the first group over the shoulders and upper chest. On either side, parallel with the right and left arms, was a gold amuletic knot of unknown meaning. On the right and left of the lower part of the thorax, there were three amuletic gold bangles: two of which bear large barrel-shaped beads of lapis lazuli and carnelian respectively, the third, an emblematic Eye-of-Horus, in iron, making the second of three examples of this rare and all important and, I might say here, historical metal found upon the king. In the *Urs* head-rest found near the king's head, this *Uzat* bracelet, and in a third and far more important example I have yet to describe, we have our first decisive proof of the introduction of that very important metal, iron, into Egypt—a metal whose properties, as Ruskin says, play, and have played, so important a part "in Nature, Policy and Art."

By removing several more thicknesses of linen wrappings we reached the eighth layer, which consisted of a very large pectoral-collar of the serpent Buto, also of chased sheet-gold. It covered the whole of the lower part of the thorax, its huge wings extending over the shoulders, the tips of its flight feathers being bent round the neck bandages. Like the other collars of this kind it had the usual tag or *mankhet*, fastened by wire at the back. This latter specimen was the last of a series of eight of the simple metal collars found upon the neck and chest of the king, all obviously of purely amuletic nature designed for eternal inertia. Concealed under it, with just a slip of plain papyrus between, were two magnificent collars or breast-plates, one covering the other, but of a totally different workmanship. These were in the form of the two goddesses, Nekhebet and Buto, but made up of numerous gold plaques of cloisonné work, like the "Collar of Horus" just mentioned.

These breast-plates, or to call them by their real names: "The Collar of Horus," "The Collar of Nekhebet," and "The Collar of Nebti" (.ie. Nekhebet and Buto), are devised in such a unique manner as to merit special attention. Each is composed of a very large number of separate gold plaques, engraved on the back and minutely inlaid on the front with opaque coloured glass in the manner of cloisonné work; the glass imitating turquoise, red jasper, and lapis lazuli stones. "The Collar of Horus" is composed of thirty-eight plaques; that of Nekhebet of 256 pieces; and of Nebti 171 pieces. Each plaque is fundamentally similar in make, differing only in modification of form and colour, in accordance with the feathers of the "district" of the wing it belongs to, or, as the case may be, the particular feather or part of feather it represents. These plaques are divided up into groups which form the principal "districts" of the wing, i.e. the primaries, secondaries, coverts, lesser coverts, and the so-called "bastard wing"; each plaque of cloisonné of the group or "district" having tiny eyelets on their upper and lower margins by which they were threaded together with bead borders. The various parts of the wings being thus firmly held together, make both gorgeous, intricate, and at the same time flexible collars.

We now arrive at the eleventh and twelfth layers of objects, which comprise a series of more personal jewellery. Hanging over the upper part of the chest and secured around the neck by

Objects found within the wrappings of the mummy

means of lapis lazuli and gold flexible straps, was a small pectoral ornament fashioned to represent a sated vulture. This exquisite example of goldsmith's work, perhaps the finest of all found upon the king, inlaid with green glass, lapis lazuli and carnelian, seems with little doubt, to be intended to symbolize the Southern goddess—Nekhebet of El Kab; for the characteristics of the bird, so beautifully rendered here, are certainly those of the sociable vulture, and are identical with the vulture insignia of Upper Egypt belonging to the diadem. The clasp of its suspending straps takes the form of two miniature hawks, but even more charming is the finely chased under surface of the pectoral itself, where, as a sort of *quid pro quo*, around the neck of the bird goddess, in high relief, a tiny pectoral is represented in the form of the king's cartouche. Still lower on the chest of the mummy was another pectoral, in form, three scarabs of lapis lazuli, supporting above the symbol of heaven, disks of the sun and moon. Their posterior legs hold the *Neb* emblems of sovereignty upon a horizontal bar, from which marguerites bloom and lotus flowers pend.

The beetles here, no doubt, have some mysterious connexion with the solar and lunar disks they hold in their fore-legs. The association of the scarab with the disk is a common occurrence in religious texts. In all probability the lunar disk—in this case the older orb growing out of the younger crescent—symbolizes the god Thoth, who personifies the moon. Both disks were in great part the original sources of Egyptian mythology, and no matter what system of religious worship on the part of those ancients prevailed, behind that veil or cult the sun was always the principal, not alone with the living, but even more with the dead. In the "Book of the Dead" (Chapter XV) we find: "O thou Radiant Orb, who arisest each day from the horizon, shine thou upon the face of Osiris [the deceased] who adorneth thee at Dawn, and propitiateth thee at the Gloaming."

We have in such specimens of private jewellery, the culminating style of the Eighteenth Dynasty in ornamental art—natural forms and symbolism associated to gratify and attract. In this case, and in other examples to come, the execution of the beetles is remarkable to a degree. Though conventionally treated, each essential detail of the insect is observed and its most striking features shown: the horny prothorax, and elytra (wing-cases) are rendered in deliberate manner; the *clypeus* or shield, that is the edge of the broad flat head, is notched with angular teeth arranged in a semicircle; the fore-legs, bow-shaped, are properly armed on the outside with five strong teeth, and like the four long and slender hinder limbs, are carved free; the last pair, slightly bowed, end with their sharp claw. Even the articulation of the underparts of this famous dung-beetle are shown, and their different functions equally realized.

Immediately below, under bandages of gossamer thickness, were three more pectorals, one placed over the centre of the thorax, and one on each side, slightly lower down. The two outer ones were suspended from the neck by gold chains terminating with lotus flowers, carnelian beads, and heart-shaped pendants at the back, below the nape of the neck. The central pectoral, also hung from the neck, had, at the ends of its three-string necklace of faience and gold beads, a small pectoral-shaped clasp of *Ded* and *Thet* symbols. The pectoral on the right side takes the form of a solar-hawk of gold—the body of open-work enclosing a peculiar green stone. That of the left side, also of gold and brilliantly inlaid, seems so devised as to incorporate a play upon the king's name: it is composed of a winged scarab beetle holding in its fore-legs a lunar disk and crescent, in its posterior legs the plural determinatives and the *heb* festival sign; thus reading, "Kheperuhebaah" in place of "Kheperunebre." The central pectoral, an *uzat* eye, having in heraldic fashion the uraeus of Buto in front and the vulture Nekhebet behind, has its under surface of finely chased gold and upper surface inlaid with lapis lazuli and an unidentified stone of pale green colour somewhat suggestive of epidote. All these pectorals show traces of actual wear such as would be caused by use during lifetime, and were, no doubt, personal ornaments.

The heart pendants of carnelian encased in gold and minutely inlaid with the king's name, recall the chapter in the "Book of the Dead" upon the heart "of carnelian," where it says: "It is granted to the soul of Osiris [the deceased] to come forth upon the earth to do whatsoever his genius willeth." From the disposition of the latter three pectorals—that of the eye in the centre, the solar orb on the right, and the lunar disk on the left—it is tempting to connect them with the "Pair of Eyes" considered as the Sun and Moon, attributed to Osiris as well as Re and other deities: "His right eye is the Sun and his left is the Moon." I should also mention here that the lunar disks on the jewellery of this tomb are always of gold-silver alloy, in contradistinction to the gold solar disks which have a copper alloy.

Below these five pectorals came the lowest layer of all, next to the flesh, though not in actual contact with it; for there were several thicknesses of linen underneath, charred almost to powder. This last layer consisted of an elaborate collarette of minute blue glass and gold beads, threaded after the manner of a bead mat, and having all the appearance of a bib. In design it was so made that the gold beads, worked into the blue glass beads, formed yellow chevrons or waves of water upon a blue background; the collarette having flexible golden hawk clasps as shoulderpieces, a border of gold sequins and an outer margin of gold drop pendants.

Included in the wrappings of the thorax and abdomen were two groups of finger-rings: over the wrist of the right hand a group of five, and beside the wrist of the left hand, a group of eight rings. These were of massive gold, lapis lazuli, cloudy-white and green chalcedony, turquoise, and one of black resin. Often, even when the devices upon the bezels included the king or his cartouches, his name was also engraved on either side of the loop of the ring, or on the under surface of the bezel; a distinguishing mark by which finger-rings may be identified as personal property of the Pharaoh. This suggests an early form of the hall-mark.

Before dealing with the several objects that were placed upon the abdomen, I will next describe the arms, forearms and hands, which, though included in the bandages of the body, were first separately wrapped. The forearms were flexed over the upper part of the abdomen, the left being placed slightly higher than the right. The right hand was over the left hip, the left hand reaching the lower right side of the thorax. Enclosed in the wrappings of the arms were two quite small amuletic bangles, which broke away with the decayed fabric during our examination of the mummy, but from the positions in which they fell, on either side, they had evidently been placed just above the elbows. That of the right arm took the form of a thick gold wire bracelet bearing a large rough green stone bead, and six finely made *uzat* eyes of various materials. The one belonging to the left arm, was a small gold bangle with swivel joint secreted under three beads and, on the opposite side of the circle, an exquisitely carved carnelian *Ment* bird. This *Ment* bird, with the solar orb upon its rump, probably represents one of the mythical transformations of the Sun-god, mentioned in the "Book of the Dead" (especially in Chapter LXXXVI), "whereby one assumeth the form of a swift." There can be little doubt that this *Ment* bird is of the family of the swifts (*Cypselidae*), though it is sometimes confused in those religious texts with the *wr* bird, of the family of swallows and martins *(Hirundinidae)*, but it could never be of the genera of doves and pigeons (*Columbidae*), as I have seen mentioned. Though it is not dissimilar to the little grey swift (*Cypsellus parvus*, Licht.) of the southern provinces of Egypt, in all probability it is intended to represent the ordinary Egyptian swift (*Cypsellus pallidus*, Shelley). The peculiar feature of the Egyptian swift is that it makes its abode in large colonies in the cliffs, far back in the hills that border the desert plain, whence it comes down to the Nile Valley at early morn and returns late in the evening. For the reason that it comes forth screaming at sunrise and returns, with even shriller notes, when the sun sinks, it may be that the ancient Egyptians connected it in some way with the transformation of the Sun-god, or the souls of the departed which came forth by day with the sun and returned at night. The chapter says: "I am the *Ment* bird . . ." and at the

Bracelets on the king's forearms

end, "If this chapter be known he will re-enter after coming forth by day."

Both the forearms were smothered from elbow to wrist with magnificent bracelets, seven on the right and six on the left forearm, composed of intricate scarab devices, granular gold-work, open-work carnelian plaques, rich gold and electrum work; some having wrist-bands of flexible bead-work, others of elaborate geometric and floral design, inlaid with semi-precious stones and polychrome glass. Their diameter shows that they had encircled a very small arm, none of them was of sepulchral nature, but all were obviously once personal ornaments that had been worn during life.

Each finger and thumb, having been primarily wrapped in fine strips of linen, was enclosed in a gold sheath. Upon the second and third fingers of the left hand was a gold ring: upon the bezel of one is the lunar barque on a deep blue ground, upon the bezel of the other, that of the second digit, the king, minutely engraved in intaglio, is represented kneeling and offering the figure of Truth.

We now come to the abdomen, distributed over which, in almost as many layers, were ten objects which I will record in the order they were found, beginning with the uppermost layers. At the left flank, within the first few outer bandages, was a curious Y-shaped amulet of sheet-gold and an oval gold plate, placed one immediately above the other. The meaning of the Y-shaped amulet is not clear. A similar object depicted in the Middle Kingdom coffin texts carries the name *abt* or *abet*, which seems to convey something of the nature of a baton, but as this symbol forms in shape part of the hieroglyphic determinative *mnkh* for clothing or linen, it would seem more likely to have some reference to the bandages, or bandaging of the mummy, the more so, as the second object—the oval metal plate found with it—has direct relation with, and was intended to cover, the incision in the left flank of the mummy, through which the embalmers removed the internal organs for separate preservation. The next object in sequence was a T-shaped symbol made of sheet-gold resembling a draughtsman's T-square. It was placed in the wrappings over the left side of the abdomen and extended down the upper part of the left thigh. So far as I am able to judge it has no parallel and its meaning is unknown. Encircling the waist, the two front ends as low as the hips, was a narrow chased gold girdle, to which, in all probability, belong a ceremonial apron and a dagger found over the thighs, the description of which will be given later. Then came a plain dark blue faience collar made up of minute beads, which had been included in the wrappings over the left side of the abdomen, as high up as the umbilicus, and reaching down over the pudenda. It has semicircular shoulder-pieces, but its distinctive name is difficult to identify among the painted texts devoted to collars on the Middle Kingdom coffins; although it is of dark blue faience it may possibly be intended to take the place of the "Collar of Lapis Lazuli," which apparently can have either rounded or hawk-headed shoulder-pieces. Over the middle of the abdomen was a circlet, such as an armlet or anklet, of gold, inlaid with coloured opaque glass. It belongs to a series of eight of similar kind (four pairs), varying only in their inlay, found elsewhere on the mummy, mostly over the thighs down to the knees. They are of purely sepulchral nature.

Having carefully removed the above objects found upon the abdomen, together with a few more layers of bandaging which were in a very decayed state, another chased gold waist-band or girdle was exposed. Tucked under it obliquely—the haft to the right of the abdomen, the point of the sheath over the upper part of the left thigh—was a most interesting and handsome dagger that certainly calls for admiration. It has a handle ornamented with bright yellow granulated gold decoration, encircled by alternate bands of cloisonné work of semi-precious stones and glass, and terminating at the hilt with a rich chain-scroll, applied in gold wire with rope pattern border. In contrast to its ornate handle, the blade of the dagger, of especially hardened gold, is simple and of beautiful form. Its surface is unadorned save for deep grooves down its centre, which converge at the point, and are surmounted with a finely engraved lily "palmette" design below a narrow band of somewhat archaic geometric pattern. The blade is housed in a richly ornamented gold sheath. On the front it has a frieze of "palmette" ornament, and the whole of the field covered with a feather-pattern in cloisonné fashion, which terminates at the lower point with a jackal's head of embossed gold. The design on the back is in many ways more attractive; for it has embossed in high relief on its gold surface, an extremely interesting scene of wild animals, suggesting that the dagger was for the chase. Here the subjects are: below a frieze of inscription and scroll-pattern, a young male ibex attacked by a lion; a male calf galloping with a slughi hound upon its back, biting its tail; a cheetah (tail annulated) having sprung on to the shoulder of an adult male ibex, is mauling its neck, whilst from underneath a lion attacks the antelope; below, is a galloping bull worried by a hound; and lastly a quite young calf is represented in full retreat. Between the exquisitely rendered animals, are various plants treated conventionally; the scene terminating at the bottom by an ornate floral device which, like the whole scheme of decoration upon the dagger and sheath, suggests affinity to the art of the Aegean or Mediterranean islands. However, the character of the hieroglyphs of the king's cartouche upon the knob, and of the short legend "the Good God, Lord of Valour, Kheperunebre" (Tutankhamen) upon the frieze of the sheath, as well as the general treatment of detail, and of the animals in the attempt at the picturesque and ornamental, suffice to show that this admirable piece of workmanship is the handiwork of an Egyptian and not of an alien, whatever the influence may be. In this superficial study it may suffice here to say that those islands, once governed by the Egyptians of the fifteenth century B.C., and called by them "The-islands-in-the-midst-of-the-sea," formed the link between the art of the Nile, Asia Minor and European civilizations.

The girdle under which the dagger was tucked is similar in type to the first example already mentioned, save for difference of the pattern chased upon it. It had attached to the front fastening or name-plate, stamped with the king's cartouche, an apron composed of some twenty strings of different faience and glass beads, connected at intervals by gold spacers or connectors. The beads had to a large extent fallen away from their decayed threads, but from our photographic records and notes, their original order can be recovered. On the centres of the backs of the two girdles are projecting cylinder-like attachments for ceremonial pendent tails, such as you see depicted hanging from the waist-bands of kings on the monuments, and which, in this case, were actually discovered under the mummy extending down between the legs. Unfortunately, by being the lowest of all the objects in the coffin, these most interesting ritualistic tails suffered considerable damage by becoming embedded, like a fossil in its matrix, in the thick hardened mass of congealed unguents that was poured over the mummy. They had to be extricated by means of hammer and chisel and, as they are composed of beads—one of them of a close mesh of minute faience beads woven over a core of fibre—restoration to their original state will be a very difficult task. They appear to be quite similar to those found by Mace and Winlock (*The Tomb of Senebtisi*, p. 70 ff.) and in this case both the examples of girdles, the apron and the tails, seem to have been made for tomb use only, though there can be little doubt that they are replicas of those used for ceremonial purposes during life.

Coinciding with the lowest layer of ornaments—the last three pectorals and the bib-like bead collarette—found on the thorax, and in reality belonging to that group, were two more pieces of jewellery: (1) a pectoral in the form of an *uzat* eye of brilliant blue faience, suspended by a necklace of equally bright blue faience, plain yellow gold and red granulated gold cylindrical beads, which from their brilliance have an almost barbaric effect; and (2) around the waist a girdle of closely strung cylindrical and discoid beads in gold and faience, which has yet to be cleaned and remounted. The interest of this latter peculiar segmented worm-like bead girdle, is that it interprets the use of the quantities of beads prominent among the famous discoveries of Egyptian jewellery of the Middle Kingdom at Dashur and Lahun.

Having seen the material that decked the king's head and neck, body and arms, we have now to see what was placed over his legs. The first object revealed to us, while removing piece by piece the masses of padding and bandages that the embalmers found necessary to pack and bind the thighs into orthodox mummy form, was the ceremonial apron belonging, in all probability, to the first chased gold girdle that we found around the waist. This is made up of seven gold plates inlaid with opaque polychrome glass, the plates being threaded together by means of bead borders. It extended from the lower portion of the abdomen down to the knees, corresponding in position and size to the aprons depicted on the dress of Egyptian monarchs pictured upon the monuments. Beside the apron, along the right thigh, and I believe also belonging to the same girdle as the apron, was an extraordinarily fine and unique dagger housed in a gold scabbard. The haft of the dagger is of granulated gold, embellished at intervals with collars of cloisonné work of coloured rock crystal; but the astonishing and unique feature of this beautiful weapon is that the blade is of iron, still bright and resembling steel!

This astounding and historical fact, to digress from the main subject, marks one of the first steps in the decline of the Egyptian Empire—the greatest empire of the Age of Bronze. This metal, iron, of which we have found three examples upon the king's mummy, was in all probability introduced by the Hittites into Egypt from Asia Minor at the time of Tutankhamen, probably in small quantity when, no doubt, it was looked upon as a speciality. Rather more than a century later, when iron began to overtake bronze in Syria, a tablet records how one of the Hittite kings undertook to supply Rameses the Great with a shipment of that metal, and that a sword of iron was sent as a gift to the Pharaoh. With regard to Egypt, iron is one more indication of foreign influence at this period. If the history of Egypt be studied, from that moment gradual foreign intrusion becomes more and more noticeable, ending eventually in foreign domination. Bronze could not fight against the superiority of iron, and as bronze took the place of copper, so iron took the place of bronze—just as in our day iron has been superseded by steel.

Both daggers—that found on the abdomen and this specimen—like those of Aahhetep and Kames in the Cairo Museum, dating from the beginning of this dynasty, are foreign in shape. They are of a style introduced into Egypt during the Hyksos invasion. Before then the handle of the dagger was of a different style. It was held between the second and third fingers, the knob against the palm of the hand, and therefore thrust instead of being used, as was the later form, with a downward stroke from the elbow.

Tucked in the hollow of the left groin was a broad barrel-shaped wristlet or anklet, typical of those ornaments represented on the wrists and ankles of figures in the mural decorations of private chapel and tomb. This was the only specimen of its kind found on the king, whereas, judging from the mural paintings, one would have expected, at least, one or three pairs, for the arms, forearms and ankles.

It was here we found the royal insignia of the diadem. That of Upper Egypt, the Nekhebet vulture head, on the right thigh near the knee, and that of Buto, the uraeus of Lower Egypt, along the left thigh; they being placed in correct orientation in accordance to the country to which they belong. The remainder of the ornaments, disposed over the legs, were seven circlets included in three distinct layers of wrappings over and between the thighs, and four collarettes of cloisonné work which were folded and crushed over the knees and the shins. The single circlet found over the abdomen with these seven specimens makes up a series of eight, i.e. four pairs; the four collarettes with their tags or *mankhets* make two pairs of a kind, each pair differing only in the number and system of cloisonné plates of which they are made up. They answer in the lists upon the coffins of the Middle Kingdom, to those which have a metal basis worked in cloisonné inlay of semi-precious stones, though in this case, they being of the New Empire, opaque coloured glass imitates and takes the place of the real stones.

Lastly, upon the feet were gold sandals made out of sheet metal, embossed to imitate rush-work. Each digit was enclosed in a separate gold stall, having details, such as the nails and first joints of the toes, engraved upon them. Around the right ankle was a gold wire bangle of somewhat crude workmanship.

These last items complete the 143 objects that were carefully disposed over the head, neck, thorax, abdomen, and limbs of the young king, in 101 separate groups.

I have described them, beginning with those on the head downwards, ending with the feet, and have dealt in each case with the uppermost object first, and have ended with the lowest nearest the mummy itself last. But it must be remembered that in the original order of sequence of the wrapping of the mummy, the lowest objects, that is those nearest the king, were the first placed upon his mummy, and those included in the uppermost wrappings last.

The objects may be divided into two categories: those which are real and personal property; and those which are purely religious and amuletic. Those of a personal character are of a much finer and more permanent nature; the others, in general, are of less permanent make and of simpler kind—they were for sepulchral use only and amuletic in meaning.

The beautiful pectorals, possibly the finer examples of the cloisonné collars, the majority of the rings and bracelets, the daggers and diadem, were—there is little doubt—personal jewellery; while the various other collars and amulets of chased sheet-gold, the inlaid amulets, the bead

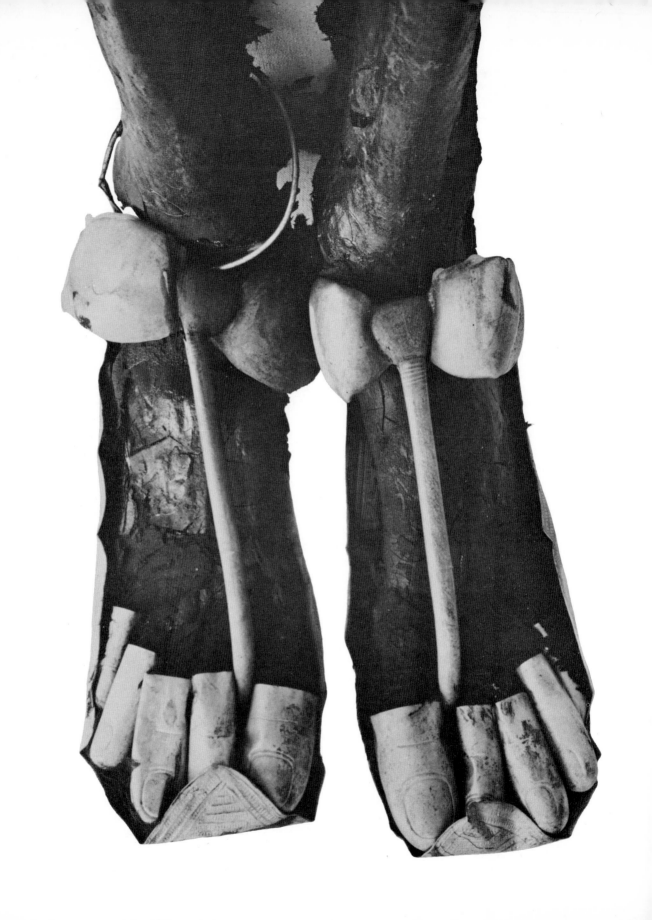

collarettes, the toe and finger stalls, the sandals, the apron and the symbolical tails, were only intended to be beneficial for the dead king.

The beautiful objects give us a vivid insight into the work of the skilled craftsmen of Thebes. The Theban court artisans were naturally picked men, and here, in this discovery, we can discern the refinement of their art. I say refinement, for the actual technique in many ways is perhaps not so fine as regards finish or simplicity as that of the Middle Kingdom jewellers, but if the technical skill be not so good, the taste displayed surpasses all our expectations. Especially when we remember that we are dealing with material belonging to the very end of the Eighteenth Dynasty. A certain ornateness and lack of high finish that may be here visible, are but steps in a decadence creeping in with iron and other foreign influences. Nevertheless it would tax our best goldsmiths and jewellers of to-day to surpass the refinement which is found in those royal ornaments.

From the mass of material upon the mummy, of which space has only allowed a cursory description, we can begin to realize the profusion of wealth with which it seems to have been customary to adorn the mortal remains of the ancient Pharaohs buried in the Valley. It impressively conveys to us the inner feelings of that ancient people for their dead—feelings which, though in many ways latent, are exhibited from time to time, among the fellahin today. The dead are generally first in their thoughts at all their festivals. They assemble in the early morning after prayer to visit the graves of their relatives, especially on the occasion of the commencement of *El Eed E' Sugheiyir* (The Small Festival), the first day of the month of *Showwal*, after *Ramadan* (the month of abstinence) when they carry, as I have witnessed at Thebes, palm-branches to lay upon the tombs, and are also provided with various foodstuffs to distribute to the poor in honour of their dead. Later, clad in their best and newest clothes, they visit their living friends.

Before I bring this chapter to a close I should mention that the charred remains of the mummy itself show no traces of the cause or causes of the young king's death, but the masses of swathings, ornaments and amulets, at least conveyed to us the care that was taken with his mortal remains and for his future life. A feeling, a sense and a care, that cannot be better expressed than in the words of Sir Gardner Wilkinson, who did so much wonderful research work in Egypt during the early half of the last century:

"Love and respect were not merely shown to the sovereign during his lifetime, but were continued to his memory after his death; and the manner in which his funeral obsequies were celebrated tended to show, that, though their benefactor was no more, they retained a grateful sense of his goodness, and admiration for his virtues. And what, says the historian [meaning Diodorus], can convey a greater testimony of sincerity, free from all colour of dissimulation, when the person who conferred it no longer lives to witness the honour done to his memory?"

The feet with their gold toe sheaths and sandals

19

The room beyond the Burial Chamber—a Treasury

THE TIME CAME in the sequence of our work to direct our energies towards the Store-room beyond the Burial Chamber, perhaps in this case better named "the Innermost Treasury."

This room is not more than 15 feet 8 inches by 12 feet 6 inches square, and 7 feet 8 inches in height. Ingress is by means of a low open doorway cut in the northern end of the west wall of the Burial Chamber. It is of extreme simplicity, there being no attempt at decoration. The four walls and ceiling are unsmoothed, the marks of the final chiselling being still visible upon the rock surfaces. In fact, it is just as those ancient Egyptian masons left it—even the last few flakes of limestone from their chisels lay on the floor.

Small and simple as it is, the impressive memories of the past haunt it none the less. When, for the first time, one enters a room such as this, the sanctity of which has been inviolate for more than thirty centuries, a sense of reverence, if not of fear is felt on the part of the intruder. It seems almost desecration to trouble that long peace and to break that eternal silence. Even the most insensitive person, passing this inviolate threshold, must surely feel awe and wonder distilled from the secrets and shadows of that tremendous past. The very stillness of its atmosphere, intensified by the many inanimate things that fill it, standing for centuries and centuries as pious hands had placed them, creates the sense of sacred obligation which is indescribable and which causes one to ponder before daring to enter, much less to touch anything. Emotions thus aroused, of which the sense of awe is the root, are difficult to convey in words; the spirit of curiosity is checked; the very tread of one's foot, the slightest noise, tends to increase a fear and magnify an unconscious reverence—the intruder becomes mute.

That appeal of the past made one hesitate before venturing to enter and explore, until one remembered that, however much one may respect it, an archaeologist's duty is to the present, and it is for him to interpret what is hidden and note whatever steps may lead him to his goal.

The doorway of this room, unlike the others, was not bricked-up or sealed; from it we had a clear view of the contents of the room. Within a few days of its discovery (17 February 1923), after we had made a brief survey of its contents, we purposely closed the doorway with wooden boards, in order that, whilst dealing with the vast material in the Burial Chamber, we might not be distracted or tempted to disturb any of the objects in this little room. That wooden hoarding is now removed, and after four years' patient waiting, our attention is once more directed within. All it holds was again revealed—objects many, both of mystic and of absorbing interest, but mostly of purely funerary nature and of intense religious character.

Placed in the doorway, practically preventing ingress to the room, was the black figure of the jackal-like dog Anubis, covered with linen, and couchant upon a gilt pylon resting on a

Anubis guarding the entrance to the innermost Treasury

sledge with long carrying-poles. On the ground within the threshold, and in front of the pylon of Anubis, was a small reed torch with clay brick-like pedestal bearing an incantation "to repel the enemy of Osiris (the deceased), in whatever form he may come," and behind Anubis, a strange head of a cow—emblems these of the tomb and of the world beyond.

Along the south wall, extending from east to west, stood a large quantity of black, sinister, shrine-like chests, all closed and sealed save one, the folding doors of which had fallen apart revealing statuettes of the king, swathed in linen, standing on the backs of black leopards. Since the discovery, imagination faltered at the thought of what those other chests might contain. The time has come when we are soon to know.

Stacked on top of those black chests, without any apparent order, save that their stems all pointed west, were a number of model craft, equipped with cabins, look-outs, thrones and kiosks, upon the poop, the amidship, and after-decks; and in front of the chests, resting upon a wooden model of a granary filled with grain, was another and more elaborate boat with rigging and furled sail. And underneath those black chests, in the south-west corner, was a huge black oblong box containing a figure of Osiris swathed in linen.

On the opposite side, placed parallel with the pylon and sledge of Anubis, was a row of treasure caskets beautifully ornamented with ivory, ebony and gesso-gilt, and some vaulted boxes of plain wood, painted white. They contained jewels and other treasures, but one of them, the simplest of all, the lid of which I raised when we first entered the room, contained an ostrich-feather fan with ivory handle—a pathetic but beautiful relic of the boy king, to all appearances as perfect as when it left his hands.

Packed along this north side of the room were a number of divers objects: more model craft; a richly ornamented bow-case; two hunting chariots, their dismembered parts stacked one upon another in a similar manner to the chariots found in the Antechamber; in the farthest north-east corner, piled on top of one another, were more wooden boxes, miniature coffins, and ten black wooden kiosks undoubtedly housing the *Shawabti*-figures—the answerers for the dead. Many of these objects had been disturbed.

Unquestionably the thieves had entered this little room, but in their predatory quest they seem to have done little further harm than to open and rifle the treasure caskets and some boxes. Some beads and tiny fragments of jewellery scattered on the floor, the broken seals and displaced lids of caskets, folds of linen hanging from the mouths of the boxes, and here and there an overturned object, were the only evidence visible at first sight of their visit. The robber, or robbers, must have been aware of the nature of the contents of this room, for, with rare exception, only those boxes which held objects of intrinsic value had been disturbed.

Such were the general contents of this little room beyond the Burial Chamber. But a single glance sufficed to show that the principal object of all was at the far end, facing the doorway. For there, standing against the east wall, and almost reaching the ceiling, was a large gilded canopy surmounted with rows of brilliantly inlaid solar cobras. This canopy, supported by four square posts upon a sledge, shielded a gilt shrine-shaped chest inscribed with formulae pertaining to the four genii, or children of Horus. Surrounding this shrine-shaped chest, free-standing on the four sides, were statuettes of the guardian goddesses, Isis, Nephthys, Neith, and Selkit. The shrine-like chest shielded the Canopic box, which in turn contained the four receptacles that held the viscera of the dead king.

It is obvious that this collection of objects placed within this room formed part of one great recondite idea, and that each of them has a mystical potency of some kind. As Dr. Alan Gardiner rightly says: "It is necessary to admit without hesitation that the idea of a mystical potency inherent in the image of things is a characteristically Egyptian conception . . ." It is for us to discover what were the respective meanings of these objects and their intended divine mystical powers. Scientific research demands the closest investigation, therefore I trust that I may not be misunderstood when I say that it was no question of showing disrespect to the burial ritual of a vanished theology, and still less of gratifying the excitement of a morbid curiosity, when one disturbed this religious paraphernalia. Our task was to leave nothing unexplored which might add to the sum of our steadily growing knowledge, both archaeological and historical, of this deeply interesting and most complicated funerary cult.

However strange, however extensive, this funerary outfit may be, it doubtless belonged to a more or less organized system for the common good of the dead, and was a system of defence against human imaginations, the results of obscure ideas. This association of equipment, in more ways than one, had been created to achieve unknown ends, and very much like the innumerable cells of a living body, they possessed, or were supposed to possess, powers to intervene, should they be called upon, in obedience to an order, who knows whence. They constituted, in fact, a form of self-protection for the future. They were a thoughtful people who made them, and, owing to their age, could not escape from the blinding influence of traditional custom. Ultra-religious as most of the emblems are, there is to be found among them evidence of the splendid capacities of the race that created them.

To endeavour to grasp the meaning of this little room, I will refer to a papyrus now in Turin: a royal tomb plan discovered in the last century, which is no less than a project for the tomb of Rameses IV. Although that document belongs to a reign some two centuries later than Tutankhamen, it does throw light upon his tomb. The document is a sketch ground-plan for a Pharaonic tomb, giving elevations of the doorways, the names and dimensions of the different corridors and chambers, with specifications such as: "*being drawn with outlines, graven with the chisel, filled with colours, and completed.*" On the back of the papyrus, among other notes, are more measurements with apparently an initial line or title: "*The measurements of the tomb of Pharaoh, Living, Prosperous, Healthy.*" The difference of certain minor details in this ancient sketch-plan, which do not agree exactly with the tomb of Rameses IV—although the plan coincides with the main details—may be explained by the fact that it was but a project modified when making the actual tomb. Among other details of interest the document refers to "*The House of Gold, wherein One rests,*" meaning the Burial Chamber where the deceased Pharaoh is placed to rest; and we find mention of that chamber "*being provided with the equipment of His Majesty on every side of it, together with the Divine Ennead which is in Duat*" (the Nether World).

The golden or yellow hue of the sepulchral chambers in all the royal Theban tombs, doubtless symbolizes the setting of the Sun-god behind the mountains of the west, hence the appellation "*The House of Gold*" given in the document to that part of the tomb—the Burial Chamber— "*Wherein One rests.*" The mention: "*provided with the equipment of His Majesty on every side of it,*" evidently refers to the great shrines and to the supports for the pall, that were to be erected over the sarcophagus, which are carefully drawn on the plan in exactly the same order as the golden shrines and pall found in Tutankhamen's tomb. The final phrase: "*together with the Divine Ennead which is in Duat*" seems to refer to the series of figures of divinities such as we discover contained in those numerous black shrine-like chests placed in the room beyond the Burial Chamber. Judging by the tomb of Seti II, where these figures are depicted, they may either be painted on the walls of the tomb or, as in the case of the Eighteenth Dynasty tombs, be represented in plastic form.

In the more developed plan of the Eighteenth Dynasty royal tomb, the Burial Chamber comprises a hypostyle hall with steps at the end leading down to a kind of open crypt for the sarcophagus, and four small rooms or treasuries—two of which adjoin the pillared portion and two adjoin the so-called open crypt. In the project of the Burial Chamber of Rameses IV, as well as in the tomb itself, these parts have been modified into one large rectangular chamber with a small corridor at the back having niches and recesses. In the document the small corridor with niches and recesses beyond the Burial Chamber are named: "*The corridor which is as Shawabti-place; the resting-place of the Gods; the left* (and right) *hand treasury; and the treasury of the Innermost.*" Upon the walls of the latter—"*the treasury of the Innermost*"—in the tomb of Rameses IV, canopic-jars, kiosks for *Shawabti*-figures, and other funerary furniture are depicted. However, in the earlier Eighteenth Dynasty tombs the canopic equipment was generally placed at the foot of the sarcophagus.

It therefore becomes fairly clear from the data quoted, and from the collection of material found in this little room beyond the Burial Chamber, that it combines several chambers in one: "*The Shawabti-place; the Resting-place of the Gods*"; at least one of the two "*Treasuries*"; and "*the Treasury of the Innermost.*"

This accounts, more or less, for the heterogeneous collection of objects crowded into this little room. In it we find the canopic equipment belonging essentially to the tomb; safeguards for the deceased's passage through the Underworld; and objects that the deceased required for his use in daily life, and hence would continue to require in his future life; jewellery for his adornment, chariots for his recreation, and servants (*Shawabti*-figures) to carry out any irksome work he might be called upon to do in the Hereafter. Housed in those black shrine-like chests there were statuettes of the king representing him in the act of divine pursuit and various forms of his renewed existence; figures of the gods pertaining to "the entire Ennead" since Pharaoh, like the divinity, must have a college of divine persons to help him through the dangers to which he may be exposed. While the little flame lying at the threshold of the doorway was supposed to hinder "*the sand from choking the tomb and repel the intruder,*" there were boats to render the deceased independent of the favours of the "*celestial ferrymen,*" or to enable him to follow Re, the Sun-god, on his nocturnal voyage through the interconnecting tunnels of the Underworld, and in his triumphal journey across the heavens. There were also barques, fully rigged and equipped with cabins, symbolizing the funeral pilgrimage; there was a granary filled with grain; a saddle-stone for grinding corn; strainers for the preparation of the exhilarating beverage, beer; and natron for the preservation of mortal and immortal remains. There was even a mock figure representing the regermination of Osiris, the revered god of the dead, who like man suffered death, was buried, and who afterwards rose again to immortal life. There were many symbols, the intention of which is obscure, but they, too, had their uses in some superstitious purpose.

Besides the material just recorded there must have been a wonderful display of riches in those treasure caskets, and would still have been, were it not for the selective activities of the dynastic tomb-plunderers.

20

The funerary equipment found in the room beyond the Burial Chamber

A FIRM CONVICTION among those ancient Egyptians (says Professor Steindorff) was that life did not end at death, but that man continued to live just as he had lived upon this earth, provided that measures for his protection to usher him through the labyrinth of the Underworld and necessaries for his future existence were assured him. We shall now see from the equipment placed in this room beyond the Burial Chamber at least part of what was considered necessary for his protection and for his future existence.

The magical torch and clay-brick pedestal found at the entrance of this room, must not be confused with the four brick pedestals with figures that were sealed within recesses in the four walls of the Burial Chamber, for those magical figures were found intact hidden in niches in the walls of that chamber. This little clay brick with its tiny reed torch and a few grains of charcoal seem not to have been dropped by mere chance on the floor within the threshold in front of Anubis. The magical formula scratched upon the brick tells us that: "It is I who hinder the sand from choking the secret chamber, and who repel that one who would repel him with the desert-flame. I have set aflame the desert (?), I have caused the path to be mistaken. I am for the protection of the Osiris [the deceased]."

The figure of the god Anubis, who takes upon himself the form of a kind of black jackal-like dog without gender, who not only presided over the burial rites, but also acted as the vigilant watcher over the dead, was appropriately placed in the open doorway, facing outwards towards the west, to guard against the intruder. His position in the tomb was evidently not the result of mere convenience, but was intentional. It enabled him to watch over the Burial Chamber and its occupant, while he also guarded his domain the "Treasury of the Innermost."

This watchful, life-size recumbent figure of the Anubis-animal, carved of wood, and varnished with black resin, rests upon a gilded pylon supported by a gilt sledge with four carrying-poles. He was protected with a linen covering—actually a shirt dated in the seventh year of the reign of Akhenaten. Under this covering his body was draped in a thin gossamer-like linen shawl tied at his throat, and fastened around his neck was a long leash-like linen scarf. This was adorned with a double fillet of blue lotus and cornflowers woven upon strips of pith, twisted into a bow at the back of the neck. Under these, gilded on the neck of the beast, is a collar and another long scarf in facsimile of the linen one just described. His eyes are inlaid with gold, calcite and obsidian; the pectinations of the erect pointed ears are gilt; his toe-nails are of silver.

We have already noticed (on page 99) his curious emblems, like skins full of solutions for preserving or washing the body, hung upon poles, and stood behind the great sepulchral shrines in the Burial Chamber. Here, within his gilded pylon, carefully wrapped in linen and deposited in separate compartments, are further strange symbols belonging to his cult: four blue faience forelegs of a bovine animal, which recall the *whm* word-sign to "repeat"; two small wooden mummiform figures, like the determinative *wi* for "mummy"; an anthropomorphic figure of Horus, or maybe Re, in blue faience; a blue faience squatting figure of the ibis-headed god, Thoth; a blue faience *wadj* "papyrus column," which may signify to "pour out" from the word *wdjh*; a wax *bahi*-bird; some pieces of resin; and lastly, two calcite cups, one inverted over the other, full of an intimate mixture of resin, common salt, sulphate of soda, and a very small proportion of carbonate of soda (natron).[1] Such objects, if my interpretation be correct, seem to signify the perpetuation of, or belong to, the ritual of mummification. In a fifth and much larger compartment in the pylon were eight large pectoral ornaments. These had originally been wrapped in pieces of linen and sealed, but they, like the symbols in the four smaller compartments, had been disturbed by the thieves in search for more valuable loot. The pectorals possibly comprise the god's jewellery, or perhaps they were worn by his eight priests who carried him in procession to the tomb?

To depart for a moment from the main subject; what was the origin of this very interesting Anubis-animal? To explain it, we are driven to conjectures of varying degrees of possibility. It is possible that it originates from some form of domesticated jackal-dog of the primitive Egyptians. It presents characteristics of several of the sub-orders of the canine family. It is represented black; as having a smooth coat; the attenuated form of the greyhound; long, pointed muzzle; long, erect, pointed ears; eye-pupils round; the fore-feet have five toes, and the hind-feet only four; and it has a very long, straight, drooping, bushy, and club-like tail. The majority of these characteristics are those of the domestic dog, but in place of the recurved tail peculiar to the dog, it has the long, straight tail of the fox, club-like in form, which it carries in drooping position like the wolf, jackal, or fox. The numerous representations of this Anubis-animal upon the Egyptian monuments resemble largely the bearing of the jackal, and this specimen gives reason to entertain the idea that it may have been a domesticated form of the jackal crossed with another sub-genus of the canine family. The collar and the scarf-like leash that are invariably represented round its neck also suggest an animal brought under human control. And when one takes into account the qualities of the domesticated canine family—devotion to its master, knowledge and defence of his property, attachment to him until death—it may be the reason why those ancients selected this jackal-like dog as the vigilant watcher over their dead.

I have witnessed two animals resembling this Anubis form of jackal-like dog. The first example was seen by me during the early spring of 1926, when in the desert of Thebes I encountered a pair of jackals slinking towards the Nile valley, as is their custom, in the dusk of the evening. One of them was evidently the common jackal (*C. Lupaster*) in spring pelage; but its mate—I was not near enough to tell whether the male or the female—was much larger, of lanky build, and black! Its characteristics were those of the Anubis-animal, save for one point —the tail was short, like the ordinary jackal. In fact, with the exception of its tail, it appeared to be the very counterpart of the figure found in this room. It may possibly have been a case of melanism, or sport deviating in both colour and form from the normal type, but I must admit that its extraordinary likeness to the Anubis beast brought to my mind the possibility of a throwback or rare descendant of some earlier species in Egypt (for similar animal see upper register, north wall of the tomb of Baqt; Newberry, *Beni Hasan*, Part II, Plate IV). The second example that I saw was in October 1928, during early morn in the Valley of the Kings. It had precisely the same characteristics as the former example described, but in this case was a young animal from about seven to ten months old. Its legs were lanky; its body greyhound-like; it had a long pointed muzzle, large and erect, pointed, ears; but its drooping tail was comparatively short and of ordinary jackal shape. Long hairs of a lighter colour (greyish) under the body could be detected.

I have made inquiries among the inhabitants of Gurna (Western Thebes) regarding these animals. They tell me that individual examples of this black variety, though very rare, are known to them, and that they are always far more attenuated—"of the Selakhi [a kind of greyhound] form"—than the ordinary species.

Characteristics of the Anubis beast are often very noticeable among a black species of the native Egyptian dogs, but like all the Egyptian pariahs they have a curled tail, coiled tightly over the rump, and never straight and drooping like that of the Anubis jackal-like dog.

The fact that this animal is invariably represented genderless suggests the possibility of its being an imaginary beast. On the other hand this want of gender may derive origin from certain precautionary measures "to prevent indignities from being offered" to the dead, mentioned by Herodotus (Book II, p. 89) when describing the ancient Egyptian method of embalming and the embalmers.

Anubis, whose cult was universal in Egypt, was the totem god of the XVIIth nome, Cynopolis, of Upper Egypt, as well as in capitals of the XVIIIth and probably the XIIth and XIIIth nomes of the same kingdom. And as the custom of embalming the dead gradually developed, he became the patron divinity of that art.

Placed between the fore-feet of this figure of Anubis was an ivory palette inscribed: "*The royal daughter, Mertaten, beloved and born of the Great-Royal-Wife, Neferneferunefertiti.*" Mertaten was married to Smenkhkare, who preceded Tutankhamen. It contained six partially-used colours: white, yellow, red, green, blue, and black. Although samples obtainable without damaging so precious an article were insufficient for confirmatory tests to be applied, Mr. Lucas was of the opinion that the white was probably calcium sulphate, the yellow of the nature of orpiment (sulphate of arsenic), the red an ochre, and the black carbon. The green was not examined and the blue was mostly used up.

Immediately behind the pylon of Anubis, and facing west, was the golden head of the Mehurit cow, called "*The Eye of Re.*" This, apparently, is a form of the goddess Hathor as Mistress of Amentit, the "Land of Sunset," who receives in her Mountain of the West the sinking sun and the dead. Around her neck was tied a linen covering, knotted at the throat. She is carved of wood; her horns are made of copper; and her inlaid eyes of lapis lazuli glass take the form of the "Eye of Re," from which she derives her name. Her head, ears and part of her throat are gilded, symbolizing the golden rays of the setting sun; the remainder of her neck, like the pedestal upon which she rests, is varnished with black resin, representing the gloom of the vale of the Underworld out of which her head protrudes.

Standing on the floor behind the head of the cow and before the Canopic equipment, were three alabaster (calcite) *tazzas* supporting shallow alabaster dishes, two of which were covered with similar inverted bowls. The central dish, which may have contained water, was empty, but the covered dishes on the right and left contained, according to Mr. Lucas, a mixture in powder composed of fine crystals of natron, some common salt, and a small proportion of sulphate of soda. Their significance is not understood, but the materials they contained suggest that they had something in common with the ritual of mummification.

The next in sequence of the arrangement of objects in this little room, and also the most effective, was the Canopic equipment—a monument not easily forgotten, that stood before the centre of the east end wall, immediately opposite the entrance doorway. It was some 6 feet 6 inches in height, and it occupied a floor area of some 5 by 4 feet. Even though it was possible to guess the purport of this monument, its simple grandeur, the calm which seemed to accompany

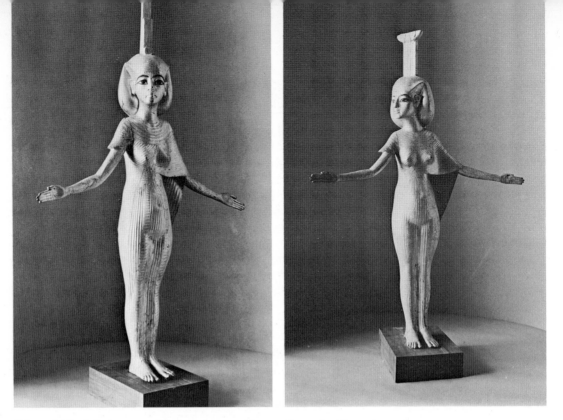

Isis and Nephthys—two of the tutelary goddesses from the Canopic equipment

the four little gracious statuettes that guarded it, produced a mystery and an appeal to the imagination that would be difficult to describe. The shielding canopy overlaid with gold was supported by four corner posts upon a massive sledge, its cornice surmounted with brilliantly inlaid solar cobras; on each side was a lifelike gilded statuette of a tutelary goddess, guarding her charge with outstretched protective arms. The central portion—a large shrine-shaped chest—also completely overlaid with gold and surmounted with solar cobras, concealed a smaller chest hewn out of a solid block of veined semi-translucent alabaster (calcite). This alabaster chest, with gilt dado, covered with a linen pall, and standing upon a silver-handled gesso-gilt wooden sledge, held the four receptacles for the viscera of the king. The viscera, wrapped in separate mummiform packages, were contained in four miniature gold coffins.

These observations bring us to consider the meaning of this elaborate Canopic equipment. In the Egyptian process of mummifying the body, the viscera were separately preserved in four receptacles associated with the genii Imsety, Hepy, Duamutef, and Qebehsnewef, who were under the special protection of Isis, Nephthys, Neith, and Selkit. Each of these four tutelary goddesses was supposed to have possessed within herself a genius, which it was her duty to protect. Hence we find Imsety guarded by Isis, and Hepy by Nephthys; the guardians of Duamutef and Qebehsnewef were Neith and Selkit respectively. An ancient myth connected with the four genii, said to be the sons of Horus, tells us that they arose from water in a lily, and that the crocodile god, Sebekh, commanded by the Sun-god Re, had to catch them in a net. However, it is also said that Isis produced them, and that they succoured Osiris in his misfortunes, and saved him from hunger and thirst, and hence it became their office to do the same for the dead. From the myth, and from the logical procedure in mummification, came the peculiar conception, which already shows itself in the Old and Middle Kingdoms, and was universally accepted in the New Empire. By the intervention of these genii the viscera were prevented from causing the deceased any unpleasantness. The viscera were removed from the

The Canopic equipment

The alabaster Canopic chest

body and placed in the charge of these genii guarded by their respective goddesses whose actual spirits they were. Hence, after the mummy, its coffins, sarcophagus, and covering shrines, the most important among the funeral appurtenances was the Canopic equipment for the viscera. And in this instance the Canopic chest, with its protective goddesses and coverings, was in keeping, both in richness and in glory, with the exalted station of its owner.

The alabaster Canopic chest certainly proves to be one of the most beautiful objects among the funerary equipment of the king. Shrine-like in form, it has the usual entablature common to the design, its sides have a slight "batter" and on the corners the four guardian goddesses are carved in high-relief—Isis on the south-west corner, Nephthys on the north-west corner, Neith on the south-east corner, and Selkit on the north-east corner. On each side are their respective formulae in bold hieroglyphics, incised and filled in with dark blue pigment. The massive lid, which forms the entablature, was carefully secured to the chest by means of cord bound to gold staples and sealed with the design: a recumbent figure of the Anubis jackal-like beast over the nine races of mankind in prisoner form, in fact, the device of the royal necropolis seal. The dado, overlaid with thin sheet-gold, is embossed with *ded* and *thet* symbols probably denoting the protection of both Isis and Osiris. The interior of the chest was only carved out some five inches deep, but sufficiently to give the appearance of four rectangular compartments containing each a jar. Covering the tops of each of the imitation jars were separate human-headed lids, finely sculptured in alabaster in the likeness of the king. The two on the east side faced west, and the two on the west side faced east. The rebated flanges of the human-headed lids fitted into the openings of the counterfeit jars: that is to say they covered the mouths of the four cylindrical holes in the chest which took the place of real jars. In each hollow, wrapped in linen, was an exquisite miniature gold coffin, elaborately inlaid and resembling the second coffin of the king.

They were placed upright, facing in the same direction as the alabaster lids; they had been subjected, like the king's mummy, to unguents which had solidified and stuck them fast to the bottom of the hollows. Whether this anointing took place in the tomb or elsewhere, we were unable to find sufficient evidence to make any final decision. The only possible suggestion that it might have taken place beforehand was the fact that the human-headed lids were slightly displaced—a displacement which might have occurred from jolting during transport to the tomb. There was, however, sufficient evidence to show that the anointing commenced with the south-east coffin, thence to the south-west coffin, the north-west coffin and ending by the north-east coffin, when a very little of the unguent was left.

These miniature coffins which held the viscera are wonderful specimens of both goldsmith's and jeweller's art. They are replicas of the second coffin that enclosed the king, but far more elaborately inlaid in feather design, the burnished gold faces being the only part of the figures that has been left plain. Each bears down the front the formula pertaining to the goddess and her genius to which it belongs, and each has on the interior surfaces beautifully engraved texts pertaining to the rite.

But in spite of all this care and costly expenditure to preserve and to protect the mortal remains of the young king, the sumptuous funerary equipment, and what must have been elaborate religious rites at the time of entombment, we find gross carelessness on the part of those people who undertook the obsequies. They must have known better than we do now, that the goddess Nephthys should be on the south side of the chest, and that her charge was the genius Hepy. And that Selkit should be on the east side, and her charge was the genius Qebeh-snewef. Yet in erecting this Canopic equipment, even though it bears distinct marks as well as distinguishing inscriptions upon each side, they placed Selkit south in the place of Nephthys, and Nephthys east where Selkit should have been. Moreover, the carpenters, who put together the sections of the canopy and fitted the wooden covering over the alabaster chest, left their refuse (chips of wood) in a heap on the floor of the chamber.

We will now turn to those sinister black chests and boxes that were stacked along the whole of the south side of the room. Hitherto, imagination faltered at the thought of what they might contain; with suppressed excitement we opened them one by one: they each enclosed one or more figures of gods or of the king.

No pains were spared in making and housing these figures. They were placed in twenty-two black wooden shrine-shaped chests constructed upon wooden sledges. Each chest had folding doors carefully closed and fastened with cord and seal. Their seals, made of Nile mud probably mixed with a small quantity of oil, bore an impression of the necropolis seal in miniature: a recumbent figure of the jackal-like dog, Anubis, over nine prisoner foes, disposed in three rows of three, which, according to Dr. Alan Gardiner, represent the nine races of mankind, called by the ancient Egyptians "The Nine Bows"—a device signifying the protection of the vigilant Anubis against all human enemies. Each statuette was enveloped in a piece of linen from the looms of Akhenaten, which date back as early as the third year of that reign—rather more than twenty years before the burial of Tutankhamen. But although each statuette was enveloped in linen, their faces without exception were carefully left uncovered, and many of the gods had tiny fillets of real flowers fastened round their heads. These fillets in many instances had fallen from decay over their shoulders.

The statuettes themselves are beautifully carved of a hard wood, overlaid with gesso and thin sheet-gold; their eyes are inlaid with obsidian, calcite, bronze, and glass; the details of their head-dresses, collars, and garments, are carefully wrought; the insignia upon the crowns and emblems in the hands of the figures of the king are made of bronze plated with thin sheet-gold; and each statuette, whether of the king or of a god, stands upon an oblong pedestal

varnished with black resin. The gods have their names painted in yellow upon their pedestals, and these figures display all the charms of the Eighteenth Dynasty art. The statuettes of the king are realistically sculptured; some show a physical likeness to Akhenaten.

Including the two that were found in the Antechamber, there were thirty-four in all: twenty-seven of divinities and seven of the king.

The exact meaning as well as the presence of this series of figures in the tomb is not clear to us. It may be that some, if not all of the divinities comprise "*the Divine Ennead which is in Duat*" (the Nether World), or it may be they represent the Ennead—the divine tribunal or synod of gods—associated with the struggle between Horus and Seth, for two of the statuettes of the king obviously pertain to that myth, while the others seem to represent him in various forms of his future existence, to show that he "*die not a second time in the Nether World.*"

The figures of the divinities include the Sun-god Atum; Shu, the god of the atmosphere; the Earth-god, Geb; the goddesses Isis and Nephthys; Horus the Elder; Horus within the shrine; Ptah, the patron deity of Egypt; Sekhmet, the lion goddess of war; Tatenen, (?) a special form of Ptah; Khepre, regarded as a form of the Sun-god; Mamu, Sent, and Tata; the children of Horus, Imsety, Hepy, Duamutef (? two figures), and Qebehsnewef; Menkaret, who holds the king above her head; two standards of Seshet, the goddess of writing; the falcon standard of Spedu; the falcon standard of Gemehsu; a serpent divinity named Neterankh; all by whom the king is beloved, and two Ihy-musicians.

The only black figures (i.e. covered with a black resin), so numerous in the preceding royal tombs of this dynasty, were the two (?) Ihy-musicians resembling the infant Horus. They bear no inscriptions, but they hold in their outstretched right hands a gilded emblem of Hathor, and may possibly be identified with the Ihy-musicians of Hathor in the Nether World, who worshipped that goddess and the name of her son. This Ihy being is mentioned in the "Book of the Dead" in connexion with the "*Negative Confessions*," numbering forty-two, "*Said on arriving at the Hall of Righteousness*," so that the deceased may be freed of his sins and that "*he may look upon the Divine Countenance.*" A parallel to these two figures may be found in a scene in a tomb in the necropolis of Meir and in the tomb of Amenemheb at Thebes, where not only female musicians of Hathor but Ihy-musicians participate in the festival of Hathor in some connexion with the deceased. Another remarkable group represents the Osirian king being held above the head of the god, or goddess, Menkaret. The king is here attired as Osiris wearing the crown of Lower Egypt. His close-fitting winding-sheet confines his arms, hands, body, legs and feet. The divinity, Menkaret, seemingly lifts him up to enable him to greet the Sun-god. Underlying this group is the character of that ancient nation, living as it was under the influence of an innocent form of superstition, the worship of the glorious luminary, their symbol of both the might and beneficence of the Master of the Universe.

The statuettes of the king show the influence of the El Amarna school. In the modelling of these particular figures, even though they be of repeated traditional type, there is a direct and spontaneous feeling for nature. The feeling here exhibited is beyond the formalized conventions learnt by rote; they show both energy and grace, in fact, the divine and the human have been brought in familiar touch with one another. Two of them depict the young Pharaoh standing with left foot forward. He wears the crown of Lower Egypt, the *usekh*-collar with *mankhet*, the pleated *shendyt*-kilt, and sandals. In one instance he holds in his left hand the long crooked *awt*-staff, and in his right the flagellum; in the second figure, in place of the crooked staff, he holds a long straight stick. In a third and slightly larger example, the king, in precisely the same attitude and holding the crooked *awt*-staff and flagellum, wears the crown of Upper Egypt. Another pair of statuettes represent the king upon papyrus-reed floats, and appear to symbolize a mythical pursuit: Tutankhamen as the youthful warrior Horus killing the Typhonial

Statues of divinities in their black wooden chests

animal, the hippopotamus, in the marshes. These two figures, exactly similar, are remarkable for the vigour and animation they display. They picture the king in the act of hurling a javelin. He wears the Lower Egyptian crown and in his left hand holds the coil of cord used with the javelin or harpoon.

From the myth of Horus, sculptured on the walls of the temple of Edfu, we gather some knowledge as to the meaning of these two figures. Apparently the divinity took upon himself the form of a young man of superhuman stature and physique, who wielded a javelin twenty cubits in length with chain of over sixty cubits, as though it were a reed. Horus hurled this mighty weapon and struck the great hippopotamus, Seth, who lurked in the waters to destroy him and his followers, when the storm came that would wreck their boats. Thus did Horus, the avenger, defeat the abominable one, the enemy of Osiris. However, we also glean from the myth that the great battle is not yet, but that Horus will destroy Seth, when Osiris and the gods will again reign upon this earth. Moreover a passage from the account of "*the Contendings of Horus and Seth*," in a recently discovered papyrus, dating from the reign of Rameses V, throws further light upon this representation of the king impersonating, in divine attribution, Horus: "*Therefore they went into their ships in presence of the Ennead. Thereupon the ship of Seth sank in the water. And Seth changed himself into a hippopotamus, and he caused to founder the ship of Horus. Thereupon Horus took his barb, and threw it at the Majesty of Seth.*"[2] It is also of interest to observe that at a much later date—the Hellenistic period in Egypt—we find Horus as a warrior, represented on horseback attacking his foe, a crocodile, with a lance, very similar to and possibly the prototype of St. George and the Dragon of the Christian era. The frail reed float upon which the king stands, is painted green and has gilt calices and bindings at the stem and stern. Such floats were obviously made of bundles of papyrus-reeds or rushes lashed together —a primitive form of craft used both for hunting in the marshes, and for ferrying purposes, in past ages as well as by the inhabitants of the upper reaches of the Nile today.

Perhaps even more mysterious are the two figures representing the king upon the backs of leopards. In both cases Tutankhamen wears the White Crown of Upper Egypt, the *shendyt*-kilt, sandals, and in his hands he holds the straight-staff (with umbel) and the flagellum. He stands upon a pedestal which is fixed upon the back of a black leopard, having its facial markings and internal pectinations of its ears gilt. Fragments of similar figures found in the tombs of preceding Eighteenth Dynasty monarchs clearly show that these extraordinary figures are not unusual in Pharaonic funerary equipment, but no light as yet has been thrown upon their meaning. The leopards are rendered in the attitude of walking, hence suggesting movement, as if the king was about to enter, or pass out from, the Underworld.

There was a flotilla of model craft. Fourteen were put on the top of those twenty-two black shrine-shaped chests that housed the statuettes, a fully rigged model was stood upon a miniature granary in front of the chests, another rigged model in the north-west corner, and two others were placed in convenient places on the north side of the room. All the model craft on the south side had their bows towards the west. Two on the north side of the room had been overturned by the thieves. The remainder of this group were discovered in the Annexe—unfortunately these were almost entirely broken up through ill-usage at the hands of the plunderers.

Among these craft we find models to follow the voyage of the sun; canoes for hunting the hippopotamus and fowling in the Hereafter, symbolizing the mythical pastimes of Horus in the marshes; vessels for the holy pilgrimage to and from Abydos; and craft to render the deceased independent of the favours of the "*celestial ferrymen*" to reach the "*fields of the blessed,*" that are surrounded by seething waters difficult to traverse. Some, we are told, would hope to be carried over by the favour of the divine birds—the falcon of Horus, the ibis of Thoth—others pray to the four heavenly spirits, Imsety, Hepy, Duamutef, and Qebehsnewef, to bring them a

The king on the back of a leopard

ferry-boat; or they turn to the Sun-god himself, that he should carry them over in his barque. But here, by the mythical potency inherent in these models, the king is rendered independent.

These models are made out of logs of wood, pinned together, shaped and planed with the adze. They are painted and gilt and in some instances highly decorated with brilliant ornamentation. With the exception of a model reed canoe, they appear to represent carvel-built boats, with planking flush, i.e. planks or blocks of timber laid edge to edge so that they present a smooth surface without, fastened on the inside with tree-nails, having no ribs, but thwarts or cross-ties to yoke the sides, the side planking being fixed fore and aft to the stem and stern pieces. They have a steering-gear consisting of two large paddles which operate upon upright crutches and overhanging cross-beams before the poop-deck.

The four ships (two large and two small) to follow the divine journeys of the sun, represent a kind of light craft probably developed from the primitive reed-float. They have a round bottom, slightly flattened under the bow and stern; their two ends gradually rise in a fine curve, the stem turned up and ending in an upright papyrus shaped post, the stern-post bent back and terminating in a papyrus pillar; in fact, in their general shape, they remind one of the Venetian gondola. Amidships is the gilded throne of the royal passenger, named on the larger barques "Beloved of Osiris," "Beloved of Sokar," and on the smaller "Like Re," "Giving Life." Thus the deceased journeys as companion of Re, the Sun-god, by day over the heavenly ocean, by night through the realms of Osiris.

> "During the daytime, [says Professor Maspero,] the pure Soul was in no serious danger; but in the evening, when the eternal waters which flow along the vaulted heavens fall in vast cascades adown the west and are engulfed in the bowels of the earth, the Soul follows the barque of the Sun and its escort of luminary gods into a lower world bristling with ambuscades and perils. For twelve hours, the divine squadron defiles through long gloomy corridors, where numerous genii, some hostile, some friendly, now struggle to bar the way, and now aid it in surmounting the difficulties of the journey. Great doors, each guarded by a gigantic serpent, were stationed at intervals, and led to an immense hall of flame and fire, peopled by hideous monsters and executioners, whose office it was to torture the damned. Then came more dark and narrow passages, more blind gropings in the gloom, more strife with malevolent genii, and again the joyful welcoming of the propitious gods. At midnight began the upward journey towards the eastern regions of the world; and in the morning, having reached the confines of the Land of Darkness, the sun emerged from the east to light another day."

The two craft (?) for the celestial ferry are very similar in type to the last, but they have the stem and stern turned inwards: the two ends, which rise high out of the water in a beautiful curve, are bent back and end in the familiar papyrus umbel. They have a broad beam and would seem to be capable of navigating shallow water with minimum draught and maximum load. The gods of the four cardinal points are said to have placed four such craft, called "*sekhen*," for the ascent of Osiris to the sky. The barques for the divine journeys of the sun and these craft for ferrying to the fields of the blessed, by being intended for divine purpose, were towed or propelled by supernatural agency, and therefore did not require sail or oar.

The canoe for the mythical pastimes of Horus is a model of a very primitive form of craft, since from its details it was evidently made of bundles of papyrus stalks lashed together at intervals into canoe-shape. The bow and stern rise slightly and end in conventional umbels of papyrus. The primitive reed-float from which this kind of craft is derived, although no longer found in Egypt proper, still survives in Nubia and in the upper reaches of the Nile. A form of reed craft similar to our model is invariably depicted in fowling, fishing, and harpooning scenes, found among the mural paintings of private tomb-chapels of the Old and Middle Kingdoms, and of the New Empire, where it is called the "*wsekhet*"-boat. Such scenes, I believe, are as mythical as the pastimes of Horus. However, "Plutarch tells us that the hippopotamus was a Typonian animal, so that the hunting of the hippopotamus would naturally evoke the memory of the struggle between Horus and Seth."[3]

Four of the series of funeral boats have a midshipmast, rigging, and a square sail. Amidships is an ornately decorated cabin, and on the forecastle and poop-decks a gilded pavilion. Although these vessels have a peculiar pointed stem and a fish-tail stern, they recall to mind the "*Nagga*" still plying on the Nile in Nubia, which is constructed of blocks of acacia wood pinned together with tree-nails on the inside, and is no doubt the direct descendant of these older craft. The remaining seven craft belonging to this series are without sail or oar. They also appear to be models of carvel-built boats; the stem and stern pieces are curved upward and terminate with blunt ends. Upon the overhanging forecastle and poop-decks are small "look-outs," and amidships a large double roofed, elaborately decorated cabin showing doors and windows. This last series of eleven craft was evidently intended for the pilgrimage to the holy spot, Abydos, where the deceased king should take some part in connexion with the funerary festivals of Osiris. By causing him to enjoy similar funeral rites he was identified with that great god of the dead; in the same manner, the king, by following the solar course, was identified with the Sun-god. It is problematical whether the procession up and down stream ever occurred, or whether it had any objective reality; for if it did occur, why were these models placed in the tomb?

Perhaps one of the most curious objects among this funerary equipment was found in a large oblong box in the south-west corner of the room, under some of the shrine-shaped chests. This object, commonly known to us as a germinated figure of Osiris, or Osiris-bed, comprises a wooden frame moulded in the form of that god, hollowed out, lined with linen, filled with silt from the Nile bed, and planted with corn. This was moistened; the grain germinated, and the inanimate form became green and living; thus symbolizing the resurrection of Osiris and of the deceased. This life-size effigy was completely wrapped in linen winding-sheets and bandaged in the like manner as a mummy. It is but another example how, in that ancient funerary cult, the virtuous dead were identified in every possible way with Osiris.

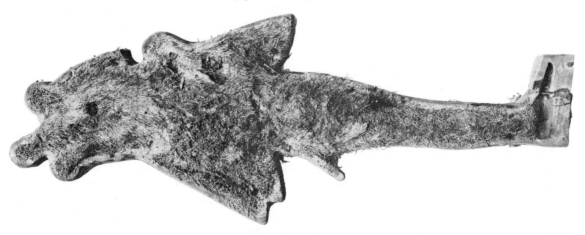

The germinated figure of Osiris

Symbolical of brewing the divine beverage, beer, for the god, were two strainers that were placed upon one of the chests. These are made of wood, covered with a coat of gesso, and have central disks of copper pierced with numerous small holes for straining purposes.

Doubtless the ancient and modern Egyptian process of brewing, or making "Booza" as it is now called, was much the same. This primitive form of beer seems to be made as follows: yesterday's bread—wheat, barley or maize—is crumbled into a large vessel, and covered with water, and left for a period of three days. A comparatively small measure of grain is placed in a bowl and covered with hot water, and left for a day. After this, the water is removed by straining, and the grain is dried in the sun for one day, when a milky-white exudation caused by incipient germination occurs. The grain at this stage is then powdered into a meal, and is mixed with the first preparation, and left for a period of about ten hours. This mixture (i.e. the first and second preparations) is afterwards vigorously kneaded, the liquid being strained from it into a fresh vessel ready for drinking, thus forming in its completed state a turbid alcoholic liquor rather stronger than common beer. The solid refuse is generally thrown away, although occasionally it is eaten by the lower classes, flavoured with red pepper, or sometimes given pure to horses.

In a rough wooden box was a model "*Mola Trusatilis*" or thrusting hand-mill for grinding corn into a coarse meal. It consists of a saddle-stone and muller made of yellow quartzite (a sort of crystalline sandstone); the saddle-stone is let into a wooden seat with a trough to receive the meal, and is coated with gesso; the muller, oval and flat-bottomed, was used for rubbing the grain upon the saddle-stone into meal.

Burchardt in his *Travels in Nubia* (1822), while mentioning the people of Berber says:

> "As they have no mills, not even hand-mills, they grind the dhoura (a local millet) by strewing it upon a smooth stone, about two feet in length and one foot in breadth, which is placed in a sloping position before the person employed to grind. At the lower extremity of the stone, a hole is made in the ground to contain a jar, wooden bowl, or some such vessel, which receives the dhoura flour. The grinding is effected by means of a small stone flat at the bottom; this is held in both hands, and moved backwards and forwards on the sloping stone by the grinder, who kneels to perform the operation."

This lucid description of what was no less than a saddle-stone and muller, such as we have before us, and the method adopted for grinding the corn, leaves little doubt that this ancient model is, though less primitive, a prototype. Women are shown using this form of hand-mill in the chapel of Amenemhet, and men similarly occupied in the chapel of Baqt, at Beni Hasan.[4] This kind of hand-mill was obviously employed for grinding flour for bread, and although the grinding of the flour was the peculiar duty of women and menials, I believe I am right when I say it was the privilege of the Pharaoh to prepare the meal for the deity. He was, moreover, actually the divine triturator.

It is remarkable how this funerary equipment retains survivals of earlier burial customs, which have long ceased to exist in private tombs, namely, models of boats, figures and implements of domestic nature—here possibly for divine purpose. Another of these models takes the form of a miniature granary, showing a doorway to an enclosure with entrance yard and sixteen separate compartments for cereals, which were found filled to the brim with grain and seeds. Large "*Shunas*" of this kind, built of sun-dried mud bricks, are the mode for storing cereals in Egypt today. Their external architectural details are precisely the same as this very model of thirty-three centuries ago.

As this completes the material that was placed on the south side of the room, I will now turn to the objects placed on the north side.

Here, placed parallel with the pylon of Anubis and reaching as far as the Canopic equipment, was a row of treasure caskets and plain white boxes. Unfortunately this group had been attacked by the dynastic tomb-plunderers for the more valuable gold and silver articles that the caskets and boxes had contained. Their seals were broken, their contents ransacked, their pieces of greater value stolen; moreover, the remainder of their contents was left in utter disorder.

It may be here remarked that valuable woods and ivory, natural stones, faience, glass and metals were employed by the ancient Egyptians for the manufacture and decoration of their caskets. Throughout the East, through all ages, these highly ornamental boxes were used to hold the more valuable and personal belongings—trinkets and clothes—or as repositories for cosmetics in costly vessels. In fact, to this day, the pride of the fellah is the gaudily bespangled and more than often trumpery box, in which he keeps his most treasured articles.

With the ancient Egyptian examples of boxes there was never any attempt at secret contrivances—hidden compartments or false bottoms—such as are often found in chests of the sixteenth and seventeenth centuries of our era. They have always simple interiors which are sometimes divided by partitions for special purposes. Such boxes rank among the most ancient domestic furniture, and in all probability precede the bedstead, couch and chair. They may be said to be the ancestors of the "chest-of-drawers," of which the later Oriental spice and inlaid medical chests enclosing sets of small drawers are but the transitional form. Boxes and caskets were in dynastic times an almost universal possession; with the rich they were often, as we see, of great value, with the poor accordingly plain and simple. They were almost invariably for domestic purpose; nothing in the nature of an ancient Egyptian "strong-box" has been found. There were no locks, therefore anything like a "strong-box" was useless, since the means of closing it depended on string and seal.

Although hinges were known to the Egyptians—several examples having been found on boxes in this tomb—they were rarely employed for attaching the lid to the box. A movable lid, separate from the box, was generally the fashion. The substitute for a hinge employed to hold the lid to the back of the box is ingeniously simple: two small holes, a slot, or a rebate, in the interior of the upper part of the back of the box, were made to receive corresponding projections on the cross-battens of the underside of the lid, which when lowered and slid into position prevented the back of the lid from being raised. The forepart of the lid was then held down by means of cord tied round the knob on the top of the lid and on the front of the box, which in turn was secured by a seal. Thus, unless the seal was broken and the cord severed, the lid was held firmly to the box at the back and front.

As a result of this ancient custom of securing goods, it is not surprising to find the more valuable and personal equipment of the king, whether it be funerary or otherwise, stored in highly ornamental caskets and boxes. Many magnificent examples have been found in this tomb, and in this treasury, among a group of six, we have before us four specimens showing very fine workmanship, especially so in the manner of marquetry-inlay, in which over 45,000 pieces of inlay have been employed in the ornamentation of a single specimen.

The first casket, which stood nearest the doorway, is embellished with an ivory and ebony veneer and marquetry-inlay: namely, a great number of small pieces of ivory and ebony arranged to form diamond, criss-cross, and herring-bone patterns within panels formed by a veneer of broad and narrow strips of ivory and ebony. The casket is oblong in shape, stands upon four square feet, and has a vaulted lid. As is usual in all such cases of cabinet-maker's art, the basic wood of the casket is of poorer quality, possibly of the genus tamarix, and over this inferior body the valuable ivory and ebony veneer and marquetry-inlay have been laid by means

A chest ornamented with ivory and ebony marquetry

of an adhesive: that is to say, the external surfaces of the body were prepared, made perfectly smooth, and a film of glue applied and the veneer and marquetry laid on. After these had been pressed and allowed to dry thoroughly, their upper surfaces were, in turn, smoothed and polished. This class of decoration is also found on ceremonial "snake" sticks, made probably by the same artisan. A docket written in hieratic upon the lid of the casket reads: "*Jewels of gold of the procession made in the bed-chamber*[5] *of Nebkheprure* (Tutankhamen)." It contained a lot of mixed jewellery, some of which may have belonged to other caskets, the thieves having taken the pieces of greater value and left the rest in disorder.

The second casket is of unusual shape, as it takes the oval form of a cartouche. It is constructed of a reddish-brown wood of possibly coniferous nature and is bordered in veneer fashion with strips of ebony. Around its sides are three horizontal bands of hieroglyphic script, engraved and filled in with blue, giving the titulary and other designations of the king. But the lid is its real and striking feature: it is one huge cartouche bearing finely carved ebony and stained ivory characters of the nomen of Tutankhamen; and these characters are laid upon a rich gold ground bordered with black ebony, which in turn is inlaid with ivory-white details and designations of the king. Like the first casket its contents had been ransacked. We found in it but a confused residue of jewellery, a mirror-case, and some sceptres of sovereignty; the sceptres probably belonged to it.

The third was but a plain whitened wood box with vaulted lid. It was empty save for a pair of fancy leather sandals of slipper-like form, and a stone anklet. It possibly contained vestments, parts of which were found in the other caskets.

The fourth and larger casket is made of a coniferous wood and ornamented with broad rails and styles of veneered ivory. Its panels formed by the rails and styles are decorated with an applied fretwork of gilt wood symbols—*ankh*, *uas*, and *neb* signs—a formula meaning "All Life and Good Fortune." The gilding of these open-work symbols in contrast to the dark brown colour of the basic wood and the white ivory rails and styles gives a very rich and elegant effect. Each rail and style is engraved with bold hieroglyphic script, filled in with black pigment, which give the titulary consisting of the five "Great Names" assumed by the king on his accession; namely, "The Horus-name," "The Nebty-name," "The Golden-Horus-name," the Prenomen and Nomen. The queen's cartouche and her titles are also included on one of the rails. The four square feet upon which the casket stands are shod with silver caps. The interior of this casket is divided into sixteen rectangular compartments, each measuring $4\frac{3}{8}$ by $3\frac{1}{2}$ inches. The compartments were evidently made to receive a similar number of gold or silver vessels for cosmetics. These were all missing—pilfered—and in their places were cast a small rush basket, a stained ivory bowl, two palettes, an ivory and gold burnisher, an ornamental case for writing-reeds, and an empty mirror-case, all of which obviously came from some other box or casket.

The fifth box is of plain whitened wood similar to the third example referred to. Upon this box is a docket in hieratic reading: "*The . . . procession of the bed-chamber.*" Lying on the bottom of the box were a few dried fruits and a beautiful but very fragile ostrich-feather fan of the king. This simple but touching relic is made up of white and dark brown ostrich feathers inserted into a semi-circular piece of ivory, to which the handle of the fan is attached. The handle, also of ivory, takes the form of a papyrus umbel and stem; it is bent at right angles to increase the movement caused by the turn of the wrist when in use; it is ornamented with gold collars, and has a lapis lazuli coloured glass knob at the end. Such charming relics seem to elude time; many civilizations have risen and died away since that fan was deposited in this treasury. Such a rare, but in many ways familiar, object provides a link between us and that tremendous past. It helps us to visualize that the young king must have been very like ourselves.

The sixth casket stood behind the first, near the doorway. It is the smallest among this group; it is of simple rectangular shape; it stands on four square legs, and is ornamented with an ivory and ebony marquetry-inlay and ivory veneer, as in the case of the first casket. We found it empty with its lid on the top of the second casket. A hieratic docket written upon it reads: "*. . . of gold in* (?) *the place of the funeral procession.*" The interior of this casket is divided into equal compartments to take four vessels, which, in all probability, explains the lacuna at the beginning of the inscription.

By the dockets written upon some of these caskets, e.g. "*Jewels of gold of the procession made in the bed-chamber of Nebkheprure,*" "*The . . . procession of the bed-chamber,*" "*. . . of gold in* (?) *the place of the funeral procession,*" "*Gold rings belong to the funeral procession,*" and from scenes of funeral processions in private tomb-chapels of the New Empire, we glean that the jewels, etc., in these treasure caskets were regular features in the funerary ceremony.

Our investigations establish the fact that the material missing from these boxes was at least sixty per cent of the original contents. What was left of the actual jewellery comprises: some ear-rings, a necklace, a number of pectoral ornaments, some bracelets, and a finger-ring. There were also a lid of a small open-work jewelled box, some sceptres, two mirror-cases, the residue of some vestments, and a writing outfit—forty-three pieces in all. The exact amount of jewellery taken is of course impossible to tell, although the remaining parts of some of the stolen orna-ments enable us to conjecture that it must have been considerable, but we can tell that two mirrors, at least twenty vessels from two of the caskets, four of which are stated to have been of gold, were stolen.

Apparently, jewellery in ancient Egyptian days had not served and completed its purpose with death, for we find it in all its forms deposited in the tomb for after-life. It becomes apparent that, with those ancients, its purpose was not only in the service of the living, but in that of the gods; it was also made for burial with the dead. In the latter case it is generally recognized by its flimsier character.

In this tomb, jewellery (amuletic and otherwise) had been deposited in large quantities. One hundred and forty-three pieces were placed upon the king's mummy, some pieces were found within the portable pylon of Anubis, and the remainder stored in these and other treasure caskets. The king's mummy, with all the personal and amuletic ornaments upon it, was untouched. But, as we have just seen, the greater mass, probably those of more intrinsic value, had been stolen from the caskets. Thus we have found only a portion of what was originally placed there. Moreover, it is apparent that the "sergeants of the necropolis," who reclosed the tomb after the raid, must have found what was left in extreme disorder; they seemed to have carried out their duty in a careless and perfunctory manner. What was left had evidently been gathered up and put back into the caskets regardless of the original order. We found parts of an ornament in one casket, parts in another, and the whole mass in confusion.

Although probably not forty per cent remained of what was originally there, from our point of view there was more than enough to enable us to study the skill of the jeweller, as well as the goldsmith's work in the royal workshops of the late Eighteenth Dynasty.

As a prefatory remark, it may be here said that in many ways these New Empire specimens do not exhibit the same perfection of finish as we find in the workmanship of their Middle Kingdom predecessors. There is shown, however, by the Theban jewellers, excellent skill in execution, a marked decorative sense, and much inventiveness in symbolical device. Their craft included that of the lapidary and the glass-cutter, inlaying, chasing, repoussé-work, embossing, twisted gold wire filigree-work, and granulated gold-work. The last craft is a prominent feature in this jewellery, and it comprises a decoration of minute spherical grains of gold, in all probability fused or sweated to the curved or flat gold surfaces of the objects thus treated. In all these arts great ingenuity and mastery of handicraft is exhibited. Many of these ornaments, in fact most of them, are worked à jour, upon which various semi-precious stones and polychrome glass were inlaid, either in high or low relief, or quite flat after cloisonné fashion. It must, however, be understood that the term "cloisonné," applied to ancient Egyptian jewellery, may be misleading. It really means that stones and their glass substitutes were cemented into the metal cells or cloisons, and that the encrustation was not enamel, as in the case of true cloisonné-work. Enamel was unknown to the ancient Egyptians.

The metals employed were gold, electron, silver and, in a lesser degree, bronze; the natural stones were amethyst, turquoise, lapis lazuli, calcite, carnelian, chalcedony, green felspar, semi-translucent and translucent quartz often backed with pigment for brilliance and imitative effects, serpentine, and an obscure hard olive-green stone not identified. In addition to these were composite materials such as faience (glazed pottery), hard vitreous paste, semi-translucent and opaque coloured glasses, used in the place of some one or other of the above-mentioned stones. But perhaps the most remarkable material used in the composition of this jewellery was a dark coloured resin, both on ornaments and as beads. Another peculiarity in these ornaments is a brilliant scarlet-tinted gold, produced by a method which is at present unknown. This, when overlaid with bright yellow gold ornamentation, such as the granulated gold-work, and in combination with the dark coloured resin, imparted a strange and somewhat barbaric effect.

The theme of the various devices employed in these ornaments has, in great part, some subordinate connexion with the state religion. Of these designs Re, the Sun-god, and Aah (Thoth), the Moon-god, are the nucleus, if not the principal. Re, the sun itself, "Lord of Heaven," "The Sovereign King of all Life," takes many forms in this jewellery, such as Khepre, Horus, Herakhte, and Atum, each being a local representative of some phase of the sun. With the ancient Egyptians, especially at this moment, there was no god of higher standing than Re. They regarded him as the Master of the Universe, who, from his sacred barque in the heavens, governed all things. To speak of God was to think of Re.

Khepre, the scarab, is a transformation of the Sun-god in the form of the famous dung-beetle, who scrupulously constructs the maternal ball provided with a cavity in which the egg will hatch and be nourished. It was in this form that the newly-born sun issued from the "Cavern of Dawn" to begin his diurnal career. On his awakening in the east he enters into the Morning barque to ascend the heavenly vault, when he is identified with Horus, either as a youth or as a Hobby-falcon (*Falco subbuteo*). A prayer refers to Re with these words: "*Beautiful is Thine awakening, O Horus, who voyagest over the sky . . . The fire-child with glittering rays, dispelling darkness and gloom.*" As he triumphantly hovers in mid-air, he is conceived as a great disk with multi-coloured wings ready to pounce upon his foe. During his heavenly course he also takes the shape of Herakhte, either in anthropomorphic form as a falcon-headed man, or as a peregrine falcon (*Falco peregrinus*)—a highly courageous bird of prey that kills its quarry upon the wing. Finally he becomes the old man, Atum, "The Closer of the Day," and enters into the Evening barque, descends behind Manun, the sacred Mountain of the West, into the Underworld to begin again his nocturnal journey through the twelve caverns—the hours of the night. There, we gather from a song, he gives light to the great god Osiris, "The ruler of Eternity." "*Give me light, that I may see thy beauty,*" is also the prayer of the dead.

From such mythological considerations as these, there can be little doubt that Pharaonic jewellery was looked upon as sacred. They may have believed it to have possessed magic powers; it may be, too, that priestly orders attached to the court had special charge of it. Underlying its themes of design there certainly appears to lurk an ulterior idea. Thus we find these jewels of Tutankhamen, though they may be made for daily use, designed so as to serve a purpose in the world to come.

But associated with these ornaments there is a problem of some intricacy—how much of it is real and intended for daily use, and how much of it was made solely for sepulchral purpose? It must be remembered that more than often sepulchral and real jewellery are so closely alike, that the distinction, if any, is far from easy to recognize. In fact, in most cases the only criterion would be flimsiness or evidence of use. There are some examples, however, which are clearly sepulchral. For instance, the eight pectorals discovered in the pylon of Anubis. Three of them are inscribed with funerary spells which have direct relation to the heart and limbs of the deceased, the others bear epithets such as:—"*Osiris, the King, Justified,*" the equivalent to our word "deceased."

The ear-rings seem to have belonged to Tutankhamen in his earlier youth.

When examining the mummy of Tutankhamen, it was found that the lobes of his ears were perforated, but among the numerous ornaments that we discovered within his wrappings there was nothing of the nature of an ear-ring. The gold portrait mask that covered his head had also the lobes of the ears pierced, but the holes had been carefully filled in with small disks of thin sheet-gold, suggesting an endeavour to hide the fact. Among the representations of kings upon the Empire monuments, perforations in the lobes of the ears are often marked, but I am not aware of any instance of actual ear-rings being depicted on a king's ears. Osiris is represented wearing collars and bracelets, but never ear-rings. On Arab boys in Egypt ear-rings (*halak*) are often worn up to the age of six and seven years, when they are generally removed and given to the lad's younger brother or sister; in rare cases of an only, or favourite, child they are worn up to the age of twelve to thirteen. Therefore, when taking into consideration the evidence afforded by the king's mummy, his mask, the monuments, and the modern custom which is probably a survival of an earlier practice, it would seem that wearing ear-rings was not customary after the age of manhood. Ear-rings were not an early form of Egyptian ornament. They apparently begin to appear among the inhabitants of the Nile about the commencement of the New Empire, and were probably introduced into Egypt from Asia during the preceding Intermediate Period, under the domination of the Hyksos kings.

There are two types of ear-rings represented here—the rigid and the flexible. In both cases they were fixed to the ears by means of studs passed through the perforations of the pendulous lobes. It is of interest to note that the solar falcon, Herakhte, represented on one of the pairs of ear-rings, has, for some unaccountable reason, the head of a mallard (*Anas boscas*) in semi-translucent blue glass.

The principal and most popular articles of jewellery in ancient Egypt, whether for kings or commoners, were bead-necklaces and broad bead-collars. Many forms of collars and necklaces were prescribed for the funerary equipment. Their popularity as ornaments among all classes of people proved, in this case, to be our loss, for, with the exception of one crude string of alternate dark resin and lapis lazuli beads, they were all taken. They were stolen, probably, not so much on account of their intrinsic value, which cannot have been very great, but on account of their universal popularity. We found beads dropped here and there on the ground from this treasury to the entrance passage of the tomb, particularly at the spot where the thieves had to pass through a small hole, made by them in the masonry that blocked the doorway of the Burial Chamber; there we found broken portions of necklaces hanging on the jagged edges of the stones and many beads dispersed in the cracks of the masonry—parts of at least two necklaces and some falcon-headed "shoulder"-pieces from broad bead-collars.

The "pectoral" is a kind of ornament which Egyptian kings wore in great variety, but almost all of them are similar in the following particulars. A breast ornament suspended from the neck either by chains of contiguous ornamental plaques, by strings of beads, by plain gold chains, or by simple twisted linen cords ending in tassels. In the case of the first three forms of suspension, they almost invariably have a "dorsal" ornament which acted not only as a counterbalance at the back of the neck, but as an ornamental fastening; these dorsal ornaments are often made to open and close, and thus they served as the clasp. Many magnificent examples of pectorals were found in the caskets, some complete, others having parts missing. Some might even have been honorific orders; for example, see the pectoral ornament representing "The Birth of the Sun", which eclipses anything of the kind hitherto discovered.

Bracelets were perhaps the most constant articles of jewellery among all Egyptian classes. Here, unfortunately, we found only three examples left by the thieves. From these specimens it will be seen that they fall into two categories: of solid metal hoop type, with pin-hinges, pin-fastenings, and encrusted with ornament; or of wrist-band type composed of beads arranged by means of "spacers" into a definite pattern, with a centre-ornament and pin-fastenings.

The only finger-ring that we found in these caskets was of somewhat poor type, composed of blue faience mounted with thin electron. The small but beautiful ivory box bearing a docket in hieratic on its lid, reading: "*Gold rings belonging to the funeral procession,*" and the massive gold rings tied up in the corner of a scarf, that were recovered in the Antechamber during our first season's work, very probably came from here.

Perhaps the most important objects among this collection of jewellery are the insignia of royalty; the two crozier-sceptres and two flagella. The crozier, or kind of pastoral staff, was one of the insignia of Osiris. It was held in the left hand of both the god and the king. It takes the form of a short staff ending at the top in a crook bent inwards and outwards, and in this case it is made up of sections of gold, dark blue glass, and obsidian, upon a bronze core. It was called "*hekat*" by the ancient Egyptians, and it may be said to have given origin to the pastoral staff used by cardinals and bishops. Both the specimens found here bear the cartouches of the king engraved upon their gold-capped ends. The flagellum, a kind of whip or scourge commonly known, especially in the Vulgate, as the "flail," was the complement to the crozier-sceptre and the second of the insignia proper of Osiris. It was held both by the god and by the king in the right hand, and was called "*nekhekhw.*" It consists of a short handle, bent at an acute angle at the top, to which are attached three "swingles" by means of beaded thongs, in such a manner as to enable them to swing freely. These two specimens are made in similar manner to the croziers, save for the swingles which have wooden cores in place of bronze. The larger example bears the prenomen and nomen of Tutankhamen; the smaller one bears his Aten name in place of the Amen name, suggesting that it belonged to the earlier part of the young king's reign, before he was converted to the worship of Amen. Its smaller size is also in keeping with this hypothesis. It becomes fairly evident that these insignia were but symbols of authority over the two principal factions in early times: the Husbandmen and the Shepherds.

With regard to the mirror-cases and their mirrors, we have the same tale to record. Their reflectors were made of solid metal and in consequence were stolen. Some fragments of the ivory portion of the handle of one of them were discovered in the Antechamber, where the thieves broke it off and cast it away. The mirror-case in the form of the symbol of "life" is lined with silver-foil; the second case, in shape symbolizing eternity, is lined with gold-foil; the mirrors were probably made of the corresponding metals.

The simpler whitened wood boxes held objects of the nature of vestments, like official garments, which were taken apparently for the value of their costly adornment. All that was left was a pair of sandals, some much deteriorated linen wraps, and a most interesting bead and gold ceremonial scarf suggesting an early form of a liturgical vestment like the modern stole. It is made up of seven rows of flat disk-shaped blue faience beads which, at intervals, are held in place by gold "spacers." The ends terminate in gold cartouches of Tutankhamen, "beloved of Ptah" and "beloved of Sokar," and, have fringes of "ankh" symbols. It is curved, so as to fit round the neck and must have been worn scarf-wise.

As previously mentioned the writing-outfit that was found thrown into one of the larger ornamental caskets, must have belonged to one of the other boxes in this room, but it is impossible to say definitely which of them it came from.

According to the funerary spells, known to us as the "Book of the Dead" (Chapter XCIV), the palette, or the scribe's outfit, was essential for the deceased. They were the implements of Thoth, the god of speech, writing and mathematics, and therefore were considered divine. A large number of funerary palettes, with imitation colours and reeds, obviously for ritualistic purposes, were discovered in the Annexe—another chamber in this tomb. The palettes and writing-outfit found here, I believe, were actually the private property of the king. One of these palettes is plated with gold and has its colours and reeds intact. It bears the Aten nomen of the king, who is "beloved of the great god Thoth," showing that it may have dated from the earlier part of the king's reign, and that the god Thoth was accepted during the so-called monotheism of Aten. The second palette, made of solid ivory, with its colours and reeds complete, bears the Amen form of the king's name, "beloved of Atum of Heliopolis," "Thoth," and "Amenre," which suggests it belonged to the later part of the reign. The colours, red and black, in both cases show evidence of having been used.

The complement of the palette, the pen-case, or to be more accurate, the reed-holder, is a

charming relic of the past, reminding one of the schoolboy of today. It takes the form of a column with palm-leaf capital; its elaborately decorated shaft and drum are hollowed out to receive the reeds, and the abacus, turning on a pivot, acts as the lid. It contained a number of fine reeds.

The palette and the reed-holder illustrate the composite hieroglyphic ideogram *sesh* for "writing," "scribe," and related words, which represents a palette, water-bowl and reed-holder. The ivory bowl found in our group, although it is not of the same shape as the vessel depicted in the ideogram, evidently served as the water-bowl. This bowl, turned out of a solid block of ivory, is $6\frac{1}{2}$ inches in diameter and shows the size of tusk that could be procured in those days in the upper reaches of the Nile.

The use of the elegant but curious mallet-like ivory instrument is not so easily recognized; however, its gold-capped top suggests that it is a burnisher, for smoothing the rough surfaces of the papyrus paper. It is evident that it belongs to this group, as a similar instrument was found with a scribe's outfit discovered by us some years ago in a Theban tomb.[6] The basket, made of papyrus-pith, lined with linen, and dedicated to Amenre, Herakhte, Ptah, and Sekhmet, also belongs to this outfit. Perhaps an idea of its original contents may be gathered by referring to that far less regal scribe's equipment previously mentioned.

But to return to the palette, the reed-holder and the little burnisher, it is of interest to notice the refinement, and exquisite delicacy which pervade them. They furnish a striking and beautiful instance of simplicity, as well as being mementoes of quaint antiquity which impart the charm of the Dynastic Ages. When one discovered the little basket, one hoped, upon opening it, to find some writing, perhaps a specimen of the boy's calligraphy; but it was void, like the whole tomb, of any form of document.

However much the deceased was identified with Osiris, it would appear that the dead feared the *corvées* (forced labour) for that deity, who, as king of the dead, would continue to till and irrigate the land and plant corn in the *fields of the blessed*, and would deal with his subjects in that world even as he did when he was their great king and agricultural teacher on this earth.

Hence, to escape future destiny, and to protect the deceased from such irksome duties as might be entailed by a *corvée*, we find stored in this room, as well as in the Annexe, large numbers of sepulchral-statuettes called *Shawabti*-figures, representing the king swathed in linen, mummiform. Such figures were originally made of *Shawabti*-wood, whence they derive their name; and their function, according to the sixth chapter of the "Book of the Dead," was to act as substitutes for the deceased in the Nether World, if he be called upon to perform any fatiguing duties, "*even as a man is bounden, to cultivate the fields, to flood the meadows, or to carry sand of the East to the West*." Upon the deceased being summoned, these figures are bidden: "*Then speak thou, 'Here am I.'*"

Their implements—the hoe, the pick, the yoke, basket and water-vessel—either depicted upon them, or as copper and faience models placed with them, clearly indicate the duty which they were supposed to perform for their deceased lord in the future life. That in this case these figures are effigies of the Osirian king becomes manifest from the names and titles upon them, and, in the finer examples, the attempt at likeness to Tutankhamen.

They were housed in numbers of wooden kiosks resting on sledges, wherein 413 figures and 1,866 model implements were packed. The vaulted roof (i.e. the lid) of each kiosk was carefully tied down with cord and sealed. The figures themselves were made of wood, wood painted, wood gesso-gilt, wood covered with gesso on linen and painted, quartzite, alabaster (calcite), white, yellow and crystalline limestone, grey and black granite, light, dark blue, violet, and white glazed pottery; some carved in the finest style, others modelled in almost primitive form. In the finer specimens, by their own symbolism is expressed the perfect serenity of death.

Mertaten's ivory palette, Tutankhamen's ivory and gold palettes, ivory burnisher and reed case

Engraved on the soles of the feet of six finely carved wood specimens, are dedications indicating that they were especially made and presented for the funeral by high officials and, no doubt, personal friends of Tutankhamen. These dedications were:

"Made by the true Servant who is beneficial to his Lord, the King's Scribe, Minnekht, for his Lord, the Osiris, Lord of the Two Lands, Nebkheprure, justified."

"Made by the King's Scribe, the General Minnekht, for his Lord, the Osiris, the King, Nebkheprure, justified."

"The Osiris, the King, Nebkheprure, justified, made by the Servant who makes to live the name of his Lord, the General Minnekht."

"Made by the Servant beloved of his Lord, the General Minnekht, for his Lord, the Osiris, the King, Nebkheprure, justified."

"Made by the Fanbearer on the right hand of the King, . . . Min[nekht], for his Lord, the Osiris, Nebkheprure, justified."

"Made by the Servant who is beneficial to his Lord, Nebkheprure, the Overseer of the Treasury, Maya."

Such dedications confirm Professors Spiegelberg's and Newberry's suggestion that figures of the kind were dedicated by servants of the deceased, who devoted their services to their master both in this life and that beyond the grave.

Minnekht is possibly the same man who excavated the tomb for King Ay in Wadyein, who is mentioned on an unpublished stela at Akhmim of the reign of Ay, and there are stelae of the same official in the British Museum and at Berlin.

Related to the *Shawabti*-figures and reminiscent of Osiris, is a kind of miniature effigy of the dead king that was found in this room in a small oblong chest, carefully padded with linen. Carved of wood, it represents a recumbent figure of the king, mummiform, as the divine prototype, lying on a funeral bier of lion-form. This "Osiride" figure of the king lies stretched out at length upon the bed; his head, covered with the *nemes*-headdress, bears the royal uraeus; his hands, free from the wrappings, grasp the emblems of Osiris—the crozier and flagellum sceptres, now unfortunately missing. On the left side a figure of the *Ba*-bird or "soul" protects the mummy with its left wing; opposite, a figure of a falcon, the (?) *Ka* or "spirit," protects the mummy with its right wing, and they seem to be no less than manifestations of divine protection on the part of the "Soul" and the "Spirit" of the deceased king. Placed with this effigy was a set of miniature implements—a pick, a hoe, a yoke and two baskets, of copper— similar to the equipment found with and belonging to the *Shawabti*-figures.

The dedications engraved upon the bier read: "*Made by the Servant who is beneficial to His Majesty, who seeks what is good and finds what is fine, and does it thoroughly for his Lord, who does [or, makes] excellent things in the Splendid Place, Overseer of Building-works in the Place of Eternity, the King's Scribe, Overseer of the Treasury, Maya.*"

"*Made by the Servant who is beneficial to his Lord, who seeks out excellent things in the Place of Eternity, Overseer of Building-works in the West, beloved of his Lord, doing what he [his Lord] says, who does not allow anything to go wrong, whose face is cheerful, when he does it [sic] with loving heart as a thing profitable to his Lord.*" "*The King's Scribe, beloved of his Lord, Overseer of the Treasury, Maya.*"

The inscriptions upon the effigy are: "*Words spoken by the justified King Nebkheprure: Descend, my Mother Nut, and spread thyself over me, and cause me to be the Imperishable Stars that are in thee.*" "*In honour with*"—Imseti, Hepy, Anubis who is in the place of embalmment, Anubis, Duamutef, Qebehsnewef, Horus and Osiris.[7]

An interesting and historical point regarding this effigy is that it was made by the Overseer of the Works in the Place of Eternity (i.e. the tomb), Maya, who, as we have just seen, also dedicated a *Shawabti*-figure to the king. He was in all probability responsible for the excavation of the king's tomb, and, in the eighth year of Horemheb, was commanded, with "his assistant the Steward of Thebes, Thothmes," to renew the burial of King Thothmes IV, which had suffered in the hands of the tomb-plunderers. This must have been some eleven years after the interment of Tutankhamen, and about the time, it would appear, when his tomb was resealed after the sundry plunderings that it had suffered. It is thus possible that Maya was also responsible for the resealing of Tutankhamen's tomb, for the seals employed on the tomb of Thothmes IV have a peculiar likeness to those used when Tutankhamen's tomb was reclosed.

During the reign of Tutankhamen, Maya bore the titles: "*Overseer of the Building-works in the Place of Eternity, Overseer of the Building-works in the West, Overseer of the Treasury, the King's Scribe.*" But in the reign of Horemheb we gather that he reached the dignity: "*The Fanbearer on the left of the King, the Leader of the Festival of Amen in Karnak,*" and that he was "*Son of the Doctor Aui, born of the Lady Urt.*"

A plain wooden box of oblong shape, which stood on the north side of the Canopic canopy, had its contents completely cleared by the tomb-plunderers. Its gable-shaped lid had been replaced the wrong way on, and only the packing material in its eight rectangular compartments was left. This material comprised pieces of papyrus reeds, shredded papyrus-pith and, at the bottom of each division, a small bundle of linen matting of long pile. There was not a trace of evidence as to what the original contents were, save that the careful arrangement of the packing suggested that the objects were of fragile nature—possibly glass.

Hitherto the discoveries in this tomb have been little more than a succession of objects, or series of objects, forming a brilliant funerary equipment, but here we come across unlooked-for surprises.

Placed on the top of the kiosks of *Shawabti*-figures was a small wooden anthropoid coffin, about thirty inches in length, fashioned like a coffin for a noble of the period. It was covered with a lustrous coat of black resin, gilded with bands of formulae pertaining to the guardian divinities and genii of the dead. It was tied with strips of linen at the neck and ankles, and sealed with the necropolis seal. It contained a second coffin of gesso-gilt wood, ornamented after the fashion of a royal coffin, but neither of these two coffins bore royal emblems, although the formulae inscribed upon them give the names of Tutankhamen. The second coffin contained a third small plain wood coffin, and, beside it, a solid gold statuette of Amenhetep III, rolled up in a separate piece of mummy cloth. Within this third coffin was a fourth, also made of wood, of anthropoid form, but not more than five inches in length. This last coffin was wrapped in linen, tied at the neck with a band of minute bead-work, sealed at the ankles, and was profusely anointed with unguents, as in the case of the king's burial. It bore the titles and name of Queen Tyi, and, within it, carefully folded in linen, was a plaited lock of her hair.

Such heirlooms as these—a lock of auburn hair of the Great Hereditary Princess, the Great Royal Wife, the Lady of the Two Lands, Tyi, and a statuette of her sovereign husband, Amenhetep III—are evidence of devotion. They were in all probability pieces of personal property that had been in the family, chattels descending by due succession. Tutankhamen, the ultimate heir, was the last of that ruling Amenhetep house; hence these heirlooms were buried with him. The gold statuette, suspended upon a chain ending with tasselled cords, to fasten it at the back of the neck, was a trinket and was treated as such; the lock of hair was human, the remains of a royal personage, for which reason it received the prerogative of a royal burial.

But even more extraordinary were the contents of two miniature anthropoid coffins that were placed, head to foot, in a wooden box beside the last-mentioned coffins. These were also fashioned in the manner such as would be used for a high personage. They were coated with a black lustrous resin, and ornamented with bands of gilt formulae pertaining to the tutelary

The coffin and mummy of a still-born child

divinities of the dead, but dedicated only to a nameless "Osiris" (i.e. deceased). The coffins were carefully fastened with strips of linen in three places—at the throat, at the centre, and at the ankles, and each fastening was sealed with clay bearing an impression of the necropolis seal. Each coffin contained an inner gilt coffin of similar design. In one case there was a small mummy preserved in accordance with burial custom of the Eighteenth Dynasty. It had a gesso-gilt mask (several sizes too large for it) covering its head. The linen wrappings enveloped a well preserved mummy of a still-born child. In the other case the inner coffin contained a slightly larger mummy of a child of premature birth, also wrapped in the prescribed fashion of the period.

These pathetic remains give much food for thought. With little doubt they were the offspring of Tutankhamen, and, although there is nothing to tell us emphatically, the probabilities are they were the issue of Ankhesenamen. Possibly, these *two* premature births were due merely to chance: the outcome of an abnormality on the part of the young queen. However, it must not be forgotten that: an accident to the expectant mother would have rendered the throne vacant for those eager to step in. But interpretation is the exclusive property of the historian, and an investigation of this kind calls for methodical, scientific and disinterested treatment.[8]

As I have mentioned, the coffins were placed side by side, head to feet, in a box. It is interesting, however, to know that the toes of the foot of the larger coffin had been hacked off because they prevented the lid of the box from closing properly. We noted a similar occurrence in the case of the king's outer coffin (page 133). Moreover, another curious fact lies in the absence of a mask over the mummy of the larger child. In the cache discovered by Mr. Theodore M. Davis, wherein remnants from the burial ceremonies of Tutankhamen were found, there was a gesso-gilt mask of similar dimensions and character to that found here on the smaller child. Could it be the one intended for this larger mummy, and that it was omitted owing to its being too small to fit over the head?

The contents of another box in this group certainly call for description. The box had been sealed in the usual way, but this fastening was broken and its lid left partially open, indicating that it had been ransacked by the robbers. The box was empty save for sixteen small model implements, one of which was found dropped on the floor beside the box. Unexpected surprises are often the fate of an archaeologist: these miniature model implements, fixed into hard, dark-grained wooden handles, proved to be of iron.

Two of the instruments are lancet-shaped, two are twisted at the point into graver-form, two are of chisel type with a slight waist in the shank, three are shaped like an ordinary chisel, three others are similar to those of the third group, but have longer handles, lastly, four comprise fan-shaped chisels set in short, flat handles. The blades are approximately half a millimetre in thickness, their length and breadth vary from 2·7 to 1·5, and 0·85 to 0·30 centimetres, respectively, and they are coated with the familiar red rust. Mr. A. Lucas, who examined them, adds:

> "They have all the appearance of iron coated with oxide; they are attracted by the magnet and fragments of the corroded surface give the usual chemical reaction for iron. The corrosion may be removed (and in one case was partially removed), by the means of strong nitric acid, leaving a bright surface of metallic iron."

Such objects seem to be out of place among ritualistic material belonging to a funeral cult of a king, nor is it conceivable that so large a chest could have contained only these small implements. Their frail and somewhat flimsy make suggests them to be models and not actual tools for use. And, if such be the case (they were not ritualistic), it throws a totally different light upon their significance in the tomb, as well as their historical value with regard to the use of iron in Egypt during dynastic times. By their being models, their presence here might be on account of the new or unusual metal; perhaps they were gifts to the king, to record its arrival or discovery in Egypt. In any case, while recognizing their historical importance, a warning at least is necessary, lest we rush into absurd revelations with regard to that metal and its use by the ancient Egyptians.

Although iron ore is fairly plentiful in the eastern desert of Egypt, and in the Sinaitic Peninsula, and although the extraction of copper required greater metallurgical skill, the Egyptians were almost entirely metallurgists of copper and bronze. It is not until this period that we have any real authentic proof of the use of iron by them, and even in this reign probably only as a strange and new metal. Copper and its successor, bronze, are the common metals through the whole of the Egyptian dynastic period, and iron objects are singularly scarce in Egypt even in the succeeding dynasties and foreign dominations.

Based upon the discovery of accidental pieces of iron, it has been claimed that iron was known and used by the Egyptians since the time of the Great Pyramid, as well as in pre-dynastic days. On the other extreme, I have noticed it mentioned that the scarcity of iron among Egyptian antiquities was due to the fact that the relics are in most cases the paraphernalia of tombs, and that iron being considered an impure metal by the ancient Egyptians was never used by them for religious purposes.

Such arguments I believe to be untenable. For, in the first case, it has been my lot to sift the dust of the plundered tombs of Amenhetep I and Thothmes I, the two tombs of Queen Hatshepsut, the tombs of Thothmes IV and Amenhetep III, and among the numerous fragments of objects, including the smallest beads and minute pieces of copper and bronze discovered in those tombs, I have not found a single trace of iron until the discovery of this tomb, wherein nineteen separate objects in that metal were found. Moreover, while excavating for many years in the Valley of the Kings, I have found in the various strata of dynastic debris numbers of bronze chisel points, that were broken off during use by the masons when they were hewing out the royal hypogaea; but I never found a vestige of iron, much less an iron tool. In the second case, if iron was considered impure by the Egyptians, why were iron emblems such as an *Urs* pillow and an Eye-of-Horus, as well as an iron dagger, placed on the hallowed remains of Tutankhamen? As a matter of fact, from his reign onwards, we find special amulets made of that material for the dead. In this tomb, two of the objects were certainly ritualistic, the others possibly being specimens—at least sixteen of them appear to be mere copies of artisan's implements.

Let us for a moment look at all the collections of Egyptian antiquities in Europe, including the outstanding collection in the Cairo Museum where there are over 50,000 specimens of every kind of object, and see what authentic examples there are of iron. It will, I think, suffice to say here that among all that material dating from the pre-dynastic period down to the last Egyptian dynasties—the result of research-work in Egypt for over a century—only twelve to thirteen instances of iron can be recorded, out of which, including this discovery, only about five can be said to be of indisputable dynastic origin. That is about all we have among—I dare not say how many—tens of thousands of Egyptian antiquities.

Surely such facts should point to the real truth. The Egyptians, excepting perhaps on rare occasions, did not deal with iron. They were a very conservative people; they were metallurgists of copper and bronze, and all their wonderful work was done with those metals.

In conclusion, the historical value of these particular specimens is, I think, more from the point of view of the introduction of iron in Egypt, than the actual use of that metal by the Egyptians. They are undoubted proof of the knowledge of iron in Egypt at this period, but not necessarily of its use to any extent in the country; and, I should here add, that with the exception of the king's dagger all the examples of iron in this tomb show crudeness in their workmanship.

To return to the box in which those iron implements were discovered, there is a possible chance that the four *Ankh*-torches and lamps, that were found on the cheetah-couch[9] in the Antechamber, came from this chest. We have, in several instances, sufficient evidence to prove that metal objects stored in this room were passed into the Antechamber by the robbers, where they evidently examined them, took or discarded them, or broke off parts of them, according to their thievish greed. Those torch-holders and lamps certainly did not appear to be in their proper place; parts of them were missing, and their wooden pedestals, coated with black resin, coincide with blotches of similar black material found on the bottom of the interior of the box. Their dimensions—the height and area they would occupy—agree with the capacity of the box. The gilding upon the torch-holders might have been mistaken for gold in an imperfect light, and the deception discovered upon a closer scrutiny in the Antechamber. This, at least, is a conjecture in the absence of any other explanation.

In the north-west corner of this chamber, leant against the wall, was the king's bow-case, ornamented with very fine marquetry decoration peculiar to the Eighteenth Dynasty, and particularly so to the reign of Tutankhamen. As a matter of fact, the decoration of this bow-case covers two provinces of ornament, namely, the relieved and the flat. The relieved ornament is rendered in embossed (thin) sheet-gold, upon a specially prepared under-surface; the flat ornament, which is the main feature of this bow-case, comprises a marquetry of different kinds of barks, applied strips of tinted leather and gold-foil, with here and there iridescent beetles' wings. It is a kind of decoration which vies in effect and quality with painting, and causes admiration for the patient and skilful workmanship of those ancient craftsmen.

On both the recto and verso of the bow-case, the scheme of ornament is symbolic as well as traditional, the principal theme being idealized hunting scenes, in which the king is the central figure. The framework of the case and the borders surrounding its panels are decorated with garland, palmette, and diaper patterns, which include hieroglyphic script. Towards the tapering ends of the case, which terminate in violet faience heads of cheetahs with gilded manes, are small symbolic scenes wherein the king, represented as a human-headed lion, tramples upon Egypt's alien foes. The central panels, of embossed gold, represent the king in his chariot, hunting with bow and arrow, accompanied by his hounds, depicted running beside or in front of his steeds, barking, or harassing the quarry. The triangular panels on either side represent, in the finest marquetry work, various fauna—denizens of the desert—stricken by the king's arrows.

This bow-case evidently belonged to one of the king's hunting chariots that were found dismantled in this room, to which it was fastened by means of copper attachments expressly made for the purpose. It contained three neatly made composite bows, now, unfortunately, in a parlous condition, their gelatinous cores at some early period having become viscid, with the result that they leaked out, and dried into a solid black mass.

A critical examination of the zoology displayed in the triangular panels is not without interest. The red antelopes with characteristic long face, and high crest for the angulated lyrate horns, with moderately long and hairy tail, are sufficiently distinctive to identify as representing one of the North African species of the hartebeest. The white antelopes with long horns are either the algazel or white oryx (*O. leucoryx*), or possibly, from the straightness of their horns, the white Arabian oryx (*O. beatrix*). The smaller sandy-coloured antelopes, with sub-lyrate horns, are probably the common dorcas gazelle, or a near allied species. They, like the larger antelope already identified, and also the desert hare depicted on the same panels, are notably inhabitants of the open desert districts, such as the scenes seem to represent. The goat-like animal, with long horns which rise from the crest of the head and bend gradually backwards, having ridges on the front surface, and terminating in smooth tips, obviously characterizes a species of ibex (*Capra ? Sinaitica*). Such antelopes inhabit elevated spots, especially the more mountainous districts. Another somewhat incompatible detail is, that hunting in a chariot with bow and arrow implies a daylight sport, yet we find in these scenes the striped hyena, nocturnal in its habits, preferring by day the gloom of caves or the burrows which it occasionally forms. Another puzzling detail is that some of the ibex are represented as having large and dark blotches—a feature, I believe, unknown among the African, Asiatic, and European species of that animal.

On the Old and Middle Kingdom monuments, both the oryx and the ibex occur domesticated, and they were fattened for the table. Young ibex kids can be brought up on goat's milk, and readily tamed, and, as ibex will propagate with the domestic goat (Cuvier), it is possible that the spotted kind depicted here is the progeny resulting from such a source. If such were the case, it throws a totally different light upon these scenes, and presents a very interesting point with regard to Pharaonic sporting pursuits. For it suggests the idea that they possibly bred and preserved animals for hunting, and that they had special sanctuaries, or enclosures, for the purpose, like the old Persian *pairidaeza*—a park, or enclosure, in which animals were kept. Hunting within kraals or zarebas, in some instances large areas surrounded by netting, is to be found represented among the mural decorations of the ancient Egyptian tombs.

Lastly, with the dismembered parts of two hunting chariots found in this chamber, was a whip bearing an inscription: "*The King's-son, Captain of the Troops, Thothmes.*" Who was this royal prince?—who, to have been "Captain of the Troops" during the reign of Tutankhamen, could not have been very young. Was he a son of Thothmes IV, or was he a son of Amenhetep III? That problem has yet to be solved. If he was a son of Thothmes IV, and was living at the time of Tutankhamen's burial, he must have reached at least sixty or more years of age; whereas, if he was a son of Amenhetep III, as one would suspect him to have been, he would not have been more than about thirty-five years of age at the time of Tutankhamen's death. Circumstantial evidence of this kind should have some bearing upon the possibility of that prince's parentage.

21

The Annexe

S TRANGE AND BEAUTIFUL OBJECTS call for wonder, conjecture and fair words, but are they not all signs of the thought and progress of the age to which they belong? Facts, too, also give food for reflection.

During the previous two seasons in the innermost Treasury we found little cause for criticism upon the general arrangement and state of the objects with which we had to deal. In this winter's work, however, we must qualify our account with a grain of question!

In contrast to the comparative order and harmony of the contents of the innermost Treasury, we find in this last chamber—the Annexe or Store-room—a jumble of every kind of funerary chattels, tumbled any way one upon the other, almost defying description. Bedsteads, chairs, stools, footstools, hassocks, game-boards, baskets of fruits, every kind of alabaster vessel and pottery wine-jars, boxes of funerary figures, toys, shields, bows and arrows, and other missiles, all turned topsy-turvy. Caskets thrown over, their contents spilled; in fact, everything in confusion.

Doubtless this confusion was the work of plunderers, but in the other chambers there had been a perfunctory attempt to restore order. The responsibility for this utter neglect would, therefore, seem to rest a good deal on the necropolis officials, who, in their task to put to rights the Antechamber, the Burial Chamber and the innermost Treasury after the robbery, had neglected this little room altogether.

To exaggerate the confusion that existed would be difficult; it was but an illustration of both drama and tragedy. While contemplating its picture of mingled rapacity and destruction, one felt that one could visualize the robbers' hurried scramble for loot—gold and other metals being their natural quarry; everything else they seem to have treated in the most brutal fashion. There was hardly an object that did not bear marks of depredation, and before us—upon one of the larger boxes—were the very foot-prints of the last intruder.

This little store-room was but another witness of the neglect and dishonour that the royal tombs had suffered. Not a monument in the Valley but bears proof of how false and fugitive is the homage of man. All its tombs have been plundered, all have been outraged and dishonoured.

During the last days of November 1927, we were able to begin this final stage of our investigations. Two days of somewhat strenuous work had to be spent in clearing the way to the little doorway that conducts to this apartment. The southern end of the Antechamber, where its doorway is situated, was then occupied by a number of large roof-sections of the dismantled shrines that had shielded the sarcophagus which, for convenience, were put there during the earlier part of our work in the tomb. These we were obliged to shift to the northern end of the Antechamber, so as to allow sufficient space for access to this store-room as well as for the transport of the material that it contained.

One of the king's shawabti's

The doorway to this room, only 51 inches high, and 37 inches wide, had been blocked up with rough splinters of limestone and was plastered over on the outside. The plaster, while still wet, had received numerous impressions of four different sepulchral seals of the king. When it was discovered, only the upper part of the blocking remained, the thieves having broken through the lower portion. This breach was never mended. The devices of the seal-impressions upon the upper part of the blocking read: (1) *"The King of Upper and Lower Egypt, Nebkheprure, who spent his life making images of the gods, that they might give him incense, libation and offerings every day"*; (2) *"Nebkheprure, who made images of Osiris and built his house as in the beginning"*; (3) *"Nebkheprure—Anubis triumphant over the 'Nine Bows'"*; and (4) *"Their Overlord, Anubis, triumphant over the four captive peoples."*

The deciphering of the very imperfect seal-impressions is mainly, if not wholly, due to the kind assistance rendered by Professor Breasted and Dr. Alan Gardiner. They spent several days studying them under somewhat difficult circumstances during the earlier stages of the discovery.

When the thieves made their incursion, as I have already mentioned, they forced a hole through this sealing of the doorway; and it was through that hole that we made our first inspection of this room.

The room, comparatively small—14 feet long, 8 feet 6 inches wide, and 8 feet 5 inches high—gave no suggestion of any kind of finish, nor paid any tribute to taste. It is roughly cut out of the bed-rock, and was intended for its purpose—a store-room.

Traces of the dilapidations of time were visible; the rock-cut walls and ceiling were discoloured by damp arising from infrequent saturations.

The history of this little room, although it may have been unfortunate, was nevertheless romantic. There was something bewildering, yet interesting, in the scene which lay before us. The incongruous medley of material, jostled in wanton callousness and mischief, concealed, no doubt, a strange story if it could be disclosed. Our electric lamps threw a mass of light upon its crowded contents, bringing out many an odd feature in strong relief among that accumulation of funerary paraphernalia heaped up to the height of some four or five feet. Our light illumined strange objects lying one upon another and protruding from remote places and corners. Close by, turned upside down, was a large chair like a faldstool, decorated in the taste of a distant age. Stretching across the room and resting precariously on their sides, were bedsteads of a form such as is used in the regions of the Upper Nile of today. Here a vase, and there a tiny figure gazed at one with forlorn expression. There were weapons of various kinds, baskets, pottery and alabaster jars and gaming-boards crushed and mingled with stones that had fallen from the hole that had been forced through the sealed doorway. In a corner opposite, poised high up, as if in a state of indecision, was a broken box bulging with delicate faience vessels, ready to collapse at any moment. In the midst of a miscellany of every kind of chattel and funerary emblem, a cabinet upon slender legs stood almost unscathed. Wedged between boxes and under objects of many shapes, was a boat of alabaster, a lion, and a figure of a bleating ibex. A fan, a sandal, a fragment of a robe, a glove!—keeping odd company with emblems of the living and of the dead. The scene, in fact, seemed almost as if contrived, with theatrical artifice, to produce a state of bewilderment upon the beholder.

When one peers into a chamber arranged and sealed by pious hands of the long past, one is filled with emotion; it seems as if the very nature of the place and objects hushes the spectator into silent reverence. But here, in this chamber, where nothing but confusion prevailed, the sobering realization of a prodigious task that lay before one took the place of that emotion. One's mind became occupied with the problem, how it could best be dealt with.

The method we were finally obliged to adopt, to remove those three-hundred-odd pieces of antiquity, was, to say the least, somewhat prosaic. To begin with, sufficient floor-space had to

An alabaster vase

The interior of the Annexe

be made for our feet, and that had to be done as best we could, head downwards, bending over the sill, which was rather more than three feet above the floor-level. Whilst carrying out this uncomfortable operation, every precaution had to be taken lest a hasty movement should cause an avalanche of antiquities precariously piled up and beyond our reach. More than often, to save an object of heavy nature, so situated that the slightest disturbance would cause it to fall, we were obliged to lean over and reach far out, supported by a rope-sling under our arm-pits which was held by three or four men standing in the Antechamber. In that manner, by always removing one by one the uppermost object in reach, we gained ingress and gradually collected the treasures. Each object, or group of objects, had first to be photographed, numbered and recorded, before they were moved. It was by means of those records that we were eventually able to reconstruct to a certain degree what had previously occurred in the chamber.

I must confess that my first impression was that the positions of those objects were meaningless, and that there was little or nothing to be learned from such disorder. But as we proceeded in our investigations, and removed them piece by piece, it became evident that many data could be gleaned as to their original order and subsequent chaos. The confusion naturally rendered evidence very difficult to interpret, and it was also disconcerting to find that our deductions, no matter how correct they may have been, could seldom be definitely proven. Nevertheless, careful examination of the facts, such as they were, disclosed one important point, and that point was: that two separate thefts of quite different nature had taken place in that little apartment. The first theft—for gold, silver and bronze—was perpetrated by the famous tomb metal-robbers, who ransacked the four chambers of the tomb for all such portable material. The second robbery was evidently by another class of thief, who sought only the costly oils and unguents contained in the numerous stone vessels. It also became clear that this Annexe was intended for a store-room, like the similar small chambers in other royal tombs of the Eighteenth Dynasty, for housing oils, unguents, wine and food. But in this case an overflow of other material belonging to the burial equipment had been stacked on the top of its proper contents.

The material that might be termed extraneous was, I believe, put there, not so much for the want of space, but probably owing to the absence of system, when the equipment was being placed in the tomb. For example, it will be remembered that below the Hathor-couch in the Antechamber there was a pile of oviform wooden cases containing a variety of meats. Those by rights should have been stored in the Annexe. But owing to some oversight they seem to have been forgotten, and, the doorway of the Annexe having been closed, they had to be put in some convenient place in the Antechamber, which, in natural sequence, was the last room of the tomb to be closed. Also, part of the series of the funerary boats and figures (*shawabtis*), placed in the innermost Treasury, were found in this Annexe.

From the facts gleaned, we may reconstruct more or less the sequence of events that took place: firstly, nearly forty pottery wine-jars were placed on the floor at the northern end of this Annexe; next to these were added at least thirty-five heavy alabaster vessels containing oils and unguents; stacked beside them, some even on top, were one hundred and sixteen baskets of fruits; the remaining space was then used for other furniture—boxes, stools, chairs and bedsteads, etc.— that were piled on top of them. The doorway was then closed and sealed. This manifestly was carried out before any material was placed in the Antechamber, since nothing could have been passed into this Annexe, nor could the doorway have been closed, after the introduction of the material belonging to the Antechamber.

When the metal-robbers made their first incursion, it is evident that they crept under the Thueris-couch in the Antechamber, forced their way through the sealed doorway of the Annexe, ransacked its entire contents for portable metal objects, and were, no doubt, responsible for a great deal of the disorder found in that chamber. Subsequently—it is impossible to say when—a second robbery took place. The objective in this case was the costly oils and unguents contained in the alabaster jars. This last robbery had been carefully thought out. The stone vessels being far too heavy and cumbersome to carry away bodily, the thieves came provided with more convenient receptacles, such as leather bags or water-skins,[1] to take away the spoil. There was not a stopper of a jar that had not been removed, not a jar that had not been emptied. On the interior walls of some of the vessels, that had contained viscous ointments, the finger-marks of those thieves are visible to-day. To get at those heavy stone vessels, the furniture piled on top of them was evidently turned over and thrown helter-skelter from side to side. Thus, by realizing the probable cause, the reader may readily guess the effect.

The knowledge of this second robbery throws light upon a problem that had puzzled us ever since the beginning of the discovery of the tomb. Why, throughout its funerary equipment, had quite insignificant stone vessels been tampered with? Why were some of them left empty lying on the floors of the chambers, and others taken out and discarded in the entrance passage? The greases, or oils, that they once contained had, no doubt, a far greater value in those days than possibly we imagine. It also gives a reason for the tomb having been twice reclosed, as traces on the sealed entrance and inner doorway of the passage signified. I believe also that the odd baskets and simple alabaster jars that were found scattered on the floor of the Antechamber came from the group in this Annexe. They are so obviously of the same class, and were probably taken out for convenience by the thieves. The same argument holds good of the solitary *Shawabti*-figure discovered leaning against the north wall of the Antechamber. It surely must have come from one of the broken *Shawabti*-boxes in this last little room—for others like it were found there.

Tradition holds that in burial custom each article belonging to tomb equipment had its prescribed place in the tomb. However, experience has shown that no matter how true the governing conventions may be, seldom have they been strictly carried out. Either the want of forethought with regard to requisite space, or the want of system when placing the elaborate paraphernalia in the tomb-chambers, overcame tradition. We have never found any strict order, we have found only approximate order.

Such were the general facts and impressions gathered during this final part of our investigations in the tomb. How much of the interpretation is absolute fact, how much the embellishment of conjecture, would be very difficult, if not impossible, to prove. It may be said, however, that it is a fair interpretation of what had occurred. If one were to record the numerous memoranda taken down at the time of the actual *déblaiement*, for the purpose of disentangling facts, the reader would be easily lost in the labyrinth of both obscure and conflicting data—the forest would be hidden by its trees. For that reason I have given what I believe to be a fair summary of the whole problem. Nothing can ever change the fact that we have undoubtedly found evidence in this tomb of love and respect mingled with want of order and eventual dishonour. This tomb, though it did not wholly share the fate of its kindred, though mightier mausoleums, was nevertheless robbed—twice robbed—in Pharaonic times, and one might here well repeat Washington Irving's words: "What is the security of a tomb?" I am also of the belief that both robberies took place within a few years after the burial. Facts such as the transfer of Akhenaten's mummy from its original tomb at El Amarna to its rock-cut cell at Thebes, apparently within the reign of Tutankhamen; the renewal of the burial of Thothmes IV, in the eighth year of the reign of Horemheb, after it had been robbed of its treasures, throw considerable light upon the state of affairs in the royal necropolis at that Age. The religious confusion of the State at that time; the collapse of the Dynasty; the retention of the throne by the Grand Chamberlain and probable Regent, Ay, who was eventually supplanted by the General Horemheb, were incidents which we may assume helped towards such forms of pillage. It must have been a considerable time before even the conquering Horemheb himself was able to restore order out of the confusion that existed at that period, establish his kingdom and enforce the laws of his State. In any case the evidence afforded by those two burials and by this tomb, prove how the royal tombs suffered even within their own Dynasty. The wonder is, how it came about that this royal burial, with all its riches, escaped the eventual fate of the twenty-seven others in the Valley.

22

The objects found in the Annexe

IN THE PRECEDING CHAPTER I have endeavoured to describe the state in which we found the Annexe, its impressions upon the spectator, and the incidents, suggested by our observations, which may have occurred after it was originally closed. In the present chapter, I propose to describe the principal antiquities that we were able to salve from the wreckage. It was astonishing how some quite delicate objects had survived almost unscathed, in spite of the ill-treatment that they had suffered. For reasons given presently I shall divide the material into two sections.

At the risk of being tedious I repeat that, apart from the exploits of the robbers, clearly there was a suggestion—one might even say demonstration—of confusion, or want of proper system, when the objects were originally deposited. Consequently, evidence as to the intended uses of the various chambers of the tomb is not absolutely clear; moreover, the tomb itself is not orthodox in plan, and is much contracted. Hence, with reference to the different kinds of funerary equipment, traditionally attributed by the ancient Egyptians to each chamber, much of the evidence gathered still requires sifting and testing. Nevertheless, it may be safely assumed that this Annexe was merely a store-room intended for provisions, wines, oils and unguents. For this reason, the objects described in Part One of this chapter may be termed "extraneous," since possibly they were not really intended for the room, but were placed in it for want of space elsewhere. The second group—Part Two—I believe to be the traditional contents of this store-room, called the Annexe. The nature of the material seems also to call for this division.

Part One

On the top of this mass of material, and stretching from side to side of the chamber, were three large bedsteads, resembling in form the modern Sudanese *angarib*. They have wooden frames, a string webbing, at one end foot-panels, and are supported by fore and hind legs of feline type. One of them, of not much account, was badly broken; the second specimen, of ebony gilt, although of not very fine work, was in fair condition; but the third specimen, of carved ebony overlaid with stout sheet-gold, was in almost its original state, save for warping due to its having rested so long upon an uneven surface. The proportions of this last bedstead are perhaps finer than any of the others found in this tomb. From its characteristics it was evidently of El Amarna make, the subject of its ornament being purely floral, namely, garlands of petals and fruits, bouquets, clumps of papyrus and red-tipped sedge, chased and embossed upon burnished gold, and signifying Northern and Southern Egypt. It is interesting to note how the strengthening transverse stretchers under its frame-work are curved, in order to be clear from

A folding camp bedstead

sagging of the webbing, when the bedstead was slept upon.

Underneath a mass of every kind of chattel at the southern end of the room, we found a fourth very interesting folding bedstead, made expressly for travelling purposes. It is constructed of a light wood painted white, and is of similar design to the specimens already described, but it conveniently folds into one third of its size by means of heavy bronze hinges.

I shall now turn to the most varied and familiar articles of domestic furniture: chairs, stools, footstools and a hassock, which were appanages of seigneurial right and, in fact, at that period the emblems of authority.

Wedged topsy-turvy in the south-east corner, between the wall and one of the bedsteads, was an elaborate chair, perhaps better named a "faldstool," which vies in rank with the so-called secular throne found in the Antechamber. There is nothing to tell us definitely its use, but its extremely elaborate detail, and its austere appearance, suggest that it is of an entirely different order from the rest of the chairs. Indeed, in character, it seems appropriate only to a "chair of state," like the specimen named "the secular throne," which is far too rich and ornate for any ordinary house use. In point of fact, it would appear to have been the king's ecclesiastical throne when presiding as the highest spiritual authority; and, in many ways, it recalls the bishop's chair, or faldstool, of our cathedrals today. It is of faldstool-form, but, while retaining its folding shape, it had at that early period already become rigid and acquired a back.

Its ample, curved seat, fashioned in the semblance of flexible leather, is made of ebony inlaid with irregular-shaped pieces of ivory, which imitate the motley markings of a piebald hide. The central portion of the seat, however, is ornamented with a series of small rectangular panels of ivory, stained to represent various other hides, including that of the cheetah. The seat is supported by cross legs of folding-stool type; these are carved in ebony and inlaid with ivory in the shape of heads of geese, and are partially bound with thin sheet-gold. Between the stretchers and the foot-bars is an openwork gilt-wood ornament symbolizing the union of the "Two Kingdoms"—Upper and Lower Egypt—the greater part of which was wrenched away by the dynastic tomb-robbers in search for loot.

The upper part of the upright curved back-panel is overlaid with sheet-gold, and richly inlaid with faience, glass, and natural stones. Here the decoration incorporates the Aten disk and names, the pre-nomen and Aten-nomen of the king, and the Nekhebet vulture holding single ostrich-feather fans. Below this device is a series of inlaid rails and stiles enclosing ivory and ebony panels inscribed with various designations of the king. Of particular interest are these inscriptions, for they give both the Aten and the Amen forms of the king's nomen, and in all cases the Aten form remains unchallenged. This faldstool is thus an important historical document with regard to the politico-religious vacillations of the reign, for, from the fact that the Aten and the Amen elements occur side by side, it would appear that the young king's return to the older faith of Thebes was gradual in transition and not spontaneous.

At the back, to give rigidity to this folding-stool form of chair, upright laths were fixed to the back-panel, the seat and the back foot-bar. The upper rail and supporting laths are encrusted with designations of the king, which include the Aten form of his name. The back of the back-panel is overlaid with sheet-gold, and upon it, finely embossed, is a large Nekhebet vulture with drooping wings surrounded by various complimentary epithets.

The strengthening framework of this chair, warped by infrequent saturations of humidity which the tomb had suffered, no longer serves its purpose, for its tenons do not now meet their mortised sockets. Thus this relic of authority offered more than one problem in the matter of reparation, even though it were only sufficient to ensure its safe transportation from the tomb to the Cairo Museum. With this chair was found its companion footstool, equally rich in workmanship. It is made of wood, overlaid with violet glazed pottery, and inlaid with ivory, glass, and natural stones. Upon the "tread" are the traditional nine alien foes of Egypt, wrought in gold, ebony, and cedar-wood, arranged so that the king's feet would rest upon Egypt's enemies.

There was something almost humorous, yet pathetic, in the situation of a small white chair possibly from the royal nursery, high-backed, animal-footed, turned upside-down among such plebeian society as oil and wine jars, and hampers of fruits, with which it was obliged to associate. Like its companion stool with gilded ornament between its seat and stretchers, it clung to the bedsteads of the royal household. Jammed down below the door-sill of the chamber, and crushed by heavy stone vessels, was another stool, also painted white, but in this case three-legged and with semi-circular seat. This somewhat ornate specimen has an open carved wood seat representing two lions bound head to tail. The rim is decorated with a spiral pattern. Like its companions just described, the space between the stretchers that brace the framework of the legs is filled in with open-work traditional throne ornament—the "Two Kingdoms"—Upper and Lower Egypt—bound together under the monarchy. In addition to its peculiar shape, it has a particular feature of its own which makes it in some ways unique. Most Egyptian chairs and stools have either the conventional bovine and feline or sometimes duck-headed legs, whereas the legs of this semi-circular stool are of canine form. Although thus fallen into decline and discoloured, these chairs and stools still bear traces of their former environment.

Opposite the doorway, on the top of the material stacked against the west wall, was a rush-work garden-chair. The seat and back were covered, and the sides of the under-framework trimmed, with painted papyrus. The painted decoration on the back consisted of petals of the lotus-corolla, and on the seat the "Nine Bows," i.e. bound Asiatic and African prisoners in elaborate costume. The rush-work (mostly split papyrus stalks) and the papyrus covering, were too far decayed to allow of more than a few fragments being preserved.

There were also several miniature rectangular footstools tucked away in sundry places. These are made of cedar-wood or ebony, one of them combining the two kinds of wood and being embellished with ivory. Their dimensions seem appropriate only for a child. Of particular interest was a hassock such as we might find in use today. Unfortunately it bears marks of

A three-legged circular stool of wood, painted white

having seen better days, but sufficient of it remains to show that it doubtless figured in some ceremony. Though of ordinary rush-work, covered with plain linen, it is enriched with compli-cated and brilliant polychrome bead-work, depicting alien captives bound and prone around a central rosette. This device, a conventional ornament usually associated in ancient Egypt with footstools and mats, is encircled with garland patterns, and the sides of the hassock are enclosed in a bead net-work of lace-like appearance. The footstools were obviously for the regal foot; maybe the hassock was intended for the royal knee.

Lodged in a very precarious position, amidst miscellanea in the centre of the chamber, was a cabinet, standing on four slim legs, and about twenty-three inches in height. It is one of those quaint pieces of antiquity which has all the peculiar charm of the lighter Egyptian furniture, as well as all the aspects of what it pleases us to call "modern" workmanship. Its rich, dark red cedar-wood panels are quite plain; its ebony uprights, rails, and stretchers are encrusted with eulogistic titulary and other designations of the king in hieroglyphic script; and between the bottom of the cabinet and the stretchers it has an open-work frieze symbolizing "All Life and Good Fortune," made up of a fretwork of alternate gilt and plain ebony emblems. The top folds back on bronze hinges fixed to the top rail of the back of the cabinet. On the top and front panel are gilt knobs, to which a cord and a seal were once attached. If one may judge by the hieratic docket written on the panel of its fellow cabinet, which was found broken in this chamber, this piece of furniture was probably intended for the fine linen raiments of the king. But its contents had been scattered, or perhaps stolen, and in it we found four very fine head-rests that had evidently been put there after the robbery.

The first of these head-rests is a magnificent example of ivory carving—perhaps the finest piece of Egyptian New Empire symbolical art we have hitherto discovered—and in addition to receiving the tint of age, it is in perfect preservation. The theme of its design seems to be an impression of the official religion, and its subject founded upon one of the early conceptions of the "cosmos," when all things fell into their places. The myth it represents conceives Geb and Nut—the Earth-god and the Sky-goddess—as husband and wife, separated by their father, Shu, the god of Atmosphere. The caryatidal figure, Shu, thrusts himself between earth and sky, and raises the sky-goddess into the heights, together with all the gods hitherto created. Nut, the goddess of the sky, took possession of the gods, counted them, and made them into stars. At the east and west extremities of earth (i.e. the foot of the head-rest) will be noticed the lions of "Yesterday and The Morrow." They probably symbolize the rising and setting of Re, the Sun-god and progenitor of all beings, mortal and immortal, or it may be that they represent the coming and going of Osiris—the deceased. The figure representing Shu (atmosphere), raising heaven into the heights and the two *arit*—lions of the East and West horizons—are full of dignity. The observer cannot but be sensible of the serenity of this little monument, inspired, it would seem, by a kindly and happy feeling that the king, when at rest, would lay his head in heaven and, perhaps, become a star in the firmament. The second head-rest takes the shape of a miniature folding stool in carved and tinted ivory. Although it is a fine example of craftsmanship, it lacks the supreme dignity of the first piece. Instead, we find in it the love of the grotesque, its main feature being the head (tinted dark green) of the hideous male demon Bes —a household god held in superstitious veneration, who was of dwarf stature, his duty being to amuse the gods with his tambourine and to tend the divine children. The third head-rest is of rich lapis lazuli blue faience. In this case the aesthetic takes the place of the symbolical, for bold form and rich colour—lapis lazuli blue embellished with gold—is its main feature. In the same manner is fashioned the fourth head-rest, which is wrought out of opaque turquoise-blue glass, with a collar of embossed gold around its stem. These head-rests belong to the ritualistic equipment entailed by Egyptian burial custom. The deceased is given them for his future benefit. The state artificers, while keeping within the limits of the convention, seem to have taken pride in rendering them for their royal master as simple and beautiful as possible. They have no sameness; each piece has some salient feature, which makes it a variety of the traditional *urs*-pillow prescribed by the "Book of the Dead," to "lift up the head of the prostrate One."

Among the series of ornamental caskets, a much ill-treated but wonderful specimen was found at the northern end of the chamber. The lid was thrown in one corner, while the empty casket itself was heaved into another, and its legs and panels damaged by the weight of material heaped upon it. Although its ornamentation comprises an ivory veneer, beautifully carved in relief like an early Greek coin, and stained with simple colours, it has borders of encrusted faience and semi-translucent calcite, and may be placed in the same category as the painted casket discovered in the Antechamber. The central panel of the lid is certainly the unsigned work of a master, but, in contradistinction to the warlike scenes upon the painted casket, the motive here is purely domestic. It depicts the young king and queen in a pavilion bedecked with vines and festoons of flowers. The royal couple, wearing floral collarettes and dressed in semi-court attire, face one another; the king, leaning slightly on his staff, accepts from his consort bouquets of papyrus and lotus-blooms; while, in a frieze below, two court maidens gather flowers and the fruit of the mandrake for their charges. Above their majesties are short inscriptions: "*The Beautiful God, Lord of the Two Lands, Nebkheprure, Tutankhamen, Prince of the Southern Heliopolis, resembling Re.*" "*The Great-Royal-Wife, Lady of the Two Lands, Ankhesenamen, May she live.*" The subjects of the side and end panels pertain to the chase, their compositions being friezes of animals, and the king and queen fowling and fishing, much like the scene upon the small shrine that was found in the Antechamber. As to the contents of the casket, when deposited in the tomb, we can only make a conjecture.

There were also three small chests, which are interesting mementoes of the king's youth. Their damaged parts were scattered here and there, they have bronze staples for suspension, like panniers, and were evidently intended to be used for travelling purposes, strapped either on the back of a beast of burden, or over the shoulders of a slave. They have a framework of ebony, panels of cedar-wood, and are inlaid with ebony and ivory. The dockets written upon their lids tell us that they were: "The linen chests of His Majesty, when he was a youth," and that they contained—I imagine this to be a subsequent docket—incense, gum, antimony, some jars and gold grasshoppers. We found pieces of incense and gum (resin), antimony powder, and small jars of faience, gold, and silver, dispersed on the floor of the chamber, but nothing in the way of gold grasshoppers!

Scarcely any object has such peculiar interest as a box especially made for the king's head-wear, that had been thrown among a lot of wine-jars at the northern end of this room. Its very domestic nature makes it at once appreciated by everyone. It is a legacy from the daily life of the past, and, one might even say, the prototype of the hat-box that is in use today. Save for a simple blue and yellow faience and semi-translucent calcite decoration bordering its panels, it is a plain rectangular wooden case, with hinged lid, containing a block-headed support for a cap. The remnants of the young king's cap were found at the bottom of the box. It was made of fine linen, embellished with elaborate beadwork of gold, lapis lazuli, carnelian and green felspar. Unfortunately, the dilapidations of time had caused the textile fabric to decay beyond recovery. There are, however, sufficient traces of its former splendour to enable us to get a record of the order of its beads, and a general idea of the original form of the skull-cap itself. Strangely enough, on the lid was a docket, reading: "What is in it," and mentioning "*shawabtis*"! This leads one to believe, that for some reason—possibly for economy—some of the funerary statuettes had been put in it at the time of burial. Or it may be, in this case, that the word has not been properly understood.

Over and above the specimens just described there were seven other broken boxes. With the exception of one chest, they are all of somewhat rough make. Of these I will mention the examples that have a particular interest attached to them. The first is a chest of far more solid make than any box we have found in this tomb, and the few remains of its contents throw not a little light upon the pursuits and amusements of a child of the Egyptian New Empire. The interior of the chest is fitted with complicated partitions, and with box-shaped drawers that are made to slide one above the other, and each provided with a sliding lid. These fittings had suffered from rough treatment; they had been wrenched open by impatient hands, evidently in search of what valuable material they may have contained. The chest was apparently for knick-knacks and playthings of Tutankhamen's youth, but, unfortunately, everything in it had been turned topsy-turvy; moreover, we found many of its trinkets strewn on the floor. A few of the things that we were able to recover were: a quantity of bracelets and anklets of ivory, wood, glass and leather; pocket game-boards of ivory; slings for hurling stones; gloves; a "lighter"; some leather archer's "bracers," to protect the left wrist from the blow of the bow-string; mechanical

The king's fire-making apparatus

toys; some samples of minerals; and even pigments and paint-pots of the youthful painter. The exterior of this chest is decorated with the names and titles of the king, as well as with dedications to various gods. Its lid opens on heavy bronze hinges; the fastening of the knob upon the lid is so notched on the inside that when the lid was closed and the knob turned, it locked the lid to the box. This contrivance, I believe, is the earliest automatic fastening hitherto known. The chest itself, some 25½ by 13 by 10½ inches in size, stands on four square feet capped with bronze, and, pegged on the centre of its back frame, is a large wooden *ded*-amulet signifying "stability."

The sense of manliness imparted by the possession of implements in connexion with fire, hunting, or fighting, such as an apparatus for making fire, and slings for hurling stones, was evidently as pleasing to the youth of those days as to the boy of our era. Those ancient Egyptians knew nothing of the combustile materials like phosphorus and sulphur, which easily take fire when rubbed on any natural or prepared rough surface, nor did they know of agents such as flint and iron with tinder. Their "lighter"—or, method of creating fire—was of a very primitive nature throughout the whole of their history, from the First to the Thirtieth Dynasty. They created fire by rapidly rotating a piece of stick in a round hole in a stationary piece of wood appropriate for the purpose. For this they applied the principle of the bow-drill, with which they were so familiar. The rotation was effected by means of a bow alternately thrust forwards and backwards, the thong of the bow having been first wound round the stock of the drill in which the fire-stick was fixed. And, in order to steady the drill, the upper end was held in a socket of stone, ivory, or ebony, or sometimes of the kernel of a *Dom*-nut, which, when cut in halves formed a ready-made drill-head. The round holes in which the first-stick was rotated were made near the edge of the fire-stock which allowed the spark to have free access to the tinder. In Tutankhamen's "lighter" the holes prepared for the fire-stick have been treated with resin, to promote friction, and thus facilitate the creation of heat.

Slings of hide for hurling stones, either for hunting purposes or as a weapon of offence, were probably the earliest device known to mankind, by which an increase of force and range was given to the thrower of such missiles. Although we first know of the sling in warfare about the seventh century B.C., it must have been in continual use in Egypt from barbaric times down to the present day, when it is still used by peasant boys employed in scaring birds from ripening cereal crops. Here, in this toy-chest of the fourteenth century B.C., this sling has already advanced. For it is no longer of hide, but of plaited linen thread, neatly made with a pouch, and a loop at the end of one of its cords, to hold it firmly on the little finger, while the second cord is left quite plain for loosing between the thumb and first finger, when dispatching the missile. Apparently, to acquire accuracy with a sling, not only a proper sized stone should be used, but the loose end of the sling must be released at the appropriate time, to ensure aim and distance. This probably explains the presence of a few smooth pebbles that we found among debris on the floor of this chamber. This type of sling is exactly the same as was used in recent years by the aborigines (Sakai) and the jungle Malays in Malaya.

Among the royal youth's bracelets and anklets there is one of particular historical interest. It is cut out of a solid piece of ivory, and carved round the upper bevel are various animals of the chase. The fauna depicted include the ostrich, hare, ibex, gazelle, and other antelope, and a hound chasing a stallion, showing that even then the domestic horse was allowed to run wild in the *pairidaeza*, much as ponies are given the liberty in our own ancient royal hunting demesne, the New Forest. There were also two pairs of bracelets, in faience, bearing the names of Tutankhamen's predecessors, Akhenaten and Smenkhkare.

The little game-boards I shall mention anon, with others of more pretentious kind that were found here.

Another box, crudely made and painted red, is worthy of mention. It was broken and bulging with a large number of delicate vessels of pale blue faience. We found it poised high up against the wall opposite the doorway, with one of its sides fallen away, but fortunately the protruding vessels were sufficiently wedged together to prevent them from falling out. They were the bane of our work when clearing that part of the room, for any unfortunate movement, before we could reach them, would have caused these vessels to fall and crash down into a hundred pieces. This box seems to have been the fellow to a box discovered in the Antechamber (No. 54), which contained similar vessels but of lapis lazuli blue faience. A similar box, without lid, that rested on the top of a lot of baskets in front of the doorway, contained a quantity of miniature light and dark blue faience fore-legs of a bovine animal. In addition, thrown carelessly in, was an odd mixture of things: two crumpled-up gala robes, a pair of gloves, a pair of rush sandals, and a ritualistic turquoise blue glass palette, which certainly did not seem to belong to the box. The amuletic significance of the faience fore-legs is unknown.

Judging from the experience gleaned from the contents of the boxes found here, and in the Antechamber, the wearing apparel came from the better-class caskets previously mentioned, and the crudely made boxes, when originally deposited in the tomb, had contained faience vases and miscellanea, discovered scattered about this and other chambers.

The two garments, which I have chosen to call gala robes, recall official vestments of the character of priestly apparel, such as the dalmatic worn by deacons and bishops of the Christian

A linen dalmatic with tapestry woven and needlework ornament

Church, or by kings and emperors at coronation. Unfortunately, their condition, or, rather, their preservation, is far from what could be desired. They had been crumpled up and bundled into the box with, as we have just seen, a whole lot of ill-sorted objects. They have also suffered deterioration set up by damp from infrequent saturations that had occurred in the tomb during the long past, but, although they were thus treated and have fallen into decay, they still bear traces of their former beauty. In their pristine state they must have been gorgeous pieces of colour. They take the form of a long loose vestment, having richly ornamented tapestry-woven decoration with fringes on both sides. In addition to this ornamentation, one of them has needlework of palmette pattern, desert flora, and animals, over the broad hem at the bottom. The opening for the neck and at the chest are also adorned with woven pattern. One of the vestments, with field quite plain, has narrow sleeves like the tunicle; the other, with the whole field woven with coloured rosettes as well as figures of flowers and cartouches across the chest,

A glove

has its collar woven in the design of a falcon with outspread wings, and it also has the titulary of the king woven down the front.

I cannot claim to be versed in the history of such garments, but from the fact that I discovered a fragment of a similar robe in the tomb of Thothmes IV, bearing the name of Amenhetep II, it may be inferred that robes of this kind were customary apparel among the Pharaohs. Perhaps they were worn on special occasions, such as religious rites—solemn consecration or coronation —and that they were symbolical of joy, very much in the manner of the dalmatic placed upon a deacon when the holy order was conferred, whereby the following words are repeated by the acting bishop: "May the Lord clothe thee in the Tunic of Joy and the Garment of Rejoicing." Moreover, these robes may well have had the same origin as the Roman garment, whence the liturgical vestment—the dalmatic—of the Christian Church derives. Vestments of the kind were in use in Egypt during the Egypto-Roman period (first to fourth centuries A.D.), and Professor Newberry has acquired a portion of such a garment, also of woven linen, dating from Arab times (Sultan Beybars, thirteenth century A.D.), which is almost identical in treatment of design with the fragment of the robe of Amenhetep II of the fourteenth century B.C.

In much better preservation were the pair of gloves, neatly folded, also of tapestry-woven linen. They were possibly intended to go with the robes,[1] and are similarly woven with a brilliant scale-pattern and have a border at the wrist of alternate lotus buds and flowers. These gloves are hemmed with plain linen, and have tape to fasten them round the wrist. Although their fabric was in a better condition than that of the dalmatics, it was nevertheless in a fragile and powdery state, but, thanks to Dr. Alexander Scott's good advice with regard to chemical treatment, both of the dalmatics were recovered from their parlous condition, and one of the gloves successfully unfolded for exhibition.

The remaining boxes of rough workmanship were found empty, and are too dilapidated to claim description.

Among this heterogeneous pile of chattels we found two curious-looking white wood cases. One of them was shaped like an attenuated shrine, about $25\frac{1}{2}$ by $2\frac{1}{4}$ by $1\frac{3}{4}$ inches in dimensions, which apparently once held a heavy metal standard cubit-measure. Naturally, the cubit was taken by the thieves on account of its value in metal, thus robbing us of valuable data as to the true linear measurement employed at that period, which, as far as we are able to estimate, must have been a unit something like 52·310 ms. having seven palms of ·07472 ms., and twenty-eight digits of ·01868 ms. The other case, from its size, shape and make, was evidently a rough chest for bows, arrows and perhaps other missiles. We found in it a number of different kinds of bows, arrows, clubs and boomerangs in a state of confusion. The bows and arrows, no doubt, belonged to the case, but it is questionable whether the boomerangs did not come from one of the boxes just mentioned. These weapons I will describe later with others which had been scattered about the room.

A most remarkable and fragile object wrought of alabaster (calcite) stood upon the floor almost unscathed. It takes the form of a boat floating in an ornamental tank. I have named it a "centre-piece" (for what else could it be?) carved of semi-translucent alabaster, engraved and painted with chaplets of fruit and flowers, as if to figure at a banquet or celebration of some kind. There is something extremely fanciful about it, as well as interesting, for is it not but another glimpse into the faded past breaking forth from the gloom of the tomb? The piece is not on a grand scale, being but 27 inches in height and 28 inches over all in length. The tank is designed as a pedestal, of pylon form, resting on four cylindrical feet, and it is hollowed out for water and flowers, with an island in the centre to support the alabaster boat. The boat represents a carvel-built barque, with round bottom, both the stem and stern rising in a curved line and terminating with the head of an ibex. Amidships is a canopy, supported by four ornate papyrus columns, which shields what appears to be an open sarcophagus; the whole representing perhaps a funeral barque for the celestial journey of the "Good God," the king. Facing forward, on the fore-deck, is a charming little figure of a nude girl, squatting and holding a lotus flower to her breast. At the helm, steering the boat, is a puny slave, which brings to mind the dwarfs at the helms of the Phoenician ships mentioned by Herodotus. This little achondroplasic female dwarf, with inward-turned feet, is as rare an example of fine art as it is in medical research. How beautifully, and how accurately, both of these female figures and the ibex heads have been rendered by the court stone-carver who wrought this fascinating ornament. With regard to the medical aspects of the dwarf steering the boat, Lord Moynihan, the famous surgeon, says:

"Achondroplasia is a congenital disease of uncertain causation. It produces a deformity so distinctive that the appearance of one man afflicted with it is character-istic of all. The achondroplasic is of low stature, of sturdy muscular and bony development. The head is large; the forehead, broad and high, bulges so much over the face as to leave a deep impression at the base of the nose; the nostrils are large and open; the lower jaw assertive. The body is long in proportion to the limbs; there is a deep incurvation in the lumbar spine, making the abdomen protrude, the arms and legs are short; the feet and hands are broad and strong. Typical examples are portrayed by artists from the earliest days. In Ancient Egypt the god Bes, 'the amuser and instructor of children,' and the god Ptah (Pataikos, son of Ptah); show all the attributes. In the Bayeux tapestry the dwarf Turold is a fairly good example. Velasquez painted many, for the achondroplasic was often a Court dwarf. Nicholas Pertusato is a flawless specimen. Artists have often shown the dwarf in charge of animals. Tiepolo shows achondroplasics with dogs and with a lion. Earliest of all, the mural sculptures at Saqqareh show an achondroplasic leading a monkey almost as large as himself. The achondroplasic seen on this alabaster boat is a female; the disease is far commoner in males. The feet are turned inwards so much that progres-sion must have meant the lifting of one foot over the other."

Lord Moynihan also adds: "the characteristic bodily and facial deformities are here exquisitely portrayed."

Nothing, hitherto, has been found to enlighten us as to the true nature of this little monument. It is a relic of times gone by; of customs and manners with which ours have no affinity. Should, by chance, it belong to the series of model funerary barques, such as were found in the Innermost Treasury, of which many damaged and wooden examples were also found here, then it belongs to the purely ritualistic objects pertaining to burial custom. But, so far as can be ascertained, it seems to be purely fanciful, much like the little silver boat discovered among the Kames and Aahhetep jewellery, and for that reason I am inclined to believe it to be a palace ornament and not really intended for funerary purpose.

An interesting piece that excites attention is a silver vase, about $5\frac{1}{4}$ inches in height, in the form of a pomegranate fruit. The vase was probably dropped or forgotten by the tomb-plunderers. The silver being slightly auriferous, the metal is preserved in almost pristine condition. Its bowl is chased with a band of cornflowers and olive leaves; the shoulders and neck with chaplets of lily and poppy petals. In aspect, the vase is modern enough to resemble the work of the silversmiths of the Queen Anne period, and, did we not know its provenance, none of us would dare to date it as belonging to the fourteenth century B.C.

The ornamental alabaster boat

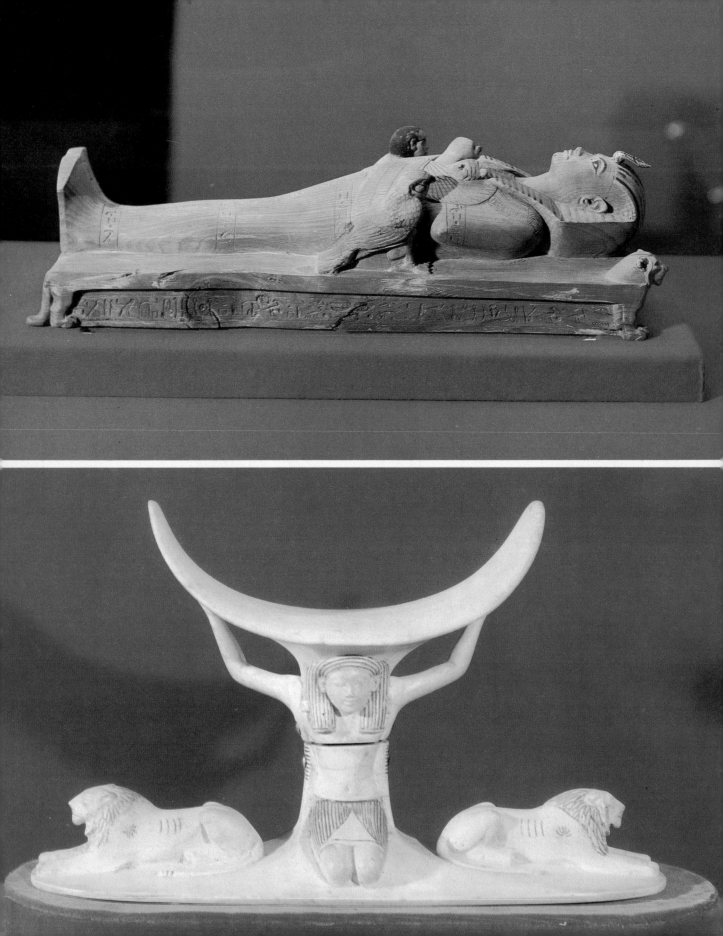

Gaming-boxes for diversion with their playing-pieces were scattered far and wide about this room, even some of their parts were discovered in the Antechamber, where they had been thrown during the dynastic plundering. They are of three different sizes—large, medium, and quite small—for the house, and of portable form for the pocket. The latter size, small and made of plain ivory, came from the knick-knack chest previously described. Their presence in the tomb is apparently justified by some mythical precedent, which the deceased hoped to enjoy in the life to come (cf. "The Book of the Dead," Chapter XVII); however, the smaller specimens, at least, seem to be chattels of an everyday pastime. The largest and most important of the games, $21\frac{1}{2}$ by 11 by 7 inches over all, rests upon a neat black ebony stand, made like a small stool upon a sledge, having the "cushions" and claws of the feet embellished with gold. The game-board—or rather, by its being purely a game of hazard, the gaming-board—is also of ebony, but faced top and bottom with ivory, and of a rectangular oblong shape. The medium-sized specimen, about 11 by $3\frac{1}{2}$ by $2\frac{1}{4}$ inches in measurement, of ivory veneered upon a basic wood body, is beautifully decorated with stained carving and gilt borders. Each game is divided into thirty equal squares, so arranged as to form ten by three—the three rows of ten squares being on its long axis. To each game there were ten playing-pieces, like pawns in chess, coloured black and white (i.e. five for each opponent), which were played by complicated chances denoted either by a kind of dice in the form of knuckle-bones, or small black and white throwing sticks, to which different values were attached according to the manner of their fall. The contest was obviously an early form of, and allied to, the modern game called "*El-Tab-el-Seega*," played almost universally in the Near East—a game of chance, from which one has been able to solve the principles of these ancient forerunners. They were played according to set rules but were decided by luck, and although they involved little or no skill they, nevertheless, afforded an amusing and exciting pastime. I would even go so far as to say that the modern games of skill, like "*Seega*," or draughts, and chess, were in all probabilities evolved from games of hazard, such as we find from time to time in ancient Egyptian tombs, and so well represented in this burial.

These gaming-boards or boxes have almost invariably each two forms of the game: the three by ten on the top, already mentioned, and three by four with an approach of eight squares on the bottom. The playing-pieces (pawns) of the large household example are missing; they were probably of gold and silver and consequently stolen in ancient times. The smaller specimens, by being of ivory, had little value in the eyes of the metal-robbers; thus we find them complete.

There were also a number of ostrich-feather fans recalling the flabella still used at a papal procession in Rome, such as was witnessed in the Eucharistic procession of His Holiness the Pope, in July, 1929. These fans, like the pontifical flabella, were carried by grooms-in-waiting in Pharaonic processions, or were held beside the throne, and appear always on either side of the king or immediately behind him. In fact the title, "Fan-bearer on the Right (or Left) side of His Majesty," was considered one of the highest offices among the court officials. The long-handled fans of this form, from their early Egyptian name *shwt*, meaning "shadow," or "shade," were probably intended more for sunshades than for agitating air, although, manifestly, they could have been, and were, used for both purposes. Curiously enough, the hieroglyphic ideogram or determinative of the Egyptian word *tay khw* "fan-bearer," shows a similar stock to these examples, but without the flabellate top and with only one ostrich-feather, of which form we find no example in this tomb. Another name for the flabellate type was *sryt*, meaning "(Military) Standard," which indicates a further use of this very decorative, and what I believe to be the royal form, of the flabellum.

Unfortunately, the ostrich feathers of all these fans were so decayed that only in a few cases the shafts of the feathers remained, and they again were in such a bad condition that it was

Above: an effigy of the dead king and below: an ivory headrest

A gaming box

almost impossible to preserve them. However, there were sufficient remains to show us that the flabellate or palmate tops of the fan-stocks, into which the quills were fixed, once held 48 feathers (i.e. 24 on each side), and that the shafts of the feathers had been stripped of their "vanes" for a short distance above the quills, so that a portion of the bare shafts was visible, like radii, and, thus, must have resembled the radiating framework ("sticks") of the modern folding fan.

The fan stocks vary from 2 feet to 4 feet in length, and they comprise a "capitulum" in the shape of a papyrus-umbel and calices, a stem, and, at the lower end, a knob in the form of an inverted papyrus umbel or corolla of the lotus. They are made of solid ivory, carved, stained and gilt; or of ebony veneered with decorative barks, and more rarely of engraved and embossed sheet-gold upon a wooden core. The gold specimen bears the prenomen, nomen, and epithets of Akhenaten, as well as the two cartouche-names of Aten, the sun-disk. The stained ivory specimen is a gorgeous piece of ornamental carving.

Another very interesting and unique specimen discovered in this Annexe, was one of the king's sceptres. It is difficult to comprehend why such a sacred object should be in a store-room of this kind, and not where one would have expected it to be, among similar insignia in the Inner-most Treasury. The only explanation that I can suggest is that, either the plunderers cast it there owing to some misgivings in stealing it, or that it belonged to a complete outfit which included the garments pertaining to religious ceremonies, such as rites in which the king con-trolled the principal parts, that were originally deposited in one of the ornate caskets found in this chamber. The latter hypothesis is perhaps the most probable, since an adze of bronze inlaid with gold (its gold blade had been wrenched off by the dynastic thieves), that belonged to ceremonies performed in front of the dead, was also discovered among the objects strewn all over the floor. This kind of sceptre is known under several names, and, I believe, always as a staff, or symbol, of authority. As a *kherp*-sceptre it was used in connexion with offerings; this is indicated by the embossed decoration on one side of the "blade". It is about 21 inches in length, and is made of thick sheet-gold beaten on to a wooden core. It is embossed and inlaid; the tip, "capitulum," and the two ends of the shaft are richly embellished with (Egyptian) cloisonné-work. The gold and blue faience inscription reads: "*The Beautiful God, beloved, dazzling of face like the Aten when it shines, The Son of Amen, Tutankhamen*," which is of interest, as it suggests a compromise between the Aten and Amen creeds.

The deceased was looked upon as a man in after death as in life; a king was a "Good God" both in life and in the hereafter; the illustrious of the long past were considered as divinities, and these divinities were called "Great Gods," and they and their divine families were worshipped—in fact the second life was considered but a continuation of the first. Thus we find movable possessions, such as household chattels, sceptres, fans, walking-sticks, staves, weapons and the like of daily use deposited in the tomb—they were burial offerings to the deceased, still living in memory, and through them may be visualized a picture of an ancient world.

The young Tutankhamen must have been an amateur collector of walking-sticks and staves, for here, as in the Antechamber and the Burial Chamber, we found a great number. They were, no doubt, in part, of ritualistic significance, but many of them have evidently seen daily use. There are many types: long staves with knobbed and forked tops and ferruled ends, crooked sticks, and curved sticks for killing snakes. Some beautifully mounted with gold and silver, others decorated with a marquetry of barks, or with the polished wood left plain.

The collection of weapons of offence that were found in this chamber comprise clubs, single-sticks, falchions, bows and arrows, boomerangs and throw-sticks for fowling and warfare. For defence there were real and ceremonial shields, and a cuirass.

The most primitive of the weapons are naturally the clubs, and, from the fact that they figure largely among the levies from the surrounding barbarian countries, they would appear to be more characteristic of foreigners than of the Egyptians. There were many, and they were mostly found in the rough white bow-box. Most of them are falciform (i.e. gradually curved over at the thick end, and in shape like a sickle), with either the suggestion of a knob at the end, or with flattened blade cut like a sickle, the concave edge being the sharper. Another, but rarer, type is of cudgel form much like an elongated policeman's truncheon with a pronounced knob on the end of the handle. They are all of a heavy, dark polished wood, and some have the grip covered with a bark resembling that of the silver birch tree.

The single-sticks are the first hitherto discovered in Egypt. They had been thrown on the floor of the chamber in the south-west corner. Six of them were about 25 inches in length, and one 37 inches. They consist of a round stick, thicker at one end than the other, and were used apparently as a weapon of attack and defence. In contradistinction to the modern European form of single-stick, the thicker end of the weapon formed the point and it was ferruled with metal, and the thinner end was the handle, which suggests they descended from the club. Protection for the hand was furnished by a leather "guard," somewhat like the "basket-hilt," which was made rigid by means of wire, and adorned with an open gold-work "guard." These had been wrenched off, but parts of them were found scattered on the floor. The handle, or "grip," was packed with leather bound with string, in order to prevent repercussion from passing to the hand. They all have wire loops for (?) suspension; three have a sheet-gold mounting for a long distance up the grip; one has bark decoration; and three—quite plain sticks—have their natural bark intact.

From scenes upon the Egyptian monuments depicting a kind of "cudgel-play," or "single-sticking," guards, cuts and parries appear to have formed at least part of the play, but a short stick bound to the left forearm, like a splint, was also used to ward off strokes not parried with the single-stick, and it obviously served as an auxiliary guard against the adversary's blows. No trace of this sort of auxiliary guard was found here.

In many ways two bronze falchions are unique: a large and heavy example found with the single-sticks, and a much smaller and lighter one discovered among other miscellanea on the floor.

The smaller falchion (16 in. long) was probably made for the king when a child; the larger and heavier weapon ($23\frac{1}{2}$ in. long) was designed for the time when he reached adolescence. In both cases the blade, shaft, and handle-plate are cast in one piece; the handle-plate being fitted with side plates of ebony. The large weapon seems more fitted for a "crushing" than for a "cutting" blow, its convex edge being only partially developed, which places it hardly a step in advance of the sickle-shaped clubs first described; the blade of the smaller specimen, however, has more of a knife edge. That the larger weapon must have inflicted a severe wound is evident from its great weight, due to the thickness of the back, viz. 0·65 of an inch.

These falchions seem peculiar to the New Empire, i.e. the Eighteenth to Twentieth Egyptian Dynasties, and judging from the sickle-shaped determinative of the hieroglyphic name, it was called *khepesh*. According to Sir Gardner Wilkinson (*Manners and Customs of the Ancient Egyptians*, Vol. I, p. 213) ". . . the resemblance of its form and name to the *kopis* of the Greeks, suggests that the people of Argos, an Egyptian colony, by whom it was principally adopted, originally derived that weapon from the falchion of Egypt." It may also be a prototype of the Oriental curved sword, the scimitar, which usually broadens towards the point, but is also falciform.

The bows and arrows were very numerous, of great variety, of a high standard of proficiency, and, to be in keeping with the dignity and rank of the owner, most of them were finely ornamented.

Although among the bows there is an absence of uniformity in any of the following groups, each bow having more or less a peculiarity of its own, they may, however, be grouped into three separate classes: (a) the "self-bow," made of a single stave of self wood, without decoration; (b) the "self-bow," made of two staves (one for each limb) of self wood, joined at the centre, and the whole length bound with bark; (c) the compound-bow, having the whole length of the stave made of several strips of horn or wood glued together, the "belly" filled in with a gelatinous substance, the whole length bound with bark and minutely decorated. The barks employed to bind and decorate the bows resemble, at least in colour, the cherry and the silver birch, but neither the woods nor barks employed have yet been identified. The few self-bows of single staves are only 27 inches in length; the self-bows made in two staves are some 29 inches in length, but one of them is only 14 inches. The compound-bows are by far the most numerous, and they range from 44 to 49 inches. Needless to mention, in each case the centre of the bow is stiff and resisting; the two limbs taper gradually to the "horns" to which the "string" is fitted, but in the case of the single stave self-bows the horn is absent; the string was fixed by means of a few turns round the end of the limbs. In every case where the "string" of a bow was preserved, it was found to be made of four-strand twisted gut.

It seems that the main difference between the self-bow, which is by far the earliest in Egypt, and the compound-bow (of the New Empire, and probably of a foreign origin), is that the self-bow is more sensitive, and its work mostly done during the last few inches of the pull, while the compound-bow pulls evenly throughout. The different types and sizes of the bows, as in the case of the arrows, were, no doubt, intended for different purposes, like our firearms and ammunition: the military rifle, the sporting rifle and gun of various weights and bores, and the pistol.

Among 278 arrows found, there were some sixteen different classes varying in detail and in size. These arrows in general comprise: a shaft of reed "footed"—i.e. a piece of hard wood tanged to the reed shaft, to which the "pile" is attached; a "pile," or point, of bronze, ivory or wood, of different shapes, tanged to the foot, or of glass (in place of flint) chisel-shape, cemented to the end of the foot; the feathers; and a tanged "nock," or notch, of hard wood, or ivory. Some of the arrows are three-fletched (feathered), but most of them are four-fletched. They are all "footed" arrows, and with few exceptions of slightly "chested" pattern, i.e. the footed shaft tapers slightly from the beginning of the foot to the pile. The exception was a group of 13 four-fletched "self" arrows of "parallel" pattern. In that case the shaft and foot are of the same thickness from neck to pile, and are made of one piece of wood.

These arrows vary from 36 to 10 inches in length; one of them is only 6 inches (note the very small bow previously mentioned). The piles vary in type according to their purpose—for warfare and for the chase, for piercing, lacerating or stunning the victim.

Several batches of arrows and also some bows were found in different places in the chamber, but the greater mass of them was discovered in the large white bow-box.

The excellence of these bows and arrows make it manifest that at this period of the Egyptian New Empire, the bowyers and fletchers were adepts in their craft. The bows are of somewhat short make, even for people like the Egyptians who were of low stature, but that may be due, in this case, to the youthfulness of the king, as the weight of the bow and the length of the arrow should be adapted to the strength of the archer.

There is every reason to believe that amongst the greater peoples of ancient history, the Egyptians were probably the first and the most famous of archers, relying on the bow as their principal weapon in war and in the chase. As a weapon of the chase the bow was, in its various forms, employed even more than in war. However, it must have had immense military value. The possessor of the bow and arrow could bring down the fleetest of animals and could defend himself against his enemy. The rapidity of consecutive shots is said to average up to four to five a minute. A searching rain of arrows would certainly be a formidable thing to march against. The Egyptians used the bow and arrow in chariots, whence they seemed to have shot equally well as on foot, and for defence against arrows both shields and cuirasses of leather were employed.

In their present state of preservation it is impossible to tell the weight (i.e. the pull) of the bows. They probably had a range of something like 150 to 250 yards. The penetrating power of the self-bows and a class of "footed" arrows belonging to the Egyptian Middle Kingdom, is well illustrated in a discovery made by Mr. H. E. Winlock of a soldier's tomb at Thebes, which contained some sixty men slain in battle (Bulletin of Metropolitan Museum of Art; *The Egyptian Expedition*, 1925–27; pub. February 1928; p. 12 ff., figs. 17, 20 and 21). The dried remains of the partially mummified bodies of those men show numbers of arrow wounds such as would have been received from a height. Some had parts of the arrows actually sticking in them. Several of those arrows, coming apparently from above, struck the men at the base of the neck and penetrated the chest; another which entered the upper arm passed down the whole length of the forearm to the wrist, and one of the men, hit in the back under the shoulder blade, had his heart transfixed by an arrow which projected some eight inches in front of his chest. The range at which those wounds were inflicted is of course unknown, neither is there any record of the type of bow used by the enemy, but, as far as our knowledge goes, only the self-bow was known and used in Egypt at that period. The fragments of the arrows found in the bodies of the men show them to have been of the "chested" pattern, "footed" with ebony, and having blunt ends without "piles."

The self-bow, among the commodities brought from the Land of Punt—a country somewhere on the east coast of Africa, north of the equator, like Abyssinia or Somaliland—clearly shows whence they came.

Another form of missile-weapon was the boomerang, of which a great number were found here—both real, and for ritualistic purpose. The real boomerangs were in the bow-box.

Boomerangs and throw-sticks were used in Egypt from the earliest to the last dynasties. The boomerang was certainly used for fowling; the throw-stick probably in warfare. Both kinds are represented in this collection. Of the first type among this lot—boomerangs proper—the

A ceremonial shield of heraldic design

return and the non-return kinds are recognizable, even though the general form of both weapons is much the same, i.e. curved in sickle-shape, or two straight arms at an angle, the main, or rather the essential, difference being the skew (twist) of the arms, which are exactly opposed in the two kinds. The non-return weapon was apparently thrown like the return type, its reverse twist or skew helping it to travel a greater distance than the ordinary throw-sticks.

Our specimens of boomerangs are made of a hard wood which I am unable to recognize; they are either painted with a polychrome pattern, or bound in part with a bark resembling that of the birch tree. The ritualistic specimens are of carved ivory, mounted with gold caps at the ends.

The throw-sticks here are either of fantastic form or of simple curved shape made of a hard wood. Those made of ebony with ends of gilt are probably ritualistic, like the example made of gilt-wood capped with faience, or those solely made of faience.

For defence there were eight shields: four possibly for real use, and four of ceremonial purpose. Two of the real shields are of light wood covered with hide of an antelope, and have the cartouches of the king blazoned in their centres; the other two, also of light wood and with similar bearings, are covered with skin of the north African cheetah; the hair and markings on the hides are still in fair condition. These shields have a maximum measurement of 29 by $20\frac{1}{2}$ inches. The ceremonial shields are slightly larger; they are wood open-work and gilt. They are heraldic in design, and two have devices representing the king as a lion trampling on Egypt's foes of human form, or as a warrior with falchion smiting foes in the form of lion; and two represent him enthroned in this life and in the hereafter respectively.

Another form of defensive armour was a crumpled-up leather cuirass that had been thrown into a box. This was made up of scales of thick tinted leather worked on to a linen basis, or lining, in the form of a close-fitting bodice without sleeves. It was unfortunately too far decayed for preservation.

Among other objects of purely ritualistic significance that were found in this chamber, I should mention: sickles for reaping in the Elysian Fields; various amuletic bronze, wood and stone implements; amulets of stone, faience and gold; wood, stone, and glass palettes; a large part of the set of wooden miniature funerary boats described in Chapter 2, and a large quantity of *shawabti*-figures in kiosks belonging to the series placed in the Treasury.

Part Two

The oils, fats, unguents and wines, fruits and foodstuffs were, I believe, the contents proper of this Annexe.

The oils and unctuous materials were stored in thirty-four alabaster (calcite) vessels and one of serpentine, which are remarkable for their diversified shapes and sizes. The ten[2] alabaster jars of similar kind found lying on the floor in the Antechamber, emptied and abandoned, in all probability came from this hoard in the Annexe. With rare exception the lids and stoppers of all these vessels had been forcibly removed, thrown aside, and their contents poured out and stolen, leaving but a small amount of residue in each vessel. On the inner walls of some of the vessels that contained viscous substances, the finger-marks of the predatory hand that scooped out the precious material are as clear today as when the theft was perpetrated. Many of the vessels were undoubtedly older than the burial of the king. Some of them have their inscriptions carefully erased; others actually bear ancestral names that carry back to the reign of Thothmes III, and some of them show traces of long use, old breakages, and repairs; in fact, they appear to have contained family oils from famous presses, fats and unguents of matured kind, dating back as far as some eighty-five years before Tutankhamen.

To transgress for a moment from the main subject, these ancestral amphorae throw light upon some of the objects found in the preceding Eighteenth Dynasty royal tombs. Among the very fragmentary remains of their funerary equipment the presence of older objects has always been a puzzle, and it has been thought that they might be accidental. However, as we find sundry objects bearing the names of predecessors among those much plundered and broken funerary equipments, and similar example in this discovery, does it not show that the inclusion of ancestral material was not only customary, but had some reason? There is one other point. As the majority of alabaster vessels have been discovered in tombs—in fact, seldom is an important tomb found without the presence of such jars—it might seem that they were made for sepulchral use only. There can, however, be little doubt that they served their particular purpose in daily life, although perhaps not so much as the ordinary pottery vessels, they being more expensive, heavy, and easily shattered. Their special use was for oils and unctuous material, while pottery vessels were restricted principally to wine, beer, water and the like. The stone vessels made expressly for the tomb are more likely to be recognized among the very ornate examples, which by being of elaborate design were rendered, in the utilitarian sense, of little practical use.

These stone vessels range from seven to twenty-six and a half inches in height, and have a capacity from about 2·75 to 14 litres, showing that at least 350 litres of oils, fats, and other unctuous materials were stored in this room for the king. Two of the vessels bearing the names of Thothmes III have their actual capacities marked upon them, namely, $14\frac{1}{2}$ and $16\frac{3}{4}$ *hins* respectively. As the *hin* at that period was about 460 c.cs., they probably contained 6·67 and 7·70 litres of some matured unctuous material. A pair of vases bearing the cartouches of Amenhetep III have the Amen nomen of the king erased and altered to his prenomen. This shows that the two vases were in use during Akhenaten's reign. Another interesting point is that a vase bearing a carefully erased inscription, faintly shows the previous existence of the prenomen and nomen of two kings upon it, possibly those of Amenhetep III and Amenhetep IV, in which case we have indication of a coregency of those two Pharaohs.

The largest vessel of all is the amphora, designed after the shape of the pottery wine-jars. Another amphora, resting on its original "tazza," or circular support, stands 26 inches high. At the bottom of this vessel a small quantity of its oil was left by the thieves; beneath the hardened crust the oil has remained viscid to the present day. Among the more remarkable vessels the following examples call for mention. A vase in the form of a mythical lion, standing upright in an aggressive attitude, quaintly heraldic like a "lion gardant"; his right fore-paw is clawing at the air in noble rage, while his left rests upon a symbol *sa*, meaning "protection," and fitted on to the crown of the head of the lion is the "neckpiece" of the vase in the form of a coronated lotus flower. The decoration of this lion-vase is incised and filled in with pigments; the tongue and the teeth are of ivory. Another vase represents a bleating ibex, rendered realistically. A third vase takes the form of a crater upon a "tazza"-stand; it is finely carved with fluted ornament, incised inscription, coloured with pigment. A fourth vase, also of crater form, is embellished with an elaborate open-work envelope of semi-translucent calcite. The workmanship of these vessels is fairly equal in quality. In designing them, the stone-carver gave free play to his fancy, borrowing forms of flowers and animals for their shapes. Some may be heavy and clumsy, while others are distinguished by their elegance and diversity of form. Especially interesting are a pair of attenuated vases with slender necks and pointed bowls; they are ornamented round their necks with simulacra of floral garlands, made of polychrome faience, embedded in the surface of the stone.

The pottery wine-jars (amphorae), three dozen in number, have an historical interest. Naturally the wines they contained had dried up long ago, but each of the jars bears a docket, written in hieratic, which gives the date, place and vintage of the wine. From these dockets we learn that the choice wines of the royal cellars came from the Aten, Amen, and Tutankhamen domains situated in the Delta—some at Kantareh on the east, but mostly on the west branch of the River Nile. We also learn from these dockets that by far the larger quantity of wine came from the Aten Domain, and dates from the IIIrd to the XXIst years, thus showing that the Aten estates were maintained for at least twenty-one years. The wine next in quantity came from the domain of Tutankhamen, and it is dated as late as the IXth year, viz.: "*Year 9, Wine of the House-of-Tutankhamen from the Western River,*" followed by the name of the Chief Vintner. This indicates that the king must have been married to the Crown Princess Ankhesenpaaten, and was enthroned at the tender age of nine years, for the balance of evidence afforded by his mummy shows him to have been about eighteen when he died. The smallest quantity of wine came from the domain of Amen, and is dated "year i," which suggests that the reversion to the worship of the capital god Amen may have taken place late in Tutankhamen's reign.

From the seals upon the wine-jars we gather some knowledge as to the system practised by the ancient Egyptians when bottling, or, as it may be better described, storing wines. Apparently, when the first fermentation was completed, the young wine was transferred to pottery jars, which were closed and sealed by means of a rush bung completely covered over with a clay or mud capsule that enveloped the whole of the mouth and neck of the jar. While these immense capsules were still soft, they were impressed with the device of the domain to which the wine belonged. The second fermentation thus took place in the jars, and in order to allow the carbonic acid formed during the process of the secondary fermentation to escape, a small hole was made at the top of the capsules. These small holes were then closed with clay or mud, and were impressed with a smaller device of the domain, made expressly for the purpose. In all probability the interior of the jars was smeared over with a thin coat of resinous material to counteract the porous nature of the pottery; the broken specimens show a distinct black coating on their inner surfaces.

Although many of the wine-jars were broken, there was no evidence of the wine having been stolen. The breakage that occurred is more likely to have been the result of the rough handling by the thieves, when removing and stealing the contents of the adjacent stone vessels previously mentioned.

About a dozen of the wine-jars were of Syrian form—having an oviform bowl, long slender neck, overlapping lip, and one handle. Being of fragile make, these were mostly broken. Not one of this type bore any docket, but the clay capsules bore an impression of a similar device to the other wines, so one presumes that the wine contained was of Egyptian and not of foreign produce.

Stacked on top of the stone vessels and the pottery wine-jars were 116 baskets, or even more, if the baskets of similar make that were found discarded on the floor of the Antechamber be included. They contained foodstuffs—mostly sundry fruits and seeds, including the mandrake, *nabakh*, grapes, dates, melon seeds, and *dom*-nuts. The baskets, round, oval, and of bottle shape, vary from 4 inches to 18 inches in their larger diameter. They show by their symmetry the natural aptitude of the expert workman. The "strokes" employed in their construction appear to be precisely the same as those used today by the native basket-makers. Some of the smaller and finer weaved examples are adorned with patterns formed by interweaving stained with natural grasses. The coarser specimens are made of fibre "skeins" from the fruit-bearing stalks of the date-palm, bound with fronds of the *dom*-palm, or, as in some cases, the date-palm, which were in all probability first soaked in water to render them both leathery and pliable. The bottle-shaped baskets contained dried grapes. On certain festivals the modern Egyptians still take similar baskets of fruits to the tombs of their deceased relatives.

23

The main cause of deterioration and chemical changes among the objects in the Tomb

BEFORE CONCLUDING THIS ACCOUNT of the discovery, it would not be out of place to say a few words concerning the state in which we found the objects in the tomb, and to suggest the main cause of much of their deterioration.

The existence in the past of damp in the tomb is a subject that needs consideration, although it has been treated summarily in the previous volumes.

From every point of view it was a thousand pities that this tomb should have suffered from infrequent moisture filtering through the fissures in the limestone rock in which it was cut. This moisture saturated the air of its chambers, and caused a humid atmosphere to exist therein for what must have been considerable intermittent periods. It not only nourished a fungoid growth, and caused a peculiar pink film to be deposited everywhere, but it destroyed practically all the leather-work by melting it into a black viscid mass. It also caused extensive warping to take place among the varied woods used in the construction of many of the objects. It dissolved all adhesive material such as glue, so that the component parts of many of the articles fell apart. It also resulted in much deterioration of the textiles—an irreparable loss, for among them were rare garments and the like made of tapestry-woven linen fabric as well as of needlework.

Indeed it was this moisture that has necessitated the ten winter-seasons' work (1922 to 1932) that we have devoted to the removal of the funerary equipment from the tomb, for it was obviously necessary first to render it fit for transport, and then for exhibition. Had not this "first aid" been applied with care, not one-tenth of the many hundreds of objects would ever have reached the Cairo Museum in any reasonable form of condition. In some instances the condition of an article necessitated treatment before it could be touched—although at first sight it looked almost fresh, by experiment, the least stress put thereto, showed that it was wellnigh perished. Thus by steady application, aided by kind help and good advice, and at the price of tedium, many a problem was solved, and I am proud to record that not one quarter per cent. of those diverse and beautiful objects was lost. The Earl of Crawford and Balcarres, in his presidential address to the Society of Antiquaries (July 1929), rightly said: "the archaeologist must be very scrupulous not to destroy —indeed, his province is to recreate nor should he neglect artistic quality."

Now, in addition to the periods when those objects were exposed to an intensely humid atmosphere, there must also have been long intervals when they were exposed to drought, thus they were subjected to infrequent conditions of expansion and contraction.

When one realizes the disastrous effects of diurnal temperature variations in the open desert, causing the breaking-up of all superficial layers of rocks, the breaking away of scarp-faces and even the splitting of huge flint boulders, one is not surprised at the extent of damage caused by infrequent changes from damp to drought such as seem to have occurred in this tomb. The more so, when one knows how much of its equipment was constructed of a number of diverse materials: for example, a chest made of an inferior basic wood overlaid with a superior veneer of ivory, ebony and gold; or a chair or chariot made of several woods and leather and inlaid with different substances such as metals, natural stones, glass and ivory; or the great protective shrines built of an oak and coniferous wood, covered with gesso, and overlaid with thin sheet-gold. In fact, it is extraordinary, considering their diverse materials and antiquity, how such objects resisted as much as they did so many opposed expanding and contracting tensions. The length of the periods of damp after saturation must have been considerable within those sealed rock-bound chambers, where the prevailing temperature was about 84° Fahrenheit (29° Centigrade).

In order to have some idea of the primary source of water that affected those chambers, the past and present frequency of rainfall in the region of the Valley of the Tombs of the Kings must naturally be considered.

Although the climatic conditions in Pharaonic times were doubtless more or less the same as they are now, we must not forget to take into account the possibility of a greater quantity of morass that existed in the Nile Valley in those ancient days, attracting a greater amount of humidity, if not actual rainfall. The fauna and flora as displayed by the dynastic monuments indicate the probability of such a condition.[1] However, contrary to the Eastern desert, where almost yearly torrents pour down its ravines, the Western (Libyan) desert, especially in the Theban regions, is indeed rainless to a remarkable degree. The normal preservation of its antiquities as well as sundry inscriptions (graffiti) upon its bare rock faces are in themselves testimony of the past and present climatic conditions.

Years may pass without any appreciable rain falling. During my own experience, covering a period of more than thirty-five years in the neighbourhood of Thebes, I am only able to record four really heavy rainfalls: one in the spring of 1898; one during the late autumn of 1900; and two quite close together during the autumn (October and November) of 1916.

Notable features of these rain-storms are their comparatively small area and their abrupt borderline. Though they are of short duration—a few hours only—and generally accompanied by powerful electrical manifestation, the downpour within the storm-area is tremendous. It will fill up valleys and turn them into seething rivers. In a few moments a ravine may be foaming with innumerable cascades carrying rocks down to its boulder-strewn bed. Yet in a very short space of time the scene changes back to its normal arid aspect. The water has rushed down to the Nile Valley, the scoured beds of the stream being the sole evidence remaining of these short but destructive floods of water.

These temporary downpours of water, called by the Egyptians "*El Seil*" (pl. "*El Sayal*"), seem to occur in the Theban district (west bank) on an average at about ten years' interval, but in a particular valley or locality, owing to the comparatively small area of these downpours, it is obvious, by the laws of chance, that the intervals may be much longer.

Any record of an individual valley is of course unknown. It might, however, be calculated by careful examination of a section of the detrital materials forming the bed of a valley, like that of the Tombs of the Kings, where we have a certain amount of knowledge as to dates, by counting the consecutive strata of wind-blown and water deposits accumulated since dynastic times.

During my experience the actual necropolis of the Valley of the Kings has suffered only one of these great downpours, and that was in the winter season 1900–1901. However, there is not a ravine in that region, large or small, which has not been at some time subject to these sudden streams of water.

Needless to mention, it may occur that a ravine suddenly becomes a seething river of rushing water without a drop of rain having fallen in its immediate locality—a phenomenon brought about by a torrential rain-storm far back on the plateau above, whence part, or all, of the water drains into a ravine and rushes down in full force until it finds its level. I have myself been witness of such an occurrence, which is perhaps worthy of notice. About 4 p.m. on 1 November 1916, the Great Northern Ravine north and collateral with the Valley of the Kings and confluent at the mouth suddenly became a great torrent. This was due to a very heavy rainstorm that had taken place on the desert plateau, some fifteen miles north-west, earlier in the afternoon. It is perhaps also of interest to observe the results of that torrent. Before the rush of water had taken place no living plants were visible on the floor of that great ravine. By January the amount of growth of various flowering desert-plants that carpeted the stream-bed was remarkable. Unfortunately my ignorance of botany prevented my recording their species. The plants—some very fragrant— attracted a number of parent moths, notably of the family of *Sphingidae*,[2] where they deposited their eggs. By the middle of February the larvae in their last stages were feeding upon the plants; at the end of March the newly-hatched imago was present. However, only a few of the hardier specimens among the desert plants survived the hot summer months, and by the end of the following spring all had practically disappeared, save their dried scrub.

Now the growth of such vegetation in those arid ravines after a torrent, suggests that the intervals of drought are not longer than the germinating life of the seeds. And this brings to mind another notable fact. There are no signs whatsoever of desert plants having been present in the main Valley of the Kings, nor in its smaller tributary branches. This absence of the usual plant growth after rainfall is so remarkable that it calls for reflection. It might be inferred that the intervals between the torrents occurring in the Valley of the Kings have been, at least in the later years, longer than the germinating life of seeds of desert plants, but when one takes into considera-tion the very narrow barrier dividing this valley from the Great Northern Ravine, such an inference seems untenable, and there must be other causes. It may be due to the actual situation of the valley, for the part of the plateau immediately above the head of the Valley of the Kings is limited in extent and comparatively isolated; consequently the chance of storm-water draining into it is less. The same argument might apply to seeds of plants, whereas the neighbouring valleys are fed from the greater plateau.

Howbeit, the primary source of infrequent water in these valleys is, I think, fairly explained.

Now as to the probable cause of those intermittent saturations reaching the chambers of Tutankhamen's tomb, which are cut deep down in the heart of the bed-rock—the lower Eocene limestone. At first sight it would not be unreasonable before closer study is made to suppose that the damps were due to the low and almost central situation of the tomb in the trough of the Valley, where debacles of water from sudden torrential rain-storms would percolate, ooze through the bed-rock, and permeate with moisture the atmosphere in the chamber of the tomb. However, although the first part of the inference may seem to be logical, it proved not to be the case.

Although it is a fact that the eastern side of the trough of the Valley had been considerably affected by water from such a source, in dynastic times, on the western side, where Tutankhamen's tomb is situated, there was not a trace of past water to any harmful extent. During our excavations in the area abutting the front of the tomb (prior to its discovery), the ground and sundry anti-quities were found to be in a perfect state of preservation. In fact, it was astonishing to see the freshness of the antiquities—letters and sketches in black upon splinters of limestone, and other refuse of the dynastic workmen—that were found there. Moreover, there were no signs of moisture having been present in the rubbish-filling of the descending rock-cut stairway, nor any sign of past damp on the sealed door, nor in the rubble filling the sloping passage of the tomb, where, had water been present, it would have immediately percolated through. The surfaces of the walls, ceiling and floor of the descending passage were also unaffected by damp. The presence of moisture in the past was only visible in the chambers themselves, and there it was very evident—a bad omen that augured ill when we breached the lower sealed doorway and entered the Antechamber. However, nothing could have been freer from moisture than the air in those chambers, when we first entered.

From the above facts it becomes evident that the source of moisture was not from the trough of the Valley, and since the only evidence of past damps was in the chambers themselves, the natural surmise is that it found its way in from above, from the sides, or from the back of the small foot-hill under which the tomb is cut; or, although this is far less likely, that it originated from sources within the chambers themselves.

So far as damps from sources within the chambers are concerned, there can be little doubt that to some extent moisture had been enclosed in the tomb at the time of burial. Moisture, such as might have been present in fresh plaster upon the walls, or in the mortar used when plastering over the outer faces of the sealed doorways, or moisture present in fresh fruits, wine and various other provisions among the funerary equipment. But dampness of that kind would only cause local trouble, and could not possibly account for the extent of humidity that had so obviously existed from time to time throughout those chambers. The Innermost Treasury contained nothing among its equipment that could give out moisture to any appreciable extent, whereas it was affected just as much as the adjoining chambers. Moreover, conditions such as moisture issuing from the equipment were common to all important dynastic burials, and we know that many of the royal tombs in this necropolis had a far greater amount of moisture enclosed within them, at the time of burial, than this tomb. Large porous pottery water-jars (*zeers*) filled with water, slaughtered bullocks, wines and fruits, etc., were placed in their store-rooms, and the plastering of the walls and ceilings of their burial chambers, as well as their sealed doors, was the common practice. Yet damage from humidity, arising from such a source, was negligible among their equipment.

Although the past humidity was general, the four chambers in this tomb having alike suffered, yet in detail there were certain exceptions. The western ends of the four great shrines that shielded the sarcophagus were in a worse condition than the front (eastern) ends; the linen pall between the outermost and second shrine was in worse condition at its western than its eastern end; it was also noticeable that many objects coming from near the west walls had suffered rather more than those on the east side. A further feature from the point of view of harm caused by humidity was that the objects in the Annexe had suffered most. Moreover, minute particles of bronze from masons' chisels that adhered to the limestone surface of the walls of the Annexe were much oxidized, whereas bronze articles among the equipment were affected far less. All such facts, in the writer's mind, point towards the source of trouble coming through the rock from somewhere on the farther (inner) side of the tomb, and, as limestone rock is permeable to moisture, the clue seems to be at the place where sufficient water had collected in the past, to percolate through and have effect.

It is an established fact that water from downpours over the sun-parched ground of these arid ravines does not sink in more than a few centimetres; it at once forms torrents and flows away to the point of lowest level, which may be many miles distant. The ground is thus little affected except where water is trapped by some hindrance, forms pools, and hence seepage begins.

The foot-hill under which the tomb is cut, rises obliquely from the trough of the Valley to the height of some 70 feet, whence it abuts the scarp of the Valley. The greatest descending slope of the foot-hill is immediately above our tomb, and here the vast hypogeum of Rameses VI is excavated. The tomb of Rameses VI shows no signs whatsoever of the presence of past moisture, neither have I been able to trace any sufficiently harmful source of water on the southern side of the foot-hill that would have had effect on Tutankhamen's tomb. But the innermost chambers of the tomb of Horemheb cut transversely through the foot-hill, and situated behind, far below,

Tutankhamen's chambers, show considerable injury from expansions and contraction brought about by the presence of humidity followed by drought, whereas the entrance and forepart of that tomb (situated on the south side of the foot-hill) is in quite good condition. Those inner and lowlying chambers of Horemheb's tomb seem to localize the problem, and give us, if not the actual clue, strong pointers as to whence came all the moisture. For, if water found its way through the rock to the depth of Horemheb's sepulchre, why should it not percolate into our tomb? Our attention and inquiry is thus directed towards the back of the northern side of the foot-hill, or, in other words, to the locality above the chambers affected in Horemheb's sepulchre.

An inspection of that region of the country reveals two converging dry water-courses which had been fed during spates by corresponding water-falls over the scarp-face above. These water-courses have, in times gone by, considerably affected that area. They commence by being wide apart, but they converge and become confluent in front of the entrance of the tomb of Merenptah, whence they formed a cascade and poured into a deep tributary channel (now filled in with detritus) that joins the main trough of the Valley opposite the tomb of Rameses IX.

During our excavations in search of Tutankhamen's tomb on the northern part of the lap of the foot-hill, we discovered that a water-course on that side had been dammed in the Nineteenth Dynasty with the stone-chips (debris) thrown out by workmen employed in making the vast rock-cut hypogeum of Merenptah, with the result that water during spates had been arrested, formed a pool, and flooded Merenptah's tomb. The spates at some early date must have been considerable, for the debris and detrital material in that region were cemented together by water-action into a mass almost as hard as the superficial limestone itself. Obviously a considerable amount of water had pocketed there; the tomb of Merenptah was completely flooded, and thus formed a kind of cistern above the inner chambers of Horemheb's tomb.

Fissures of various degrees in size are abundant in the lower Eocene limestone, and especially so in this foot-hill. Some of these fissures are so regular in formation that, to the inexperienced eye, they appear of artificial origin. The fissures traversing the area in question were, I believe, the means of water having percolated down to the heart of the foot-hill. More than probable they have direct connexion with the fissures that exist in the rock of those low-lying inner chambers of Horemheb, as well as having relation with the fissures in the ceilings, walls and floors of Tutankhamen's tomb. The lips, or rather the edges, of the cracks in the rock of those chambers are water-stained. I am thus persuaded that they are the responsible agents of moisture from above reaching and saturating those underground chambers. Incidentally, the somewhat careless procedure, or want of forethought, on the part of Merenptah's workmen, was the eventual cause of the total ruin of his own tomb, and of the partial injury to the sepulchral chambers of Horemheb, and was responsible for the deterioration that took place in the sepulchre of Tutankhamen. Had those dynastic workmen taken more care, and left a free passage for water to get away during spates, the magnificent hypogea of Horemheb and Merenptah, and the beautiful paraphernalia of Tutankhamen, would have been in a far more perfect state of preservation today. Indeed, but for this ancient oversight, our work instead of taking ten years, might have been finished in one or two.

Another interesting subject peculiar to the tomb of Tutankhamen, and one which has been a puzzle throughout our work, was the existence of a pink film (soluble in warm water) deposited over all exposed surfaces within the chambers—the ceilings, floors, walls and objects—a phenomenon so peculiar to the discovery that it appears to be part result of the humidity already discussed. This deposit prevailed everywhere; it varied in density as well as in colour—pink to a bright red—in accordance with conditions, but where an object or material covered another, or where an object stood against and protected a part of any surface, the deposit, if not absent, was of a far lighter density, causing either behind or below the object a faintly indicated impression.[3]

If, as has been suggested, the coloration came from the rock through influence of water, then why is it absent on the rock surfaces that were shielded by objects?

Although damp affected the tomb of Horemheb, and many other tombs cut in the lower Eocene limestone in other parts of the necropolis, there is no trace in them of the pink deposit that so palpably prevailed here. Those tombs were found almost entirely void of their equipment; Tutankhamen's tomb had practically the whole of its funerary equipment intact. This leads me to believe that the humid atmosphere created by those infrequent saturations caused chemical changes to take place among certain materials pertaining to the equipment especially the leathers and glues which by process of evaporation deposited and formed this pink film over everything. There must have been periods when, due to condensation, a moist vapour steamed from every article comprising the equipment, and those chambers were like some infernal chemist's shop.

A funerary bouquet

Appendix 1

Report upon the examination of Tutankhamen's mummy

by Douglas E. Derry MB, ChB

I N THE MUSEUM OF ANTIQUITIES in Cairo may be seen the mummies of many of the most famous Pharaohs of ancient Egypt, kings who left behind them great monuments, magnificent temples and colossal statues, and whose names have become as familiar as those of modern monarchs, though separated from them in time by some thirty to forty centuries. Little was it expected that a king of obscure origin with a short and uneventful reign should one day attract the attention of the whole world, and that, not on account of fame attaching to himself, but to the single fact that while the tomb of every other Pharaoh yet discovered had been rifled in ancient times, that of Tutankhamen was found practically intact. In the confined space of this small tomb was contained an assemblage of royal possessions such as had never before been seen. What then must have been the contents of the tombs of Seti I, of Rameses III, and others, in one of whose halls alone all the wealth of the tomb of Tutankhamen might have been stored? But the tomb of every one of these monarchs had been entered by thieves, and that not once or twice, but over and over again until not a shred of the original tomb furniture remains. The wrappings of the royal mummies had been torn open in search of jewels and in some cases much damage had been done to the body itself. Most of the royal mummies were rewrapped at least once by the priests, many of them more than once, but the persistence of the robberies eventually necessitated the removal of the bodies of many of the kings and queens to special hiding-places which were only discovered in recent times owing to the perpetration of fresh robberies, and the mummies were then brought to the museum in Cairo. As a result of these frequent disturbances it is not surprising that some doubt exists as to the identity of certain of the mummies which had been removed from their own coffins and reburied in others often of later date. With one or two exceptions none of the Pharaohs has been found in his original tomb, few in their own coffins, and none except Tutankhamen has ever been seen in the wrappings, coffins, sarcophagus and tomb in which he was originally laid to rest.

A word may fittingly be said here in defence of the unwrapping and examination of Tutankhamen. Many persons regard such an investigation as in the nature of sacrilege, and consider that the king should have been left undisturbed. From what I have said as to the persistent robberies of the tombs from the most ancient times up to the present, it will be understood that when once such a discovery as that of the tomb of Tutankhamen has been made, and news of the wealth of objects contained in it has become known, to leave anything whatever of value in the tomb is to court trouble. The knowledge that objects of immense value lay hidden a few feet below ground would certainly invite the attempt to obtain them, and while the employment of a strong guard might suffice for a time to prevent any such attempt meeting with success, any remission of vigilance would be instantly seized upon, and objects which are now safely housed for all time in the Museum of Antiquities would have been destroyed, while others would reappear in a more or less dilapidated state in the hands of dealers through whom they would soon be dispersed to all parts of the civilized world. The value of the intact collection to scientists is incalculable, while the instruction and delectation provided for the public by the exhibition of these ancient works of art is in itself an argument of immense weight in favour of their preservation in a museum. The same argument applies to the unwrapping of the king, whose person is thus spared the rude handling of thieves, greedy to obtain the jewels massed in profusion on his body. History is furthermore enriched by the information which the anatomical examination may supply, which in this case, as will presently be detailed, was of considerable importance.

The preservation of the dead body, brought to its highest pitch by the ancient Egyptians in the art of mummification, has always excited the greatest interest. Much has been written on the subject and the methods employed at different periods have been investigated by Professor Elliot Smith[1] in the royal mummies preserved in the Museum of Antiquities, as well as in a number of mummies of priests and priestesses of the Twenty-First Dynasty.[2] From these and other researches we have a tolerably clear picture of the manner in which the embalming process was carried out. Nevertheless there can be little doubt that a large measure of its success is due to the peculiarly dry climate of Egypt, apart from which it is questionable whether the most perfectly embalmed body would have persisted unchanged, as some have, for nearly four thousand years. The vast majority of mummies examined prove to have had the internal organs removed through an opening made in the abdominal wall. By this means the most decomposable parts were got rid of, and the subsequent immersion of the body in a saline bath seemed to account sufficiently for the excellence of the results obtained. But recently a series of the most perfect mummies yet examined has been described by Mr. H. E. Winlock and myself from the tombs in the vicinity of the Eleventh Dynasty Mentuhetep Temple at Deir el Bahari, in which there is no abdominal or other incision, and from which none of the organs whatever has been taken away. Such perfect preservation without mummification is also exhibited in the remains of some of the predynastic race in Egypt, but these people were usually buried in sand without coffins and the rapid desiccation so produced, by heat and the favourable draining properties of sand, is understandable. The case of the Eleventh Dynasty mummies just referred to is at first sight entirely different, as they were bandaged with great care and placed in coffins and sarcophagi, and so might be expected to have suffered from the effects of enclosed humidity, nevertheless, as already said, they are amongst the most perfect examples of artificial preservation yet seen, and a careful examination of all the facts seems to point to the extreme dryness of the area in which they were discovered as the principal factor in attainment of this result.

Such methods, or lack of them, are however rare and in the following dynasty, the Twelfth, as exemplified in the mummies of certain nobles discovered at Sakkara, the removal of the viscera through an opening made in the abdominal wall was already practised, and there is evidence that it existed even earlier. The mode of preserving the body in the Eighteenth Dynasty, to the end of which period Tutankhamen belongs, has been described by Professor Elliot Smith in the catalogue to which reference has been made. This observer examined most of the kings of the Eighteenth Dynasty and among them some of the ancestors of Tutankhamen.

Unfortunately much doubt exists as to the accuracy of the identification of the mummy said to be that of Amenhetep III, the grandfather of Tutankhamen. Professor Elliot Smith points out that the methods employed in the preservation of this king, and in particular the curious practice of packing materials of various kinds beneath the skin of the limbs, trunk, neck, etc., with the object of restoring as far as possible to the dead body some resemblance to its appearance in life, was not introduced until the Twenty-First Dynasty nearly three centuries later. It is possible, therefore, that this is an example of the mistakes which were apt to be made, when, owing to the frequent robberies of the tombs and desecration of the bodies, the priests undertook the removal and rewrapping of the mummies. The mummy in question was in a coffin of much later date bearing the names of three kings, amongst which was that of Amenhetep III, hence the identification, but it is probably that of a person of a later period.

This statement receives further confirmation in the examination of Amenhetep's descendants, for it is improbable that had this method been introduced in the time of Amenhetep III, it would have been discarded in that of his immediate successors. The remains we now have of his son Akhenaten consist, it is true, of little else than the bones, but had his body and limbs been packed in the manner described by Professor Elliot Smith for his supposed father, some indication at least would assuredly have remained of the process. In the case of Tutankhamen, as we shall see, the methods employed were those in vogue in his dynasty and agree very closely with the descriptions given by Professor Elliot Smith for other undoubted mummies of the period. We must therefore regretfully conclude that, so far, the mummy of Amenhetep III has not been identified.

The examination of the mummy of King Tutankhamen was begun on 11 November 1925, in collaboration with Dr. Saleh Bey Hamdi. When first seen the mummy was lying in the coffin to which it was firmly fixed by some resinous material which had been poured over the body after it was placed in the coffin. Over the head and shoulders, and reaching well down on the chest, was the beautiful gold mask which is an effigy of the king's face, head-dress and collar. This could not be removed as it also was stuck to the bottom of the coffin by the resin, which had dried into a mass of stony hardness. The mummy was enclosed in a sheet which was held in position by bandages passing round the shoulders, hips, knees and ankles. At the outset it was clear that no sort of orderly unwrapping was possible, as the bandages were in a state of extreme fragility and crumbled at a touch. This seems to have been due to the inclusion of some humidity at the time of interment, as well as the decomposition of the unguents, which generated a high temperature and thus brought about a sort of spontaneous combustion which carbonized the wrappings. This has frequently been observed and has given rise to the idea that mummies so affected have been burnt. Other facts, already pointed out by Dr. Carter, bear witness to the same effect of damp. Had the tomb been absolutely dry the textile fabrics would have been in perfect condition.

As all operations had to be conducted with the mummy *in situ*, Dr. Carter suggested that the upper layers of bandages might be strengthened with melted paraffin wax in order that they might be incised and turned back with less disturbance to the original arrangement. This was done and, when the wax had set, an incision was carried down the middle line of the mummy wrappings from the lower edge of the mask to the feet. This penetrated only a few millimetres and the two flaps so produced were turned outwards. A number of objects came to view included in the layers of bandages, and hereafter it became necessary to remove the latter piecemeal in order to expose the objects, so that they might be numerically recorded and photographed before being touched. Throughout the course of this part of the work, which was necessarily slow, the increasing state of disintegration of the wrappings was noticeable. These in many places were reduced to dust, and in no case could any length of bandage or sheet be removed intact. Thus it was impossible to follow the system of bandaging, as may be easily done when the condition of the mummy wrappings is such as to allow of the removal layer by layer of the bandages, sheets or actual clothing, which may have been employed in the final stages of the ritual of mummification. So far as could be ascertained the general principles of bandaging with which we are familiar in Mummies, and which have been described in detail by Professor Elliot Smith in his Catalogue of the Royal Mummies in the Museum of Antiquities in Cairo, were followed in the case of Tutankhamen. Numerous wads of linen were so placed as to fill up the inequalities produced by the objects which were included in the bandages, in order to enable the embalmer to apply the bandages smoothly round the body and limbs.

Some of the linen used in the wrapping of the king was of the nature of the finest cambric, notably that first encountered when the examination was commenced and again immediately next to the body itself. The intermediate bandages were of coarser make, and at one stage folded sheets of linen were placed along the front of the body as far as the knees and retained in place by transverse bandages. The practice of using immense quantities of linen in the form of folded sheets appears to have been common in the Twelfth Dynasty, one such sheet, removed by myself from the mummy of a noble, measured 64 feet in length by 5 feet in width, this being folded to produce a covering eight layers thick. In his account of the removal of the bandages from the mummy styled Amenhetep III (*loc. cit. supra*) Professor Elliot Smith notes the presence of several folded sheets, as well as "a number of rolls of bandage . . . in front of the body, apparently left there inadvertently." These latter may well have been employed originally to fill up the spaces and inequalities existing between the limbs and body, a practice frequently seen in mummies of all periods, and with the same object as in the case where they were used in connexion with the funerary ornaments placed on the body. Over the thorax the bandages were made to pass alternately in crossed and transverse layers, the crossed bandages being carried over one shoulder then round the body returning over the opposite shoulder.

In the crutch the crossed arrangements of the bandages was easily visible, though the method used to produce this could not be followed out, both on account of the fragility of the wrappings and the fact that the body could not be moved at this stage from the coffin.

All the limbs were separately wrapped before being enclosed by the bandages which enveloped the body as a whole. The upper limbs were so placed that the king lay with his forearms across his body, the right forearm resting on the upper part of the abdomen with the hand on the crest of the left hip bone. The left forearm lay higher up over the lower ribs, with the hand lying on the right side of the thorax, between the latter and the right upper-arm. Both forearms were loaded with bracelets from the bend of the elbow to the wrist. All fingers and toes were bandaged individually and gold sheaths were then adjusted over each before the bandage covering in the whole hand or foot was applied. In the case of the feet gold sandals were put on at the same time as the toe-sheaths and after the first few layers of bandage had been applied, in order to allow the bar of the sandal to be adjusted between the great and second toes—the whole being then enclosed in a bandage.

When first exposed, the upper part of the bandaged head was seen to be surrounded by a double fillet which overlay a bandage encircling the head. This fillet, which somewhat resembled a Bedouin head-rope, but of a much smaller diameter, was composed of some sort of vegetable fibre around which twine had been tightly wound. The circular bandage in its turn held in place a sheet which passed over the head and face. Beneath this sheet the bandages passed alternately across the head and transversely round the head and face. When the face was finally exposed some resinous material was found plugging the nostrils, and a layer had been placed over the eyes and between the lips.

General appearance of head: The head appears to be clean-shaved and the skin of the scalp is covered by a whitish substance probably of the nature of fatty acid. Two abrasions on the skin covering the upper part of the occipital bone, had probably been caused by the pressure of the diadem which was enclosed by the tightly-wound head bandages. The plugs filling the nostrils and the material laid over the eyes were found by Mr. Lucas to consist of some woven fabric, impregnated with resin. Mr. Lucas also examined some whitish spots on the skin over the upper part of the back and shoulders, and these proved to be composed of "common salt with a small admixture of sodium sulphate" in all probability derived from the natron used in the embalming process. The eyes are partly open and had not been interfered with in any way. The eyelashes are very long. The cartilaginous portion of the nose had become partially flattened by the pressure of the bandages. The upper lip is slightly elevated revealing the large central incisor teeth. The ears are small and well made. The lobes of the ears are perforated by a circular hole measuring 7·5 mm. in diameter.

The skin of the face is of a greyish colour and is very cracked and brittle. On the left cheek, just in front of the lobe of the ear, is a rounded depression, the skin filling it, resembling a scab. Round the circumference of the depression, which has slightly raised edges, the skin is discoloured. It is not possible to say what the nature of this lesion may have been.

The head when fully uncovered was seen to be very broad and flat topped (platycephalic) with markedly projecting occipital region. Even allowing for the shrinkage both of the scalp and the posterior muscles of the neck, this prominence is still remarkable. There is pronounced bulging of the left side of the occiput and the post-bregmatic region is depressed. The general shape of the head, which is of a very uncommon type, is so like that of his father-in-law, Akhenaten, that it is more than probable there was a close relationship in blood between these two kings. Such a statement made in regard to the normal type of Egyptian skull might justly be considered to have little weight, but the reality of the comparison is accentuated when it is recalled that the remarkable shape of the skull of King Akhenaten led Professor Elliot Smith who first examined it in 1907, to the conclusion that the heretic king had suffered from a condition of hydrocephalus. Subsequent examination has not confirmed his theory, chiefly because the flattening of the cranium in Akhenaten contrasts markedly with the shape of the head in known cases of hydrocephalus. In these the pressure of fluid in the brain acting upon the yielding walls of the cranium naturally produces a globular shape, particularly in the frontal region, which is quite the reverse of the condition observed in the skull of Akhenaten.

When, therefore, we find that Tutankhamen exhibits an almost exact reproduction of his father-in-law's head it not only disposes finally of the theory of hydrocephalus, but makes the argument in favour of a very close relationship extremely convincing. This argument receives still greater weight when we compare the measurements of the two skulls. A breadth of 154 mm. in Akhenaten is, as pointed out by Professor Elliot Smith, "quite an exceptional breadth for an Egyptian skull" yet in his son-in-law we have a breadth of 156·5 mm. When allowance is made for the thickness of the scalp, over which, in the case of Tutankhamen, all measurements were necessarily made, and which by a special instrument was found to be not more than 0·5 mm. in thickness, the breadth of the actual skull is 155·5 mm. exceeding therefore that of his father-in-law, which as we have seen is "quite exceptional." Corresponding measurements in the two skulls, so far as these may be justly compared under the different conditions of examination, show a remarkable similarity, and make the probability of blood relationship almost a certainty.

The effigy of Tutankhamen on the gold mask exhibits him as a gentle and refined-looking young man. Those who were privileged to see the actual face when finally exposed can bear testimony to the ability and accuracy of the Eighteenth Dynasty artist who has so faithfully represented the features, and left for all time, in imperishable metal, a beautiful portrait of the young king.

The skull cavity was empty except for some resinous material which had been introduced through the nose in the manner employed by the embalmers of the period, after they had extracted the brain by the same route.

The right upper and lower wisdom teeth had just erupted the gum and reached to about half the height of the second molar. Those on the left side were not so easily seen but appeared to be in the same stage of eruption.

General appearance of body and limbs: The cracked and brittle state of the skin of the head and face, already referred to, was even more marked in the body and limbs. The abdominal wall exhibited a marked bulging on the right side. This was found to be due to the forcing of the packing material across the abdominal cavity from the left side where the embalming incision is situated. This opening, which had a ragged appearance, is roughly 86 mm. in length and is placed parallel to a line drawn from the umbilicus to the anterior superior iliac spine and an inch above this line. This was only exposed after the removal of a carbonized mass of what was apparently resin, and the length of the incision may therefore have been greater than is now apparent, as the hardness of the adherent mass made it difficult to define the limits of the wound. The lips of the wound are inverted owing to the forcible packing of the abdomen with a mass of linen and resin, now of rock-like hardness. The plate of gold or wax so frequently found covering the embalming wound was not present, but an oval plate of gold was found on the left side during the removal of the wrappings included amongst the layers of bandages and in the neighbourhood of the opening in the abdominal wall. The incision is situated somewhat differently from that described by Professor Elliot Smith in the royal mummies he examined; in these it was usually placed more vertically and in the left flank, extending from near the lower ribs to the anterior superior iliac spine. At a later period the incision was more often made in the lower part of the abdominal wall, parallel with the line of the groin, but always on the left side, but there were occasional reversions to the older site and it seems questionable whether the position had any significance. There was no pubic hair visible, nor was it possible to say whether circumcision had been performed, but the phallus had been drawn forward, wrapped independently, and then retained in the ithyphallic position by the perineal bandages.

The skin of the legs, like that of the rest of the body, was of a greyish-white colour, very brittle and exhibiting numerous cracks. Examination of a piece of this showed that it consisted not only of the skin but of all the soft parts down to the bone, which was thus laid bare when such a piece came away, the whole thickness of skin and tissues in this situation being not more than two or three millimetres. The fractured edges resembled glue. There is little doubt that this was produced by the combustion referred to. The left patella and skin covering it could be lifted off and the lower end of the femur was thus exposed, showing the epiphysis which was found to be separate from the shaft and freely movable. The term epiphysis is applied to that part of a bone which ossifies separately and which eventually becomes fused to the main bone. In the limb bones the epiphyses form the chief part of the upper and lower ends. During early life they are attached to the main bone by cartilage which finally becomes completely converted into bone and growth then ceases. The average date of union of all the epiphyses is known, hence the approximate age can be estimated in any case where union is still incomplete.

The limbs appeared very shrunken and attenuated, but even when due allowance is made for the extreme shrinking of the tissues, and the appearance of emaciation which this produces, it is still evident that Tutankhamen must have been of slight build and perhaps not fully grown at the time of his death.

Direct measurements made him about 5 feet $4\frac{1}{4}$ inches in height, but this is almost certainly less than his stature during life, owing to the shrinkage referred to. An estimate of living height from the measurements yielded by the principal limb bones calculated according to the formulae devised by Professor Karl Pearson[3] gives a stature of 1·676 metres (5 feet 6 inches), which is probably very near the actual truth. With the assistance of Mr. R. Engelbach, the writer measured the two wooden statues of the young king, now in the Museum of Antiquities, which stood on either side of the sealed door leading to the Burial Chamber, and which represent him as he appeared in life. Measurements were made from the root of the nose to the sole of the foot, the nasion being the only anatomical point on the heads of the statues which could be located with any degree of accuracy, as the actual height of the head is obscured in the statues by the head-dress. In the two statues this measurement gave 1·592 metres and 1·602 metres respectively, as the height from sole of foot to root of nose. It was then necessary to add to this the calculated height from this point to the top of the head. This was estimated by measurements from the actual photographs of the king, as well as from a series of observations on Egyptian skulls, to amount to between 8 and 9 cm., which, added to the height of the statues already given, yields a result within a few millimetres of the calculated stature from the bones.

The evidence for the age of the king at the time of his death was obtained from the extent of union or otherwise of the epiphyses. As already mentioned, the cracked condition of the skin and tissues overlying the femur permitted a clear view of the lower ununited portion. This part unites with the shaft about the age of twenty. At the upper end of the thigh bone the prominence known as the great trochanter was almost entirely soldered to the main bone, but on its inner side a definite gap showing the smooth cartilaginous surface where union was still incomplete, could be well seen. This epiphysis joins about the eighteenth year. The head of the femur was fixed to the neck of the bone, but the line of union was clearly visible all round the articular margin. This epiphysis also unites about the eighteenth or nineteenth year. The upper end of the tibia was also ununited, but the lower end appeared to be quite fused. As this latter portion of the tibia is generally found to fuse with the shaft about the age of eighteen, Tutankhamen, from the evidence of his lower limbs, would appear to have been over eighteen but below twenty years of age at the date of his death.

But we are not limited to these bones for evidence of age. It was possible to examine the upper limbs. Here the heads of the humeri, or upper-arm bones, which join about twenty, are still not united, but the lower ends are completely joined to the shaft. In modern Egyptians of seventeen years of age the lower end is seen to be quite fused to the shaft as well as the epiphysis capping the internal condyle, when examined by X-rays, so that if what obtains in Egypt today can be applied to the young king, Tutankhamen was evidently over seventeen when he died.

The lower ends of the radius and ulna in modern Egyptians show little or no union in most cases until the age of eighteen, after which date they fuse fairly rapidly. The union begins on the inner side of the ulna and proceeds laterally, gradually involving the radius. In Tutankhamen fusion appeared to have begun in the ulna, but the distal end of the radius is entirely free, no bony union whatever having commenced between the shaft and its epiphysis. From the state of the epiphyses above described it would appear that the king was about eighteen years of age at the time of his death. None of the epiphyses which should unite about the twentieth year shows any sign of union. There is evidence that in Egypt the epiphyses tend on the average to unite somewhat earlier than is the rule in Europe.

Mention has already been made of the epiphysis of the internal condyle of the humerus which in Egypt is joined completely to the shaft by about seventeen years of age, and of those of the lower end of the radius and ulna which begin to unite at about eighteen. The absence of any ossification here might be taken as evidence that Tutankhamen was less than eighteen at death, but against this we have the complete union of the lower end of the tibia, usually about eighteen, as well as the condition of affairs at the upper end of the femur where the great trochanter, which also joins about eighteen years of age, is, with the exception of a very small portion, fused to the main bone and the head of the same bone, although the line of union is clearly visible all round, is nevertheless joined to the neck.

There is thus little room for doubt as to the approximate age of the king, but it should be borne in mind that the dates given represent the average and that it is permissible to add or deduct about a year, so that Tutankhamen might be any age between seventeen and nineteen, but with the balance of evidence strongly in favour of the middle date, viz. eighteen.

The following table illustrates the similarity between the measurements made on the skull of Akhenaten and those from the head of Tutankhamen.

	Akhenaten	Tutankhamen
Length of skull	190·0	187·0
Breadth of skull	154·0	155·5
Height of skull	134·0	132·5
Forehead breadth	98·0	99·0
Height of face: upper	69·5	73·5
Height of face: total	121·0	122·0
Breadth of jaw	99·5	99·0
Circumference of head	542·0	547·0
Height calculated from limb bones	1·66 metres (5ft. 5¼ in.)	1·68 metres (5ft. 6 in.)

Although the examination of the young king afforded no clue to the cause of his early death, the investigation has added something at least to the few facts already known of the history of the period. The age of Tutankhamen at the time of his decease, and the likelihood that he was a blood relation of Akhenaten, are important evidence in the reconstruction of the events of the time, and will play their part when the history of that time comes to be written.

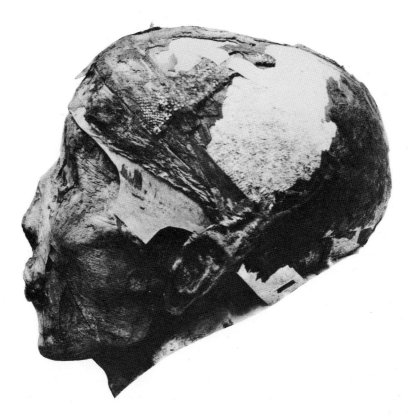

The head of king's mummy

Appendix 2

Report on the floral wreaths found in the coffins of Tutankhamen

by P. E. Newbury MA, OBE

F ROM TIME IMMEMORIAL it has been the custom to decorate the bodies of the dead with wreaths of flowers. When, in 1881, the mummies of the Kings Ahmose I, Amenhetep I, and Rameses II were discovered in the vault of a king of the Twentieth Dynasty at Deir el Bahari many floral wreaths were found in their coffins. Some of these were in an astonishing state of preservation, and Dr. Schweinfurth, who examined them shortly after they were brought to light, remarked that in some instances even the colours of the flowers were admirably preserved. Adorning the mummy of the Princess Nesikhensu, which was also found at Deir el Bahari, was a garland made of willow leaves, poppy flowers and cornflowers; of the poppy flowers Dr. Schweinfurth said that "rarely are such perfect and well-preserved specimens of this fragile flower met with in herbaria; the colour of the petals is maintained in a high degree, as in dried specimens of the present day."

The wreaths found by Dr. Carter in the coffins of Tutankhamen are, unfortunately, not in such good preservation as were those which Dr. Schweinfurth examined from the Deir el Bahari cache, but they are, nevertheless, in a sufficiently good state to enable us to determine nearly all the kinds of plants that were used by the king's florists. Most of the leaves of which the wreaths were made were too brittle to handle when taken from out of the coffins, so they were soaked in lukewarm water for a few hours before being examined. Two or three flowers fell into dust on being touched, but other specimens were selected from better-preserved portions of the wreaths and these were sufficient for me to determine their genus and species. In all, three wreaths were found.

1. A small wreath: This was tied around the vulture and uraeus insignia on the forehead of the king's second coffin. It is composed of the leaves of the olive (*Olea europea*, L.), petals of the blue water-lily (*Nymphaea caerulea*, Sav.), and flowers of the cornflower (*Centaurea depressa*, M. Bieb.). In the manufacture of this wreath a strip of papyrus pith served as a foundation; over it were folded leaves of the olive which served as clasps for the cornflowers and water-lily petals; the olive leaves were securely fastened together in a row by two thinner strips of papyrus pith, one placed over, the other under, alternate leaves. The leaves were arranged so that one leaf had its upper surface outwards, the next with its under surface outwards, this arrangement giving the effect of a dull green leaf beside a silvery one. This wreath was probably the king's "Wreath of Justification." A special chapter of the "Book of the Dead" (Chapter XIX) was devoted to this kind of wreath, and a magical formula is preserved which was to be recited when such a wreath was placed upon the coffin. These "wreaths of justification" were common from the Twenty-second Dynasty to the Graeco-Roman period.

2. A pectoral garland: This garland was made in four bands which were arranged in semicircles on the breast of the second coffin. The first and second bands are composed of the olive (*Olea europea*, L.) and cornflowers (*Centaurea depressa*, M. Bieb.). The third is of leaves of a willow (*Salix safsaf*, Forsk.), cornflowers, and petals of the blue water-lily. The fourth and lowest band is of olive leaves, cornflowers and leaves of the wild celery (*Apium graveolens*, L.). In the making of this wreath the willow leaves are folded over narrow strips of papyrus pith and serve as clasps for the cornflowers, water-lily petals and sprigs of wild celery.

3. The floral collarette: This Floral Collarette, found upon the third coffin, is composed of the leaves, flowers, berries and fruits of various plants, together with blue glass sequin beads, arranged in nine rows and attached to a semicircular sheet of papyrus pith. It is one of a type that is only known from examples[1] of Tutankhamen's reign and it is especially interesting as showing the actual kinds of leaves, flowers and fruits upon which the faience pendant-bead collarettes of the latter half of the Eighteenth Dynasty were modelled.

The first three and the seventh rows of this collarette are similar; they are composed of blue glass sequin beads and berries of the woody nightshade (*Solanum dulcamara*, L.) strung on thin strips of the leaves of the date palm. The sequins and berries are arranged in groups alternately, twenty to twenty-four sequins and four berries. The fourth row is of leaves of the willow and of a plant as yet unidentified, arranged alternately and serving as clasps for petals of the blue water-lily; these are all bound side by side with strips of papyrus pith going over and under the leaves. The fifth row consists of berries of the woody nightshade strung on a strip of the leaf of the date palm. The sixth row is composed of the leaves of a plant not yet identified, flowers of the cornflower, and of *Picris coronopifolia*, Asch., with eleven fruits of the mandrake *Mandragora officinalis*, L.[2] placed at regular intervals along the row. The fruits of the mandrake have been sliced in half lengthwise and the calices cut away; they were then sewn on to the collarette. For the seventh row see the description of rows one to three. The eighth row is composed of leaves of the olive and of an unidentified plant arranged alternately. The ninth and outermost row is made up of the leaves of the same unidentified plant as were used in rows six and eight, together with flowers of the cornflower.

Remarks on the plants identified: The wild celery (*Apium graveolens*, L.). This plant was already known from ancient Egypt from two sources. A very beautiful wreath composed of its leaves and of petals of the blue lotus was discovered in a tomb of the Twenty-second Dynasty at Thebes in 1885 and is now preserved in the Cairo Museum. Another somewhat similar wreath was found by Schiaparelli in the tomb of Amenhetep III's architect Kha at Deir el Medineh (now in Turin). Wild celery (σελινον) was also a favourite plant among the chaplet-makers of Greece and Rome (Anacreon, 54; Theocritus, 3, 23); the victors of the Isthmian and Nemean games were crowned with garlands made of its leaves (Pindar, O., 13, 46; Juvenal, 8, 226); and such garlands were also hung on tombs, whence σελινον δειτ ι was said of persons dangerously ill (Plutarch, 2, 676 D). It is interesting to note here that some wild celery seeds from an Egyptian tomb are preserved in the museum at Florence (No. 3628), and that seeds of this plant were one of the ingredients used in embalming the bodies of kings by the Scythians (Herodotus, iv, 71).

The cornflower (*Centaurea depressa*, M. Bieb.). This was one of the commonest flowers used in wreath-making by the ancient Egyptian florists, and many specimens of it have been preserved in garlands dating from the Eighteenth Dynasty to Graeco-Roman times. It is not a native of Egypt but must have been introduced from Western Asia or the Greek mainland probably at first as a cornfield weed[3] and then cultivated in the gardens of Thebes. At the present day there are no localities for it in Syria or Palestine, but it occurs in Arcadia and in the Attic plain, where it flowers in April.

The mandrake (*Mandragora officinalis*, L.) is not a native of the Nile Valley but was certainly introduced in ancient times from Palestine where it is a common plant, especially in marshy plains. It is the love-apple of *Genesis* xxx. 14 ff., and *Canticles* vii. 13; its fruit was, and still is, considered in the Near East to possess aphrodisiac properties and to promote conception. In wall-paintings of several Theban tombs of the Eighteenth Dynasty baskets of this fruit are represented, and sometimes women are depicted smelling or eating it at banquets[4]. The plant with its leaves and fruit is figured in a Theban tomb.[5] Tristram[6] says that it is a very striking plant which at once attracts the attention from the size of its leaves and the unusual appearance of its blossoms. He notes that he found it in flower in Palestine at Christmas in warm situations, and gathered the fruit in April and May. The wheat harvest is, therefore, the period of its ripening. The fruit is of a pale yellow colour, soft, and of insipid and sickly taste. The Arabs believe it to be exhilarating and stimulating even to insanity, hence their name for it, *tuffah el jinn*,—the apple of the jinn.[7] It is probable that it is the *didi*-fruit (*cp.* Hebrew *dudaim*, "mandrake"), often mentioned in Egyptian inscriptions of the New Kingdom; it is said to have been gathered at Elephantine and was sometimes mixed with beer to produce unconsciousness. It is interesting to note that the Carthaginian general, Maharbal, is recorded as having captured or slain a host of rebels whom he had contrived to drug with a mixture of mandragora and wine.[8] An extraordinary amount of folk-lore has grown up around this plant; it has been collected and discussed by Sir James Frazer in the second volume of his *Folk-Lore in the Old Testament*, pp. 372–397.

The blue water-lily (*Nymphaea coerulea*, Sav.) was the celebrated lotus of the ancient Egyptians and it was used by them for chaplet-making from the Pyramid age onwards. It is a native of the Nile Valley but is now chiefly found in ditches and stagnant pools of the Delta where it generally blooms from July to November.

The olive (*Olea europea*, L.). This tree is only cultivated in a very few gardens in Upper Egypt at the present day, but there is good evidence that it must have been more widely distributed throughout the Nile Valley in ancient times.[9] It is mentioned in the inventory of plants grown by Inena in his Theban garden in the time of Queen Hatshepsut, and Theophrastus, Pliny and Strabo refer to its being grown in Upper Egypt. The first-named writer expressly states (iv, 2, 9) that it grew in the Theban province in his day.

The *Picris coronopifolia*, Asch., is a small composite plant which is very common on the outskirts of the desert at Thebes and elsewhere in Upper Egypt. It flowers in March and April.

The willow (*Salix safsaf*, Forsk.) still occurs in the wild state on the banks of the Nile in Nubia, but in Egypt proper it was considered by Dr. Schweinfurth as only a riverine fugitive whose real home is in the south.

The woody nightshade or bitter-sweet (*Solanum dulcamara*, L.). Only the berries of this plant have been found in Egyptian tombs; they are always threaded on to thin strips of the leaves of the date palm. Berries of this nightshade are often found in the wreaths of the Graeco-Roman period.[10] Pliny (H.N., xxi, 105) mentions the nightshade being used by the garland-makers of Egypt.

Note on the season of the burial of Tutankhamen: From the blossoms and fruits found in these wreaths it is possible to indicate the season of the year at which King Tutankhamen was laid to rest in his tomb. The cornflower flowers at about the harvest time in March or April, and it is just at this time that the mandrake and woody nightshade fruits ripen. The small *Picris* also flowers in March and April. Although the water-lily blossoms in the ditches and stagnant pools of Lower Egypt from July to November, it is very probable that being cultivated in garden tanks at Thebes it would flower much earlier in the year. We may therefore safely say that the season of the year when Tutankhamen was interred was from the middle of March to the end of April.

Notes

Chapter 1
1. This stela, parts of which are roughly translated here, was subsequently usurped by Horemheb, as were almost all Tutankhamen's monuments.

Chapter 2
1. Breasted, *Ancient Records of Egypt*, Vol. IV, par. 538.

Chapter 3
1. They certainly have the appearance of houses, but actually they are façade tombs of the Middle Kingdom.
2. Pococke, *A Description of the East*, Vol. 1, p. 97.
3. From the evidence of *graffiti*, these same tombs were opened in classical times. The Greek authors refer to them as συριγγεσ (syringes), from their reed-like form.
4. Norden, *Travels in Egypt and Nubia*, translated by Dr. Peter Templeman. London, 1757.
5. Bruce, *Travels to Discover the Source of the Nile*, Vol. I, p. 125.

Chapter 4
1. Potsherds and flakes of limestone, used for sketching and writing purposes.

Chapter 5
1. From later evidence we found that this re-sealing could not have taken place later than the reign of Horemheb, i.e. from ten to fifteen years after burial.

Chapter 7
1. These are two of the attributes of Hathor. There are many others.
2. These, on our first entrance into the tomb, were mistaken for rolls of papyrus.

Chapter 10
1. Carter and Newberry, *Tomb of Thoutmosis IV*, Pls. I and XXVIII, Nos. 46526–46529.

Chapter 11
1. Lord Carnarvon died at five minutes to two on the morning of 5 April 1923. [Publisher's note.]

Chapter 14
1. For the identification of the wood as oak, I am indebted to Mr. L. A. Boodle of the Jodrell Laboratory, Royal Gardens, Kew.

Chapter 17
1. Davies and Gardiner, *The Tomb of Amenemhet*, p. 56.
2. Erman, *Egyptian Religion*, p. 127.
3. N. de G. Davies, *The Rock Tombs, El Amarna*, Part V, p. 30.
4. Meaning undoubtedly, Osiris, the great god of the dead.
5. On account of the risk of the natron corroding the flesh and converting it into the condition of pulp.
6. Davies and Gardiner, *The Tomb of Amenemhet*, p. 56.

Chapter 18
1. Knudtzon, *El-Amarna-Tafeln*, 28(=w.24).

Chapter 20
1. Analysed by Mr. A. Lucas.
2. Alan H. Gardiner, *The Chester Beatty Papyrus, No.* 1, chap. 13, ll. 9 and 10.
3. Davies and Gardiner, *The Tomb of Amenemhet*, p. 30.
4. Newberry, *Beni Hasan*, Part I, Plate XII; Part II, Plate VI.
5. In my opinion "bed-chamber" may possibly refer to "bier-chamber".
6. See Carnarvon and Carter, *Five Years' Exploration at Thebes*, pp. 75–77, Plate LXVI.
7. For these translations I am indebted to Mr. Battiscombe Gunn.
8. Dr. Douglas Derry reported on this in Appendix I of the third volume of the original edition. It is not included in this edition. [Publisher's note.]
9. I now believe that cheetahs are represented on that couch and not lions as aforesaid.

Chapter 21
1. Some abandoned water-skins were found in the descending entrance passage.

Chapter 22

1. A Roman Catholic bishop wears gloves when pontificating—also buskins, tunic and dalmatic under his chasuble.
2. This does not include the four highly ornamental examples, which were *in situ* in the Antechamber.

Chapter 23

1. The rainfall in Egypt must have been far greater in pre-historic times than in our era. Palaeolithic implements that are found distributed over the higher desert terraces bordering the Nile Valley almost certainly prove that semi-desert conditions existed during their epoch. From that time Egypt, or let us say north-east Africa, appears to have gradually reached its present state of dryness. Egypt as we know her is probably not more than ten to fifteen thousand years old. Her alluvial muds are about thirty to thirty-five feet thick. The rate of those deposits appear to have been from three to four inches per hundred years, and they, in all probability, first began when the tributary Blue Nile broke into the White Nile, bringing with it the Abyssinian alluvium. Before then it was the White Nile that brought tropical forms of African life into the Delta, and its progress north to the Mediterranean was undoubtedly marked by swamps, flooded areas and lakes. (See Meinertzhagen, *Nicolls's Birds of Egypt*, Vol. I, chap. I, 1930).
2. *Hippotion* (*Chaerocampa*) *celerio*—the Silver Striped Hawk, abd *Deilephila* (*Hyles*) *euphorbiae*—the Spurge Hawk.
3. Lately I witnessed a very interesting demonstration of a somewhat similar effect. My magazine, wherein masses of materials were stored, was set on fire by thieves to cover a theft they had perpetrated. They set fire to a heap of hemp sacks and large rolls of brown paper that were stored in the magazine (an ancient Egyptian rock-cut tomb chamber closed by a heavy modern wooden door). The fire was detected, from smoke issuing from the cracks of the door, within about an hour of ignition; in fact, in time to prevent any great harm being done, further than charring the sacks and brown paper which had only smouldered owing to insufficient air in the chamber. Having extinguished the fire and removed the charred sacking and paper, I found upon inspection, a light amber brown sticky (? resinous) deposit from the smoke all over the walls, ceiling and floor of the chamber, as well as on all the exposed materials stored therein; an effect, except for the colour and nature of the film, exactly as met with in the tomb of Tutankhamen.

Appendix 1

1. *Catalogue Général des Antiquités Egyptiennes du Musée du Caire, The Royal Mummies.*
2. *A Contribution to the Study of Mummification in Egypt* (Mémoires de l'Institut Egyptien, tome V, fascicule I, 1906).
3. Phil. Trans. of the Royal Society, Vol. 192, pp. 169–244.

Appendix 2

1. Theodore Davis in 1908 found in the Valley of the Tombs of the Kings several objects belonging to the funerary furnishings of Tutankhamen. Among these were some floral collarettes very similar to the one here described; they are now in the Metropolitan Museum of Art, New York.
2. For the identification of the mandrake fruits I am indebted to Mr. L. A. Boodle of the Jodrell Laboratory, Royal Gardens, Kew, and to Mrs. Clement Reid.
3. Newberry in Petrie's *Hawara, Biahmu and Arsinoe,* p. 49.
4. N. de G. Davies, *The Tomb of Nakht,* Plates X and XVII.
5. Wilkinson, *Manners and Customs of the Ancient Egyptians,* 2nd Ed., Vol. II, p. 413, No. 5.
6. *Natural History of the Bible,* p. 468.
7. Thomson, *The Land and the Book,* Vol. II, p. 380.
8. Frontinus, *Stratagem,* ii, 5, 12.
9. *See* Newberry in *Ancient Egypt,* 1915, pp. 97–100.
10. Newberry in Petrie's *Hawara, Biahmu and Arsinoe,* p. 51.

Index